BLOODY CONSTRAINT

BLOODY CONSTRAINT

War and Chivalry in Shakespeare

Theodor Meron

OXFORD
UNIVERSITY PRESS

Oxford University Press

Oxford   New York
Athens   Auckland   Bangkok   Bogotá   Buenos Aires   Calcutta
Cape Town   Chennai   Dar es Salaam   Delhi   Florence   Hong Kong   Istanbul
Karachi   Kuala Lumpur   Madrid   Melbourne   Mexico City   Mumbai
Nairobi   Paris   São Paulo   Singapore   Taipei   Tokyo   Toronto   Warsaw

and associated companies in
Berlin   Ibadan

Library of Congress Cataloging-in-Publication Data
Meron, Theodor, 1930–
Bloody constraint : war and chivalry in Shakespeare
/ Theodor Meron.
p.   cm.
Includes bibliographical references and index.
ISBN 0-19-512383-2; 0-19-514406-6 (pbk)
1. Shakespeare, William, 1564–1616—Knowledge—Military art
and science. 2. Knights and knighthood in literature.
3. Military history in literature. 4. Chivalry in literature.
5. War in literature. I. Title.
PR3069.M5M47 1998
822.3'3—dc21   98-14533

Parts of chapter 9 are reproduced with permission from 92 *Am. J. Int'l L.* 1 (1998),
© The American Society of International Law.

1 3 5 7 9 8 6 4 2
Printed in the United States of America
on acid-free paper

For Monique,
who made me love him

ACKNOWLEDGMENTS

I acknowledge with gratitude the helpful comments and suggestions made by Professors John Baker, John Brewer, Roger Deakins, William Elton, Robert Miller, Liam Murphy, Thomas Nagel, Benedict Kingsbury, Julie Peters, Oscar Schachter, David Sylvan and Detlev Vagts; and Monroe Leigh and Aryeh Neier. Thanks also to Ronald Brown of the NYU Law Library, my very able research assistant Laurie Rosensweig, to Alice Palmer for the preparation of the index, and my secretary Sharon Town.

I also wish to express my deep thanks to the Filomen D'Agostino and Max E. Greenberg Research Fund of New York University Law School for its generous support of this study and to Professor Philip Alston and the European University Institute in Florence for a Jean Monnet Fellowship in 1997. Finally, many thanks to my Oxford University Press editor, Thomas LeBien, for his help and encouragement.

CONTENTS

BLOODY CONSTRAINT

INTRODUCTION

I n his generous review of my most recent book, *Henry's Wars and Shakespeare's Laws*, Professor Adam Roberts of Balliol College, Oxford, triggered the idea for this book. Adam Roberts wrote that the one question I left virtually neglected is whether we have lost as well as gained by having a system of law based on the Hague and Geneva Conventions rather than on customary rules and chivalric codes. Obviously, we gained uniformity and clarity in the rules, as well as the formal assent of virtually all states. "However, we have also lost something: the sense that rules arise naturally out of societies, their armed forces, and their rulers on the basis of experience; the flexibility that came from their essentially customary character; and the value attached to honor, chivalry and mercy."[1]

In *Henry's Wars*, I tried to provide an international humanitarian lawyer's commentary on the law of war issues arising in Henry V's French campaigns. The purpose was to illustrate the law's evolution and to provide a lawyer's commentary on Shakespeare's play, *Henry V*, by examining how he used the law of nations for his dramatic purposes.

Now, in this book, I have the opportunity to respond to Professor Roberts's challenge and, at least, to address the broader significance of chivalry. I thus expand the focus from the laws of war in the strict sense to the broader system of chivalry in Shakespeare, and from *Henry V* to other plays also raising issues of chivalry.[2] A broader sequel to *Henry's Wars*, *Bloody Constraint* requires an exploration of the chivalric values and foundations that sustained and reshaped the customs of war in the

3

Middle Ages and the Renaissance, values that continue to surface in the legal, moral and utilitarian arguments configuring the laws and practices of war today.

Shakespeare's work contains a plethora of fascinating texts illuminating chivalry and the humanitarian ideal, on which I intend to draw. Perhaps more than anything else, chivalry meant the duty to act honourably, even in war.[3] But my interest in the investigation of chivalry in Shakespeare extends beyond its role in war. Chivalry, certainly as discussed by Shakespeare, implies an all-important code of behaviour for the honourable person in civil society. The legacy of this code has in turn shaped our contemporary law and values.

Not a literary critic, I do not purport to write as one. Rather, I write as a scholar of international humanitarian law who is interested in history and literature. I focus not only on Shakespeare the poet and dramatist, but also on the Shakespeare who read the chronicles,[4] Plutarch and the literature and poetry of chivalry, and had an acute understanding of the affairs of state and war; and who often recreated historical events and the mores of times past in his plays. Above all, I focus on the Shakespeare whose characters articulate a moving call for civilized behaviour, for mercy and quarter, and for humanitarian principles and moral responsibility, the Shakespeare whose protagonists censure savage comportment. I touch on the intellectual genealogy of our modern international law.

Shakespeare's writings thus constitute an early literary reflection of this law and a vast source of questions still important today. As a scholar and an advocate of humanitarian law, I recognize that great literature has both a story and a message about humanitarian principles and our code of civilized behaviour, in civil society as well as in war, that is more poignant, more powerful and more memorable than anything we can read in the language of international treaties or even customary law. Shakespeare's plays on war and chivalry can thus still do some good. His poetic texts are a powerful instrument for illuminating the humanitarian idea as an ideal for all times. I agree with Bernard Shaw, who has Queen Elizabeth acknowledge, in her imaginary exchange with Shakespeare in *The Dark Lady of the Sonnets*, that "the Scottish minstrel hath well said that he that maketh the songs of a nation is mightier than he that maketh its laws."

Shakespeare's focus on chivalry can also be explained by his wish to accommodate the interests of the Tudor Court. As Eric Mallin,[5] among others, has demonstrated, the chivalric premise and rites were central to the royal court, where they served to promote the nobles' fealty and the ideas of the monarch's glory and service to a lady, Queen Elizabeth. By reviving the literary and historical image of medieval chivalry, Shakespeare was thus serving the Queen and the Court.

In the Middle Ages, the focus of Shakespeare's Histories, chivalry was the principal normative system providing a code of behaviour for knights, nobility and the entire warring class in the endemic wars in which they were involved. As a code for the upper classes, chivalry also radiated values for other members of society. The humane and noble ideals of chivalry included justice and loyalty, courage, honour and mercy, the obligations not to kill or otherwise take advantage of the vanquished enemy, and to keep one's word—sanctity of the chivalric oath was particularly important—and the duties to protect the weak, women, widows and orphans, to help people in distress, to be gentle, to act nobly and generously, to redress wrongs, to avenge injustice and to renounce the pursuit of material gain (but not the spoils of war and ransom). Dubbing of knights thus reflected merit, courage and service to the community, in accordance with these principles. Seldom if ever realized in full, these ideals remained a source of inspiration, pervading the political, social and literary life and filling an important need as the yardstick for the mores of the period. Chivalry in the Middle Ages was thus a mix of reality, poetry and legend. While humanizing warfare, chivalry also contributed to the legitimizing of war.

Chivalry contained an important humanitarian and ethical component that attracted Shakespeare.[6] His knowledge of chivalry evolved through reading his principal chroniclers, Holinshed and Hall, and studying various medieval and particularly Renaissance literary sources, humanist English writers, and older authorities such as Plutarch, the first-century Greek biographer and historian whose *Parallel Lives* were translated into English by Shakespeare's contemporary Sir Thomas North in 1579, and Homer, in various translations and sometimes fragmented texts. Although chivalry was a concept that blossomed in the Middle Ages and was linked to the Catholic Church, creating the obligation to participate in the crusades for the liberation of the holy places, Shakespeare also derived chivalric principles from pre-Christian sources, extrapolating a few chivalric notions to extend to his mythical, Trojan and Roman plays. He tended to depict Trojans, Greeks and Romans as knights, respected citizens and patriots, and, except for the absence of Christianity, as true knights. In the period of Elizabethan absolutism, ancient material allowed Shakespeare greater literary freedom and a more politically neutral setting.

The rules of chivalry were customary, not statutory. However, various royal ordinances, including Henry V's famous ordinances of war promulgated in 1419 and earlier, codified some of these rules, including those protecting women from rape, and churches and persons belonging to the Church from assault, robbery and capture. In addition, writers on chivalry compiled treatises and manuals explaining the rules of chivalry, such as the duties to grant quarter on the battlefield in exchange for ransom, to treat prisoners humanely, to protect women, children, other noncombatants, peaceful "civilians," and so on. Apart from legal sources on chivalry, there were the more broadly cultural texts, such as the so-called courtesy books exemplified by Baldassare Castiglione's (1528; translated into English by Sir Thomas Hoby in 1561), from which the Elizabethans derived many ideas about chivalry.

Chivalry's norms were fully applicable regardless of nationality between knights and nobility, those who had the right to wage war, but did not protect commoners and peasants and were not applicable to non-Christians. On the battlefield, rules of chivalry protected only members of the knightly class: "[D]uring a given battle, gentlemen were careful to avoid surrendering to 'commoners' . . . because they expected no mercy from them; it is hardly necessary to say that the opposite was also true."[7] In effect, chivalry served as the customary law governing relations not between states, nations or peoples, but within the class of warring men.

In this sense, the system was quite international. A French knight, for example, could complain against an English knight to English military authorities or to an English court of chivalry. These authorities and courts regarded themselves as enforcing the rules of an international order of chivalry, not of any national state or sovereignty. Rules could be and often were enforced by princes, such as Henry V's order to hang Shakespeare's Bardolph, for example, for violating the sanctity of a church, by military commanders or their courts, or by the courts of chivalry. Honour and shame played an important role in enforcement; the sanction of dishonour for the knight who violated his knightly duties, thus becoming a traitor to chivalry and to his knightly vow, was quite effective.

Chivalry had many formal, vain and excessive aspects as well, often based on exaggerated notions of honour. There were jousts and tournaments, the often ridiculous vows to surmount unbelievable perils to meet the expectations of courtly love, and the silly challenges to single combat to establish the incomparable virtue of a lady, even one unknown to one of the combatants. These exaggerations and foolish rituals led some historians, especially Johan Huizinga, to consider chivalry as primarily a romance, a veneer, a dream of a beautiful life in an otherwise very harsh and brutal universe, rather than an effective system of values. Maurice Keen and others disagree, arguing that chivalry performed an important social function based on upholding justice and protecting the weak. I tend to agree with Keen and believe that without the constraining and humanizing effects of chivalry, the endemic wars of the Middle Ages would have led to even more chaos, injustice and bloodshed. Thus, despite the occasional violations, such as at Agincourt, quarter was normally granted in the Anglo-French wars dramatized in Shakespeare's Histories.

Even at its apex in the Middle Ages, chivalry only applied among Christians and did not protect non-Christians, such as the Muslims defending the Holy Places against the crusaders. The crusaders thus massacred the Muslim and Jewish populations of Jerusalem in 1099. Even distant and "different" Christians were not always spared, as the crusaders, led by the Venetians, demonstrated in the massacre and sack of Christian Constantinople.[8] Furthermore, in battles between communal troops and nobles or between the communes themselves it was not normal practice to grant ransom.[9] Perhaps there was a greater sense of community between the noble and chivalric class of various nations than between that class and lower-class compatriots, suggesting the absence of a sense of national community.

Shakespeare was aware of the decline of chivalry in his era. Largely observed in the Middle Ages, chivalric rules faced two major challenges, one military, the other religious. As the English historian Malcolm Vale observed, wars fought by larger groups using long-range artillery fire were not conducive to the pursuit and the taking of prisoners or to the once customary grant of ransom. However, the religious wars following the Protestant Reformation demonstrated that religious fanatics posed a still greater challenge to chivalry than military advances.

The emergence of Protestantism and the brutal confrontation be-tween Elizabethan England and Catholic Spain, backed by papal power, still further eroded the effectiveness of the norms of chivalry. The Reformation triggered an increasing dehumanization of those belonging to an adversary branch of Christianity, pitting Protestant against Catholic and sparking the religious wars on the European continent, marked by unmitigated cruelty and bloodshed. Throughout history, dehumanization has created a fertile environment for the physical destruction of those who have already been defined as subhuman or inhuman. The difference between non-Christians and Christians of another branch of Christianity became blurred, justifying for some even the most terrible excesses, such as the Saint Bartholomew's Day massacre (August 24, 1572), the infamous slaughter of the Huguenots in Paris, Spain's military campaign in Ireland and Elizabethan England's exceptionally bloody conquest of Ireland. Protestant England developed a siege mentality, leading to still further excesses.[10] When ships of the Spanish Armada were wrecked in a storm on the coasts of County Clare in western Ireland (1588), supporters of the English killed any sailors who managed to reach the shore. Shakespeare's contemporary, the renowned and enlightened jurist Alberico Gentili, censured this hanging of the Spanish soldiers, "as if they were robbers and pirates" and, anticipating the concept of war crimes, recommended severe punishment "in order to satisfy the enemy against whom the war was not waged according to the law."[11]

In the first part of this book, I discuss Shakespeare's treatment of war and show how his characters attempt to discourage war through legal, moral and utilitarian arguments. Irony and sarcasm are deployed to advocate prior resort to diplomatic negotiations and peaceful settlement, oppose aggressive and unjust wars, criticize self-serving and hypocritical assertions of just war, highlight the futility of war, and emphasize its inevitable cruelty and cost. Of course, it is through his characters that I try to learn their author's attitudes. Each of Shakespeare's dramatic characters expresses distinct, individual attitudes, and is not a spokesperson for Shakespeare. I believe, nevertheless, that when the preponderance of his characters express certain themes, as about the bloodiness and the futility of war, for example, it is legitimate to draw certain conclusions about Shakespeare's own attitudes.

The canon resists the glorification of war in chivalric literature and its theological justifications. Writing in the post-chivalric era marred by the savagery of religious wars, Shakespeare recognizes the continuing pertinence of ethical and protective values of chivalry. Even more, he is conscious of the inevitable human misery that all wars bring, even those considered just and necessary. He thus shows that wars are not only tragic and bloody, but also futile. In reinforcing his dramatic statements and arguments about war, Shakespeare finds it necessary, from time to time, to depart from his sources. He shows how leaders make claims to justify rule by force, and how empty versions of honour differ from true honour, chivalry and compassion. In dramatizing Greek or mythical wars, Roman wars, early British wars and medieval wars, Shakespeare's plays demonstrate the differences and the similarities in the problems that arise.

The second part of the book addresses chivalry as a system of values (originally designed just for Christians, but universalized by modern law of war) that should not only humanize the conduct of war, but instruct our daily comportment whether in peace or in war. For Shakespeare, honour and shame are the central forces that motivate and shape our behaviour. I therefore discuss such issues as quarter and mercy for the vanquished foe, treatment of prisoners and women, and chivalric oaths as the basis of a system of honour amidst the pressures of necessity and reasons of state. I show Shakespeare's sympathy for chivalry as an ideal, a sharp contrast to his sarcasm for vain and excessive chivalry and exaggerated and dangerous notions of honour.

The third part of the book addresses crimes of state and war crimes, the accountability and ethics of leaders and—much like our own recent experience—the denial of criminal orders. I highlight the relationship between leaders, their aides and their victims, often in light of Shakespeare's sources, raising legal and ethical questions.

If Shakespeare's references to chivalric values like mercy, honour and humanity in the treatment of prisoners and women appear idealized, he may have been trying to ensure the survival, or the revival, of those values for his own time. By describing a period long gone by, with its system of norms and simple, essential humanity, he was perhaps signalling the need to return to the old and tested values. In the intolerant climate that prevailed in England at the time, writing about times past was politically the safest way to articulate such statements as an appeal for the survival of humane rules of war. As I noted, he was also serving the interests of the Queen.

In *Don Quixote*, Shakespeare's contemporary Cervantes recognizes the positive in the ideal of chivalry.[12] But by writing about a knight errant in the peaceful setting of post-chivalric pastoral Spain, he satirizes chivalry as irrelevant, foolish and dangerous. Shakespeare also wrote in the post-chivalric era, and did not hesitate to debunk some of chivalry's vain and frivolous features. However, he was far more positive about the ideal of chivalry. Indeed, even today some experts on international humanitarian law believe that a better system of values had not yet been found.

I have already disclaimed any competence in literary criticism and will not directly address literary methodologies or their consequences for textual interpretation. However, inevitably in addressing historical issues, I share many of the New Historicists'[13] concerns and recognize the importance of situating Shakespeare's text in his own cultural and political environment and relating it to his public, the institutions, practices and beliefs of the Tudor and the Renaissance society, the requirements of a popular commercial theatre and court censorship. In addressing issues of such central importance to historical feminism as rape in war and representation of women in positions of power, I share many of feminists historians' concerns.

Shakespeare's plays had a strong contemporary resonance to which I sometimes allude, but on which I cannot elaborate. The fact, for example, that *Henry V* was written in 1599, during England's preparations for Essex's expedition against the Irish insurgency,[14] is important for understanding a certain jingoist spirit of the play, subverted by all kinds of ironies, but does not adulterate Shakespeare's discussion of the chivalric code.

I shall have recourse to one traditional concern of Shakespearean scholarship, the use of and deviation from his sources, to highlight his own views and contribution to debates about chivalry and its moral code. I shall also demonstrate, when necessary, the very important influence on Shakespeare of the humanist writings and concepts. My principal interest is to discuss a set of legal and moral dilemmas that arise in situations of

English Kings in Shakespeare's Histories

Kings	Accession Date	Length of Reign	Plays
John	May 27, 1199	18	*The Life and Death of King John*
Richard II	June 22, 1377	23	*Richard II*
Henry IV	September 30, 1399	14	*1 Henry IV*
			2 Henry IV
Henry V	March 21, 1413	10	*Henry V*
Henry VI	September 1, 1422	39	*1 Henry VI*
			2 Henry VI
			3 Henry VI
Edward IV	March 4, 1461	23	*Richard III*
Richard III	June 26, 1483	3	Richard III
Henry VIII	April 22, 1509	38	*All is True (Henry VIII)*

Source. Theodor Meron, 92 Am. J. Int'l Law 1, 2; some of the information in this table is taken from Black's Law Dictionary 1657 (6th ed. 1990).

tension and conflict, especially those involving military power and vio-lence. Because my approach is thematic, in some places I focus on one particular action or play, elsewhere on another. In order to maintain a thematic coherence, I am forced to isolate particular passages for discus-sion as though they were free-standing, without dwelling on their im-mediate context in a particular play or situation.

Shakespeare's characters, speak, of course, with a hundred voices. Nevertheless, certain general attitudes can be discerned, for example, to-ward such normative systems as chivalry. Each speaks for himself or her-self.[15] There is hardly a text that cannot be understood in different and sometimes contradictory ways. Certainly, by distilling concepts of chivalry and humanitarian law from Shakespeare, I shall be guilty of inevitable oversimplification.

CHIVALRY'S LEGACY

Chivalry's enduring influence stems from the ability of its ideals, such as honour, loyalty, courage, mercy, commitment to the community and the avoidance of shame and dishonour,[1] to fulfill a lasting human need. Chivalry was, as Malcolm Vale wrote, "honour in its medieval guise."[2] Its legacy was a conception of honour understood, as Maurice Keen suggests, as a nexus between the ideals of society and the actions of individuals: "honour commits men to act as they should. . . . Chivalry's most profound influence lay in just this, in setting the seal of approbation on norms of conduct. . . ."[3] The mores of the knight errant eventually developed into the code of the officer and the gentleman. The U.S. Uniform Code of Military Justice states that an officer who is convicted of conduct unbecoming an officer and a gentleman shall be punished as a court-martial may direct. Such conduct must offend so seriously against law, justice, morality or decorum as to disgrace the offender or bring dishonour upon the military profession. In *Parker v. Levy* (1974), the U.S. Supreme Court decided that this provision is neither void for vagueness under the due process clause of the Fifth Amendment nor overbroad in violation of the First Amendment.[4] In this code, the duties of the gentleman go beyond the purely military. In the British Army, an officer could be cashiered for bouncing a cheque, as an example of conduct unbecoming his status. The practitioners of the ideal and the code of chivalry, knights, were supposed to be cultivated gentlemen, rather than just professional soldiers.[5] Gentleness, faithfulness, compassion for the weak and the oppressed, honour, courage and generosity were among the standards chivalry set for the perfect gentleman.[6] Although feudalism, a social and economic system which originated in a grant, usually of land tenure ("fief") in exchange for services, especially military service, and focused on the relationship between the vassal and the lord, became hereditary, chivalry never did, remaining an ideal and a standard of achievement.[7] Of course, the very individualism of knightly ideals meant that the quest for personal glory often prevailed over that for common victory;[8] No less, material gain was at least as important as acts of glory, if not more so.[9] Divorced from its martial connotations, the conception of chivalry as the duty to vindicate justice, protect the weak and act honourably is also enormously important for every citizen as a source of values in civil society.

Chivalry's legacy appears most clearly in the principles of modern humanitarian law. Several centuries of relative neglect passed between the medieval and essentially chivalric ordinances of war[10] and the modern movement to codify the law of war, or international humanitarian law, that began in the mid-nineteenth century. Several factors triggered the latter movement, including advances in the technology of weapons, especially artillery, and the resulting horror and enormity of killing and maiming in war, particularly in the American Civil War and the Battle of Solferino between the Franco-Piedmontese and the Austrians, in which 39,000 soldiers were killed and wounded in just one day (June 24, 1859). As if to exaggerate the horror, most of the wounded were left uncared for on the battlefield.

Technology, which ended the face-to-face combats and "the individualism of combat"[11] between medieval warriors, thus precipitating the demise of chivalry, ultimately generated the need for international rules of war to humanize the conduct of hostilities, limit the killing and maiming, and ensure the humane care of prisoners, the sick and the wounded. The simplicity and quintessential humanity of the rules of chivalry, with their emphasis on honour and shame or dishonour, made them the ideal source for the new international rules. These rules would apply not only among the members of an international warrior class but among warring nations; not only among Christians, but among all nations, religions and ethnicities.

The American Civil War generated the *Lieber Code* promulgated in 1863 and drafted by Francis Lieber, a political refugee from Prussia and a professor at Columbia College Law School. President Abraham Lincoln promulgated this code as the Instructions for the Government of Armies of the United States in the Field. The *Lieber Code* ultimately spawned the branch of international humanitarian law commonly known as The Hague Law, which governs the conduct of hostilities. The Battle of Solferino, along with Henry Dunant's moving portrayal of the suffering and bloodshed at the battle, in *A Memory of Solferino* (1862), inspired the Geneva Law, the other branch of international humanitarian law, which emphasizes the protection of the victims of war, the sick, the wounded, prisoners and civilians. Nonetheless, both prongs of international human-itarian law drew their guiding principles from chivalry. Rules of modern humanitarian law such as the prohibition on the use of poison and the requirement to use fairness and restraint, mercy and compassion, in both offensive and defensive situations, have their origin in chivalric honour.[12]

In a letter addressed to James C. Conklink on August 26, 1863, President Lincoln wrote, "[C]ivilized belligerents do all in their power to help themselves, or hurt the enemy, except a few things regarded as bar-barous or cruel. Among the exceptions are the massacre of vanquished foes, and non-combatants, male and female."[13] Effectively restating the basic premise of chivalry, President Lincoln may have learned of such norms from Francis Lieber's Code, promulgated a few months earlier on April 24, 1963. Consider these statements in the *Lieber Code*:

As Martial Law is executed by military force, it is incumbent upon those who administer it to be strictly guided by the principles of justice, honor, and humanity—virtues adorning a soldier even more than other men, for the very reason that he possesses the power of his arms against the unarmed.[14]

The law of war does not only disclaim all cruelty and bad faith concerning engagements concluded with the enemy during the war, but also the breaking of stipulations solemnly contracted by the bel-ligerents in time of peace. . . . [15]

Men who take up arms against one another in public war do not cease on this account to be moral beings, responsible to one another and to God.[16]

Military necessity does not admit of cruelty—that is, the infliction of suffering for the sake of suffering or for revenge, nor of maiming or wounding except in fight, nor of torture to extort confessions. It does not admit of the use of poison in any way, nor of the wanton devastation of a district. It admits of deception, but disclaims acts of perfidy. . . . [17]

[A]s civilization has advanced during the last centuries . . . [t]he principle has been more and more acknowledged that the unarmed citizen is to be spared in person, property, and honor as much as the exigencies of war will admit.[18]

All wanton violence committed against persons in the invaded country, all destruction of property not commanded by the author-ized officer, all robbery, all pillage or sacking, even after taking a place by main force, all rape, wounding, maiming, or killing of such inhabitants, are prohibited under the penalty of death. . . . [19]

It is against the usage of modern war to resolve, in hatred and revenge, to give no quarter. No body of troops has the right to declare that it will not give, and therefore will not expect, quarter.[20]

Such chivalric principles, now regarded as the customary law of nations, clearly appear in the 1899 and 1907 Hague Convention (No. IV) on Laws and Customs of War. The Hague Convention prohibits killing or wounding an enemy *hors de combat* who, having laid down his arms, has surrendered, declaring that no quarter will be given, employing poison or poisoned weapons and arms calculated to cause unnecessary suffering.[21] The Convention contains the famous Martens clause, which provides that inhabitants and belligerents remain under the protection and the rule of the principles of the law of nations until a more complete code of the laws of war is adopted. These principles stem from the usages established among civilized peoples, the laws of humanity and the dictates of the public conscience.[22] The Martens clause requirement of submission to broad residual norms, rather than the discretion of a military commander, itself reflects medieval and Renaissance ordinances of war.[23] The Geneva Conventions and Additional Protocols further reinforce this requirement.

Chivalry continues to have a major influence on contemporary humanitarian law. The authoritative manual of the U.S. Army states that the law of war "requires that belligerents refrain from employing any kind or degree of violence . . . not actually necessary for military purposes and . . . conduct hostilities with regard for the principles of humanity and chivalry."[24] The more recent Air Force manual is more explicit in explaining the impact of chivalry:

> During the Middle Ages, chivalry embraced the notion . . . that the opponent was entitled to respect and honor, and that the enemy was a brother in the fraternity of knights in arms. Modern technological and industrialized armed conflict has made war less a gentlemanly contest. Nevertheless, the principle of chivalry remains in specific prohibitions such as those against poison, dishonorable or treacherous misconduct, misuse of enemy flags, uniforms, and flags of truce. The principle of chivalry makes armed conflict less savage and more civilized for the individual combatant.[25]

Other countries also demonstrate the pervasive impact chivalry has had on modern principles of warfare. For example, a Canadian Army manual states that the core precepts of the Army's professional ethos include

> [h]onour—[defined as] being loyal to unit and faithful to comrades; granting quarter to an opponent . . . treating surrendered enemy and

non-combatants humanely and protecting them from harm; adhering to professional values . . . ; and displaying gallantry, courtesy, dignity, and chivalry in one's everyday actions and conduct.[26]

The usefulness of chivalry's simple and elementary rules is most apparent in the frequent practice of reproducing these norms on cards and distributing them to combatants. During the conflict in Vietnam, the United States distributed to every soldier a three-by-five card, entitled "The Enemy in Your Hands," which stated these rules: "You cannot and must not: mistreat your prisoner, humiliate or degrade him, take any of his personal effects which do not have significant military value, refuse him medical treatment if required and available. [Finally,] always treat your prisoner humanely."[27] In addition, the four Rules for Combatants distributed by the International Committee of the Red Cross provide an excellent summary of chivalric principles. The first requires that all civilians, particularly women, children and aged people, be respected; the second prohibits attacking persons and objects protected by the Red Cross sign, such as the wounded and the sick; the third prohibits attacking or mistreating wounded enemy combatants or enemy combatants who surrender; the fourth requires that prisoners be respected, that wounded and sick prisoners receive medical treatment and prohibits killing, torturing and mistreating prisoners.[28] The ICRC describes these rules as the "International laws for all combatants." The fact that they not only offer a useful summary of the Geneva Conventions for the Protection of Victims of War, but also encompass the principles of chivalry, demonstrates the importance of chivalry's legacy.

WAR AND PEACE

In this chapter, I will examine attitudes towards war and demonstrate the anti-war bent of many of Shakespeare's characters. War was a major theme, perhaps the most important theme, in Shakespeare's plays, especially the Histories but also his classical and mythological plays. War provided Shakespeare with a dramatic vehicle through which his characters could highlight and praise such concepts as honour, courage and patriotism. In addition, it was the ideal setting for an articulation of ethical and humanitarian attitudes towards war. Shakespeare's treatment of war cannot be understood without taking into account both the perspective on war provided by the literature of chivalry and the immediate historical context of the period when he was writing, some two centuries after Agincourt.

As Maurice Keen has demonstrated, there was a strong pacifist tradition in the early Christian church. However, the Christian doctrine of just war, espoused as early as the fourth century by Saint Augustine (354–430), eroded this anti-war bent by emphasizing the corrective virtues of just war, punishment of sin and restoration of justice and peace.[1] Thus, balanced against the pacifist tradition were a restrictive interpretation of pacifist verses in the New Testament and the Old Testament's image of a God of hosts, ordering war against the enemies of his people.[2] The need to resist pagan enemies in northern and eastern Europe, as well as Muslims in southern Italy and Spain and elsewhere along the Mediterranean, supported the Church's militancy, along with, eventually, the desire to mobilize Christian warriors for crusades to liberate the holy places in Palestine.

Just war as a fight for justice and the re-establishment of peace and serenity (*tranquillitas ordinis*), as a campaign to avenge wrongs and to recover goods wrongly captured, and as a struggle for the defence of country and religion gained the Church's support.[3] As a result, from its early condemnation of killing in war, the Church moved to promise remission of penance to Christian crusaders. Secular knighthood thus became a Christian vocation.[4] Shakespeare's Henry IV articulates this image of the knight as a soldier of Christ:

> KING HENRY: As far as to the sepulchre of Christ—
> Whose soldier now, under whose blessèd cross
> We are impressèd and engaged to fight—
> . . .
> To chase these pagans in those holy fields
> Over whose acres walked those blessèd feet
> Which fourteen hundred years ago were nailed,
> For our advantage, on the bitter cross.
>
> (*1 Henry IV*, I.i.21, 24–27)

By discouraging wars between Christians, albeit meekly, the Church and chivalry promoted the ideal of a united Christendom fighting non-Christians. Thus, Shakespeare's Salisbury, lamenting the belligerency between England and France, wishes the war would be carried

> unto a pagan shore,
> Where these two Christian armies might combine
> The blood of malice in a vein of league,
> And not to spend it so unneighbourly.
>
> (*King John*, V.ii.36–39)

The Church then introduced the regulation of war through measures such as the Peace and Truce of God, which listed the categories of persons protected from acts of war. Independently from the Church, secular chivalry also developed rules for regulating the practice of war and establishing parameters for permissible acts.[5] In this way, the secular code of chivalry thus supplemented canonistic doctine by providing for the protection of broader categories of persons and the granting of mercy and quarter to the vanquished on the battlefield. These developments qualified the Church's toleration of war by introducing the notion that the justness of a war depended not only on the existence of a just cause, but also on the conduct of the war as evidence of conscience and motivation. Thus, carnage, pillage, excessive cruelty and rape would disprove a party's claims of just war; practices including mercy, quarter and pious conduct towards the dead and wounded would strengthen such claims.[6]

War was an endemic condition in the Middle Ages, wreaking havoc on the common people, particularly the peasants, who were the victims of ravaging mercenaries, free companies, robbers and even some knights for whom, notwithstanding the rules of chivalry, plunder of the country-side was a way of life. In an era of great economic poverty and hardship, participation in war offered serious material incentives. Adventurers and mercenaries fought for profit from pillage and ransom.

For the warring class, the knights, war was both noble and ennobling, despite its hardships and horrors. The support of the Church, the promise of salvation for knightly deeds in defence of the Church, the soothing doctrine of chivalry with its emphasis on the idea of service to the community and the duty to defend the weak and to right any wrongs combined with the quest for recognition, fame and honour to produce a society that both promoted war and depended on its continuation for its economic well-being and social status. Maurice Keen speaks of the social mystique attaching to arms, the ceremonial knightings before battles, the ennoblement of common men who demonstrated particular courage, and the attraction of "the tinsel glint of chivalry."[7] For those who aspired to enhance their social status through elevation to knighthood, fighting wars provided the primary vehicle for the achievement of their goal.

Profit was also a motive for knights and nobility to go to war. Princes had the additional lure of the prospects of recovering lost territories, acquiring additional ones, satisfying just claims and gaining glory. No less, resort to foreign wars frequently served to divert attention from internal troubles.

This glamorization of war, this glorification of knightly virtue, impressive feats of arms and honour found ample expression in poetry and literature. Jean de Bueil's biographical novel, Le Jouvencel (ca. 1465), rhapsodizes the comradeship, courage and honour of war:

It is a joyous thing, is war. . . . You love your comrade so in war. When you see that your quarrel is just and your blood is fighting well, tears come to your eyes. A great sweet feeling of loyalty and of pity fills your heart on seeing your friend so valiantly exposing his body to execute and accomplish the command of our creator. And then you prepare to go and die or live with him, and for love not to abandon him. And out of that, there arises such a delectation, that he who has not tasted it is not fit to say what a delight it is.[8]

In these circumstances, it is not surprising that medieval authors of manuals of chivalry, and such chroniclers of chivalry as the French Jean Froissart, writing for the chivalric class, articulated and rationalized a rather permissive doctrine regulating recourse to war. In many respects, they were apologists for war, masking or minimizing war's horrors, brutality, bloodiness, greed and economic motivations, the quest for lands and titles, and the hypocrisy behind the perceived glamour of chivalric sword. Justifying war served the interests of the knightly class and the nobility for whom war was both a way of life and the *raison d'être*, an opportunity to gain glory on the battlefield and to acquire wealth through pillage and ransom.

A primary example of this approach to war is Giovanni da Legnano's famous treatise written in the second part of the fourteenth century, *Tractatus de bello, de represaliis et de duello*.[9] Relying heavily on the Old Testament and Saint Augustine, Giovanni da Legnano argued that wars came from divine law, with "positive allowance" from God.[10] According to Giovanni, since the "end of war . . . is the peace and tranquillity of the world [, war] proceeded originally and positively from God."[11] This reasoning therefore justified both a declaration of lawful war and the war itself because they would lead to such peace and tranquillity. In addition, the authority to punish evil persons stemmed from God, and lawful war sought to punish evil and rebellious persons and to bring the vanquished to piety and justice. In this way, God not only permitted, but actually ordered Joshua to fight his enemies. Implicit in this premise is that the sinners, whom the war is designed to punish, will be vanquished. For Giovanni, these norms justifying and allowing war belonged not only to divine law, but also to natural law, civil law and canon law. Finally, the regulatory power of the law of nations also provided a source for such principles.[12] The just war doctrine allowed the extension of the knight's sword-arm of justice to relationship between peoples.[13]

In his authoritative treatise *The Tree of Battles* (ca. 1387), Honoré Bouvet wrote that a prince not only had a right to resort to war to defend subjects from pillage and murder, but a duty as well.[14] He regarded war as "not an evil thing, but [as] good and virtuous," because it sought to "set wrong right."[15] The aim of war was thus to "to wrest peace, tranquility and reasonableness, from him who refuses to acknowledge his wrongdoing."[16] Like Giovanni, Bouvet argued that war derived from divine law and from God because, as in the case of the biblical Joshua, God not only permitted war, but "ordained it."[17] It was also authorized by the law of nations, including canon law and civil law. Shakespeare's King John thus claims to be "God's wrathful agent" (*King John*, II. i. 87) in his war with France.

However, Bouvet could not remain entirely oblivious to concerns about the innocent victims of war. He maintained, nevertheless, that the evil things that happen in war are caused not by war, but by abuse, as in the case of a soldier raping a woman or setting fire to a church: "if in war many evil things are done, they never come from the nature of war, but from false usage."[18] The unstated premise was thus that such abuses were, in principle, avoidable.

Admitting that the innocent suffer with the guilty, Honoré Bouvet claimed that war should therefore be compared to a medicine that, while curing the disease, has some adverse effects as well. A gardener who pulls weeds inevitably plucks some good plants as well; for the fault of one man, many can be destroyed in war.

In her treatise *The Book of Fayttes of Armes and of Chyvalrye* (ca. 1408–09), Christine de Pisan followed suit: "As touchyng the harmes & euyllis that ben doon aboue the right & droyt of warre . . . that cometh nothyng of the right of warre but by euylnes of the peple . . ."[19] Thus, as Maurice Keen suggests, any "incidental . . . miscarriages of justice could be written off against the ultimate achievement of the divine purpose"[20] of war.

These chivalric authors resonate with Saint Thomas Aquinas (1225–74), who, citing Saint Augustine, regards just war as a means of meting out deserved punishment, making amends, restoring what has been seized unjustly, and achieving peace. Admitting that those who resort to arms sinfully are not necessarily defeated, Aquinas falls back on the promise of damnation: "[T]hey will always 'die by the sword' since they will be punished eternally for their sinful use of it."[21]

The Archbishop of York, a leader of the rebellion in *2 Henry IV*, voices the chivalric theme that war serves as a medicine or blood-letting, a corrective designed to cure a disease, that is, to establish a true peace:

> [W]e are all diseased,
> And with our surfeiting and wanton hours
> Have brought ourselves into a burning fever,
> And we must bleed for it.
> . . .
> I take not on me here as a physician,
> Nor do I as an enemy to peace
> Troop in the throngs of military men;
> But rather show a while like fearful war
> To diet rank minds, sick of happiness,
> And purge th' obstructions which begin to stop
> Our very veins of life.

> (*2 Henry IV*, IV.i.54–66)

The Archbishop's aim is

> Not to break peace, or any branch of it,
> But to establish here a peace indeed,
> Concurring both in name and quality.

> (*2 Henry IV*, IV.i.85–87)

The passage shows Shakespeare's familiarity with concepts of chivalry, even though York is using one of them to justify an act of rebellion, which in itself runs against chivalry.

But although Shakespeare's York (2 *Henry VI*) articulates the war-as-medicine idea, a few years later, in *Henry V*, Shakespeare parts company from the chivalric writers, and aligns himself with the pacifist scepticism about war and its motivations articulated by the humanistic tradition of Desiderius Erasmus (ca. 1466–1536) and Thomas More (1477–1535). Erasmus argued that leaders should consider the costs of a war in advance. Full accounting would show that everyone suffers ruin, physical wretchedness and abuse, the choice between cruel slaughter and being slaughtered, and that war consists of manslaughter and robbery. Humanist social criticism emphasized that offensive war was almost always unjust and that war between Christians was inherently unjust. It urged resort to alternatives to war, including exhaustion of other means and arbitration.[22]

In *Henry V*, the loss of innocent lives in war is not incidental; rather, it is inherent in the nature of war that it is bloody and evil. Moreover, this inevitability of the shedding of innocent blood is unrelated to the justness of war, but follows from the reality of war, whether it is just or unjust. Henry V's admonition to Canterbury to give him fair and objective advice regarding the justness of his war against France and, especially, whether the Salic law disqualifying women and the female line from succession to the Crown of France bars his claim, is a useful example:

> For God doth know how many now in health
> Shall drop their blood in approbation
>
> . . .
>
> *For never two such kingdoms did contend*
> *Without much fall of blood*, whose guiltless drops
> Are every one a woe, a sore complaint
> 'Gainst him whose wrongs gives edge unto the swords
> That makes such waste in brief mortality.
>
> (*Henry V*, I.ii.18–28) (emphasis added)

Viewed from another perspective, Henry is using the Archbishop to absolve himself from the bloodshed he knows will occur in the war he fully intends to wage, while the Archbishop is using Henry to forestall measures against the church. Motivations for and justifications of war are made even more suspect in *Troilus and Cressida*, where war is not a corrective to the ills of peace, but is simply a disease, an instrument of senseless, purposeless butchery, and where the justness of the war is directly challenged.

Henry VI, understood that even in a rebellion, when the king's cause is presumptively just, war must result in casualties and cause the innocent to suffer. Consequently, to avoid the loss of innocent lives, he opts for negotiations with the rebel Jack Cade:

> I'll send some holy bishop to entreat,
> For God forbid so many simple souls

Should perish by the sword. And I myself,
Rather than bloody war shall cut them short,
Will parley with Jack Cade their general.

(*2 Henry VI*, IV.iv.8–12)

If Shakespeare's characters articulate a message which is essentially anti-war, this can best be understood in the context of the post-chivalric Elizabethan era. Shakespeare was fully aware of the decline of chivalry in his lifetime. If references to war in the canon as an institution are frequently negative, if allusions to the normative and positive values of chivalry, such as the duty to give quarter, mercy, honour and humane treatment of prisoners and women, are so idealized, perhaps Shakespeare wanted to discourage war that, without the veneer of chivalric rules, appeared to be entirely barbaric. I shall return to Shakespeare's pacifism in the conclusions of this chapter.

Even with such rules, however, loss of life and tremendous suffering are inherent in war. Shakespeare's characters challenge war through a combination of legal and literary means. His protagonists insist on the exhaustion of diplomatic and peaceful remedies. In emphasizing this requirement, Shakespeare's Henry V follows the chroniclers and thus reflects an actual medieval practice. Shakespeare's characters articulate the requirement of a just cause for war and show the self-serving, hypocritical and opportunistic arguments that often drive "just war" justifications. They deride the claim that war is necessary for the sake of honour or to save face. They bring into relief the unmitigated horrors of war. Finally, they demonstrate the inescapable futility of war.

Advising the Prince on the Justness of the War

The just cause requirement first obligated a prince to ascertain honestly whether his cause was just. The absence of a just cause should *ab initio* end any thoughts of recourse to war. However, the determination whether a cause was just or not was complex, so that a prince would have great difficulty assessing the legal aspects of, for example, a complicated dynastic dispute. Obviously, princes were not thoroughly schooled in the law of nations and needed expert advice. Franciscus de Vitoria wrote that since "a king is not by himself capable of examining . . . the causes of a war," he might make a mistake that would bring "ruin to multitudes."[23] The prince therefore had a duty to consult "the good and wise and those who speak with freedom and without anger or bitterness or greed" about the justice and causes of the war.[24]

Shakespeare's Henry V pays due heed to this principle, deferring to the moral, religious and even legal and historical authority of the Archbishop of Canterbury, the senior English ecclesiastic, for assurance that the English cause is just. At the same time, Shakespeare—following Holinshed—actually presents the Archbishop's arguments as self-serving, cynical and opportunistic.

When in 1369 Charles V of France reopened hostilities against Edward III of England, he did so only after consultations with French and foreign experts on canon and civil laws confirmed the justness of his cause.[25] Furthermore, medieval princes understood the importance of convincing public opinion of the legitimacy of their wars. "[C]onstant attention was paid, if not to the *ideology*, then at least to the *phraseology* of *justum bellum*."[26] Therefore, Henry V not only consulted legal and spiritual advisors, but devoted considerable attention to preparing and disseminating legal briefs for his war against Charles VI.[27]

Medieval and Renaissance writers on chivalry and the law of nations emphasized the importance of obtaining independent and objective advice on the justness of war. Christine de Pisan urged that such advisers should be unbiased and impartial[28] and Vitoria stressed the advisers' duty to tell the prince honestly whether his cause was just.[29] However, whether it was realistic to expect counselors to give the all-powerful leader advice that would displease him was another question entirely. In his *Utopia*, More discussed the dilemma of the humanist who is solicited by his prince to become a court adviser. He is tempted to enter the prince's service, explaining his action by a higher duty to the common cause. But More's imaginary Raphael Hythlodaeus voices utter pessimism concerning the prospect that a court expert will be able to maintain his independence. Interested in status and promotion, an adviser is bound to tell the ruler what he wants to hear. Tampering with the truth is the reality of service to the prince.[30]

Shakespeare addresses this issue primarily in the context of the role and the responsibility of courtiers, offering little to reassure his audience.[31] Most medieval courtiers were wary of offending or embarrassing the king, who, anointed by God, must not be contradicted or challenged. However, Shakespeare's York pleads with Richard II not to confiscate Hereford's rights, which would not only violate the law on which the legitimacy of Richard's title depends, but would also bring untold dangers to Richard:

> Take Hereford's rights away, and take from Time
> His charters and his customary rights:
> Let not tomorrow then ensue today;
> Be not thyself, for how art thou a king
> But by fair sequence and succession?
> Now afore God—God forbid I say true!—
> If you do wrongfully seize Hereford's rights,
> Call in the letters patents that he hath
> By his attorneys general to sue
> His livery, and deny his offered homage,
> You pluck a thousand dangers on your head. . . .

> (*Richard II*, II.i.196–206)

This unsolicited advice proves useless as Richard brazenly states his disregard:

> Think what you will, we seize into our hands
> His plate, his goods, his money, and his lands.

> (*Richard II*, II.i.210–11)

Similarly, when the Bishop of Carlisle warns the future Henry IV against usurpation, predicting that tumultous wars will result from the terrible wrong, indeed treason, of subjects judging King Richard II, especially *in absentia* (*Richard II*, IV.i.105–40), he is arrested for his efforts on charges of capital treason (*Richard II*, IV.i.141–42). In another example, Buckingham's vaccilation about assisting Richard III in the murder of the two princes, the sons of Edward IV, causes Richard III to lose confidence in him and threaten his life (*Richard III*, IV.ii). Still another king, Henry VIII, rebukes his council for taking an independent position against Cranmer, the Archbishop of Canterbury (*Henry VIII*, V.ii). Finally, in *King John*, Hubert does not even try to dissuade King John from his criminal designs against Arthur. John later blames Hubert, hypocritically, for neglecting the courtier's duty to give honest advice and being guided solely by his desire to please his king (*King John*, IV.ii.204–70).

The message that emerges from each of these episodes is one that certainly would not encourage a royal adviser to counsel his prince against starting a war he is already inclined to fight. Nonetheless, the medieval system of government recognized the need for both internal and external procedures before the leader could resort to war. Christine de Pisan wrote that a prince could only take up arms if he had consulted with "Parliament," as anglicized in William Caxton's translation, and obtained its consent.[32] As early as the fourteenth century, the principle of prior consultation with the lords and the commons about a war was recognized in England and steadily expanded thereafter.[33]

Two episodes in Shakespeare directly address this issue of internal consultations about the justification for recourse to or continuation of war. The first episode, the exchange between Henry V and the Archbishop of Canterbury, focuses on ensuring recourse to a just war. Aware of the inevitable loss of blood in a major war, Henry demands an honest opinion from his adviser (*Henry V*, I.ii.9–20). Canterbury's response is categorical, stating that Henry's cause is unquestionably just (*Henry V*, I.ii.33–95). Not satisifed, Henry insists, asking, "May I with right and conscience make this claim?" and Canterbury gives the most solemn guarantee an ecclesiastic can give, invoking "the sin upon my head" (*Henry V*, I.ii.96–97). Canterbury concludes by alluding to the symbols of war, "blood and sword and fire" (*Henry V*, I.ii.131), that will serve to win Henry's right. Henry also consults with and receives enthusiastic support for the war from secular lords, such as Exeter and Westmorland, the latter referring also to the element of power—"[Y]our grace has cause; and means and might"(*Henry V*, I.ii.125). Compare York's arguments in *2 Henry IV*, I.iii.1.

The debate is over, the procedures have been scrupulously followed with perfect results, and Henry V is satisfied. But does Shakespeare satisfy his audience fully? We already know that Henry IV's lesson to his son was "to busy giddy minds / With foreign quarrels, that action hence borne out / May waste the memory of the former days," (*2 Henry IV*, IV.iii.342–44), that is, so that the father's usurpation of Richard II's Crown would be forgotten. In contrast to Paul Jorgensen, I believe that this statement was intended to stigmatize the king's motivation.[34]. Furthermore, if this invocation of *realpolitik* were not enough to cast doubt on the proceedings, Shakespeare clearly taints Canterbury's advice with an allusion to his ulterior motives, which he cynically reveals to the Bishop of Ely. The Archbishop recognizes that the Church's financial support for the war, combined with the persuasive articulation of a just cause for the war, could save the Church from being deprived of a substantial part of its possessions (*Henry V*, I. i. 70–73, 76–90).

In a way, both Canterbury and Henry use each other. Canterbury offers financial incentives and somewhat strained legal interpretations for a war Henry actually seeks—in order to fight a bill that would strip the church from a considerable portion of its temporal possessions. Henry uses the Archbishop to absolve himself of responsibility for the bloodshed he knows will occur. The fact that both Canterbury and Henry have their own agendas introduces a certain doubt in the procedures designed to validate recourse to war. Perhaps these texts indicate that legal authority for recourse to war was politically necessary, though ethically it was less important in the politics of war.

The second episode, from *Troilus and Cressida*, concerns discussions in the Trojan council after the Achaian peace proposal premised on the return of Helen and waiver of war reparations. Hector supports the proposal and takes an anti-war stand, perhaps encouraged by King Priam's apparent hesitations. Shakespeare here offers a remarkable discussion of the requirement that the war have a just cause. Hector, a Trojan, asserts that the Trojans are fighting an unjust war, insisting that Helen "is not worth what she doth cost the holding" (*Troilus and Cressida*, II.ii.50–51) and that she does not belong to the Trojans (*Troilus and Cressida*, II.ii.21). Therefore, the moral laws of nature and of nations require that Helen be returned (*Troilus and Cressida*, II.ii.172–87). No one challenges Hector's view that the war is not just. Nonetheless, other considerations trump, and despite strong reservations, Hector responds to his comrades' appeals to honour and solidarity and joins the advocates of war.

In each of these two episodes, Shakespeare demonstrates the vulnerability of the normative principle of just war. He first sets out the principle, even offering justifications for adherence to the rule. However, he then describes the subordination of the norm to more practical, but less moral, concerns, ultimately producing recourse to war without a clearly and honestly articulated just cause.

Exhausting Peaceful Remedies

In Shakespeare, as in the legal doctrine of the Middle Ages and the Renaissance, even the existence of a just cause would not warrant recourse to war unless peaceful remedies were exhausted through negotiations, defiances and ultimatums. In the Middle Ages, the requirement that a war be publicly declared was commonly met by issuing letters of defiance, which served much the same function as declarations of war, although different in form.[35] Pisan warned against resort to war before a prince had offered his adversary a chance to remedy the wrongs which he allegedly committed.[36] Francisco Suárez argued that in order to wage a legitimate war, one had to be incapable of remedying the wrong suffered in any other way; since killing was morally wrong, the king must truly have no choice.[37] It is thus essential not only that the cause be just and sufficient, but that the grave injustice could not be otherwise resolved.[38] Exhaustion of peaceful remedies was therefore both a moral-religious imperative and a legal requirement. In addition, it served important public relations and propaganda considerations.

In the Renaissance period, the law of nations required that an ultimatum be issued and war declared. Ideally, the claim should be stated, its basis in the law of nations or the law of nature invoked, and the consequences of non-compliance—recourse to war—articulated. When Shakespeare's King John rejects King Philip's claims on behalf of Arthur, the French Ambassador Châtillon warns that this refusal will trigger a "fierce and bloody war, / To enforce these rights so forcibly withheld" (*King John*, I.i.17–18). Upon John's acceptance of the French challenge, "[H]ere have we war for war, and blood for blood, / Controlment for controlment: so answer France," the Ambassador issues a formal defiance (a declaration of war with its statement of claim and ultimatum): "Then take my king's defiance from my mouth" (*King John*, I.i.19–21).[39]

Although King Philip and his ally, the Duke of Austria, are anxious to start hostilities to enforce Arthur's rights over Angers, failure to await Châtillon's return would violate the principle of exhaustion of peaceful remedies and incur heavy spiritual responsibility. Despite her role as the driving force for war, Arthur's mother, Constance, therefore insists on the cardinal importance of exhaustion of remedies:

> Stay for an answer to your embassy,
> Lest unadvised you stain your swords with blood.
> My lord Châtillon may from England bring
> That right in peace which here we urge in war,
> And then we shall repent each drop of blood
> That hot rash haste so indirectly shed.

> (*King John*, II.i.44–49)

The historical Henry V claimed to hold France in full sovereignty through inheritance. He engaged in long and substantive negotiations with France to this end, but it is difficult to believe that he did so in good faith. These negotiations were both preceded and accompanied by legal propaganda, designed to demonstrate both the French wrongs and Henry's reasons for raising his standards. In Shakespeare, Henry V's declaration of war, delivered at the court of Charles VI through Exeter's embassy, follows both Hall's chronicle[40] and the classical requirements of the law of nations. It also includes an ultimatum, threat of "Bloody Constraint" (*Henry V*, II.iv.97) and a catalogue of some of the horrors of war the French will encounter if they resist (*Henry V*, II.iv.76–110).

Going beyond the legal doctrine of his time, Shakespeare suggests that resort to a peaceful settlement of disputes is appropriate even in civil wars. Bolingbroke (through Northumberland) thus offers Richard II an honourable peaceful resolution:

> Upon his knees doth kiss King Richard's hand,
> And sends allegiance and true faith of heart
> To his most royal person, hither come
> Even at his feet to lay my arms and power,
> Provided that my banishment repealed
> And lands restored again be freely granted.
> If not, I'll use the advantage of my power,
> And lay the summer's dust with showers of blood
> Rained from the wounds of slaughtered Englishmen[.]

> (*Richard II*, III.iii.34–43)

Just War/Unjust War

The theme of just war dominates the literature of chivalry and the law of nations of both the Middle Ages and the Renaissance. This literature identifies causes justifying resort to war, such as remedying a grave offence or recapturing lands wrongfully deprived. A just cause for resorting to war was essential for both secular-legal and spiritual-moral reasons. Secular considerations included the validity of the title that a prince and his troops would acquire over the spoils of war, their enjoyment of combatant privileges, their protection by the laws of war and their entitlement to war reparations. In a just war, the unjust belligerent had the duty "not only to make restitution [of whatever it seized], but also to make good the expenses of the war to the other side, and also all damages."[41] In Chapter 4, I will discuss Shakespeare's references to war damages.

Establishing the validity of his claim was therefore vital to a prince's ability to raise troops and sustain their morale. Vitoria wrote that "[i]f a subject is convinced of the injustice of a war, he ought not to serve in it, even on the command of his prince."[42] Although a victorious prince faced few difficulties in maintaining that his war was just as a matter of *realpolitik*, this requirement could have presented a real difficulty for a knight whose right to ransom or to the spoils of war was contested before a court of chivalry, which would apply the international *jus armorum*. In the case of an unjust war, the other side could demand reparations. It was therefore important to have not only a just cause, but one that was seen to be just, and one that the knights needed to fight the war would accept as just. Following the appropriate protocol for trying to avoid war was also vital to the claim of a just war. Thus, although Exeter's embassy to Charles VI (*Henry V*, II.iv) and Châtillon's embassy to King John (*King John*, I.i) proved useless, the requirement of the exhaustion of local remedies was part of the just war doctrine and could, where successful, have some war-reducing effects. If in fact recruiting for an unjust war was more difficult, the perception that a cause was unjust might have had a deterrent effect on the prospective aggressor.

In *Henry V*, Shakespeare's most patriotic and nationalistic play, the justness of the English cause is presented as accepted wisdom, a seemingly simplistic, almost unquestioning orthodoxy. Katharine Eisaman Maus emphasized that Shakespeare's patriotic play served the cause of Essex's mobilization for the campaign against Ireland. But even in this play, the war excitement is balanced by the Chorus's allusion to the loss of France during the infancy of Henry VI, and thus to the ultimate futility of this bloody war (*Henry V*, Epilogue 10),[43] and by the opportunistic character of the Archbishop's advice. In other plays, and even in *Henry V*, Shakespeare points to a number of difficulties and doubts, ultimately leaving the reader unlikely to accept war as a desirable or even acceptable solution. With the exception of the right to war reparations, where he overlaps legal commentators, Shakespeare often emphasizes spiritual accountability rather than secular considerations.

Two plays in particular, *Henry V* and *Troilus and Cressida*, bring the right to reparations into relief. With considerable sophistication, despite its patriotic one-sidedness, *Henry V* depicts a demand for war reparations by the party that is not supposed to have a just cause but expects to win nonetheless.

> MONTJOY Bid him therefore consider of his ransom, which must proportion the losses we have borne, the subjects we have lost, the disgrace we have digested—which in weight to re-answer, his pettiness would bow under. For our losses, his exchequer is too poor; for th' effusion of our blood, the muster of his kingdom too faint a number; and for our disgrace, his own person kneeling at our feet but a weak and worthless satisfaction.
>
> (*Henry V*, III.vi.124–32)

Shakespeare seems to suggest, at the very least, that France may also have had a just cause. However, he shows that the party that appears to be stronger will thus present more far-reaching claims. In *Troilus and Cressida*, the Greeks, as the aggrieved party, would be willing to waive their legitimate right to war reparations if the Trojans would return Helen (*Troilus and Cressida*, II.ii.1–7).

Shakespeare's work suggests that compliance with the just war requirement involves important incentives. On the religious and spiritual plane, it protects the king from sin and damnation for recourse to an unjust war that causes the loss of innocent lives (*Henry V*, IV.iii). Shakespeare's plays contain many references to this essentially religious concept. Moreover, there are positive incentives, such as enhancing the prospect of victory in war, that supplement the promised immunity from eternal damnation. Shakespeare's heroes invoke this concept because they believe in the justness of their cause, and it soon becomes every leader's self-serving, *pro se* argument.

Shakespeare's Henry IV proclaims, in dispatching his officers to take command of the troops, "God befriend us as our cause is just" (*1 Henry IV*, V.i.120). After eliminating the Southampton conspiracy, Henry V encourages his lords:

"Now lords for France, the enterprise whereof
Shall be to you, as us, like glorious.
We doubt not of a fair and lucky war."

(*Henry V*, II.ii.179–81)

Being just ("fair"), Henry's war must necessarily be victorious ("lucky"). In a similar vein, the Duke of Austria expresses confidence in the outcome of the war in *King John*: "The peace of heaven is theirs that lift their swords / In such a just and charitable war" (*King John*, II.i.35–36). Invoking the divine support for his cause, Richard II assumes that heaven supports the lawful king:

"God for his Richard hath in heavenly pay
A glorious angel. Then if angels fight,
Weak men must fall; for heaven still guards the right."

(*Richard II*, III.ii.56–58)

Finally, Henry of Richmond's oration to his troops before the decisive battle against Richard III is explicit about the link between a just cause and support from God:

Yet remember this:
God and our good cause fight upon our side.
The prayers of holy saints and wrongèd souls,
Like high-reared bulwarks, stand before our forces.
Richard except, those whom we fight against
Had rather have us win than him they follow.
For what is he they follow? Truly, friends,
A bloody tyrant and a homicide;

. . .
One that hath ever been God's enemy.
Then if you fight against God's enemy,
God will, in justice, ward you as his soldiers.

(*Richard III*, V.v.193–200, 206–08)[44]

Richard III's "might is right" oration to his troops before the same battle provides an interesting contrast.

Go, gentlemen, each man unto his charge.
Let not our babbling dreams affright our souls.
Conscience is but a word that cowards use,
Devised at first to keep the strong in awe.
Our strong arms be our conscience; swords, our law.
March on, join bravely! Let us to 't, pell mell—
If not to heaven, then hand in hand to hell.

(*Richard III*, V.vi.37–43)

Whether Shakespeare actually believed that fighting a just war increased the probability of victory is unclear. He did know that each party would claim to have God and justice on its side and that some of those who invoke God and justice would lose, like Richard II.

This idea "that justice was infallibly on the side of the victor,"[45] that the just will triumph, was part of the myth of chivalry on which Shakespeare probably drew. Bouvet, for example, wrote that because just war was designed to purge the earth from sin and sinners, those who die fighting in such a war "will be saved in Paradise."[46] Notwithstanding this myth, invoking the increased prospect of victory for the just also served the moral purpose of discouraging unjust or aggressive wars.

However, although just war doctrine had an important proscriptive function, so that a war could not, or at least should not, have been resorted to without at least a colourable claim of justness, it proved largely useless as an effective vehicle for the discouragement of wars. A victorious prince faced few difficulties in maintaining that his cause was just, regardless of how hypocritical and self-serving the claim. In the absence of any system of independent arbitration or fact-finding, and because many causes justified resort to war in medieval and Renaissance legal doctrines with no clearly established hierarchy among them, the requirement of a just cause did not constitute a significant restraint on waging war. As a result, the distinction between just and unjust wars was often merely sophistry.

Under medieval legal theory, which was fairly uniform until the fourteenth and fifteenth centuries, only one party could have a just cause, as Balthazar Ayala, a contemporary of Shakespeare, maintained. Since the Romans would never begin a war except with just cause, he argued, their enemies could not have a just cause, because "the same cause of war cannot be just both for this side and that."[47] Although in theory, the justness of war depended on both a just cause and a declaration of war by a sovereign authority, in practice just war and public war—one declared by the sovereign authority—began to mean the same thing.[48] Since both belligerents could claim, as they usually did, that their war was just, *bellum nostrum justum*, the whole moral foundation of the just war doctrine lost its credibility, as reflected in Abraham Lincoln's statement: "[I]n great contests each party claims to act in accordance with the will of God. Both *may* be, and one must be *wrong*."[49] Lincoln, however, does not quite capture the Renaissance legal perception that in practice a war could be just for both sides.

Unlike Lincoln, Alberico Gentili, a contemporary of Shakespeare, could conceive of just cause on both sides. He starts from Saint Augustine's proposition that an adversary's injustice makes a war just, and, therefore, the injustice of one party furnishes the other party with a just cause, according to which it could wage just wars.[50] However, he promptly dissents, stating, "[B]ut if it is doubtful on which side justice is, and if each side aims at justice, neither can be called unjust."[51] Gentili demonstrated the complexity of just war claims, which, in practice, were not reducible to the assertion that one side must be in the wrong. He envisaged situations in which both sides might properly resort to war, and the war might, in effect, be treated as just on both sides. Since the whole structure of the medieval doctrine allowing war rested on the artificial claim that only one party could be just, questioning that premise by suggesting that the other party could also be just, could, but probably did not, serve to discourage war. Gentili notes that those who have a better cause are, in fact, frequently defeated.[52]

Shakespeare was probably not aware of these legal niceties, since there is no evidence that he knew the works of various contemporary writers on the law of nations. He was quite familiar, nonetheless, with Hall and Holinshed, whose chronicles often reflected legal discussion and analysis. As a result, he well understood the cynical and self-serving invocation of the just war excuse for the recourse to war. Implying that he doubted the value and vitality of just war doctrine, his plays reveal the emptiness of these invocations, point to the possibility that both parties may have "just war" pretensions, and suggest that wars were launched for less than acceptable reasons. By emphasizing these self-serving invocations of just cause and suggesting that both parties could be just or both unjust, Shakespeare's plays discredit the theories justifying recourse to war.

Troilus frames the issue perfectly, albeit in a different context: "O virtuous fight, / When right with right wars who shall be most right" (*Troilus and Cressida*, III.ii. 167–68). As another example of conflicting claims of just cause in a civil war, Warwick's exchange with Prince Edward is notable. The former, a supporter of York, claims that "York in justice puts his armour on," causing the latter, the future King Edward, to retort, sarcastically, "If that be right which Warwick says is right, / There is no wrong, but everything is right" (3 *Henry VI*, II.ii.130–32).

Shakespeare is also aware of the distinction between international and national wars, exemplified when Richard III says, "March on, march on, since we are up in arms, / If not to fight with foreign enemies, / Yet to beat down these rebels here at home." (*Richard III*, IV.iv.459–61).[53] He usually confines the term "enemy" to external enemies, and the term "rebels" or "traitors" to English subjects. Since treason could only be committed by a person owing allegiance to the sovereign, traitors were thus persons who breached their oath. Shakespeare's Lady Macduff defines a traitor with admirable succinctness as "one that swears and lies" and who, therefore, "must be hanged" (*Macbeth*, IV.ii.48–51). Knowingly or not, Shakespeare's distinction between foreign enemies and domestic rebels or traitors corresponded to that already made in the common law. He thus moved towards modern humanitarian law, with its distinction between international and internal wars and requirements of more humane treatment for those involved in the former.

Shakespeare knows that rebels are treated as traitors and therefore do not benefit from the protection of chivalric principles. Nevertheless, he introduces at least some elements of the just war doctrine into civil wars and shows that in such wars, as in international wars, the two parties may have competing claims of justice. For example, in offering terms to the rebel party on behalf of Henry IV, Westmoreland apparently finds it useful to invoke the just cause of the royal party, emphasizing the nobility's support of that cause:

> Our battle is more full of names than yours,
> Our men more perfect in the use of arms,
> Our armour all as strong, our cause the best.

> (2 *Henry IV*, IV.i.152–54)

The Archbishop of York, representing the rebel party, also claims to fight in support of a just cause:

> Then take, my lord of Westmoreland, this schedule
> For this contains our general grievances.
> Each several article herein redressed,
> All members of our cause, both here and hence,
> That are ensinewed to this action
> Acquitted by a true substantial form. . . .

> (2 *Henry IV*, IV.i.166–71)

In response, Prince John promises to redress the rebels' grievances and so requests that they discharge their armies. Once the rebel army disperses, its leaders are arrested for treason, perhaps reflecting the fact that promises made to rebels do not equal those made to enemies in international wars, and that the discussion of just cause in internal wars is only a matter of form. York's protestation that the arrests were in breach of good faith meets with the legalistic but not unreasonable response that the rebels also acted illegally.

When King John rejects Philip of France's ultimatum to cede his possessions and titles to Arthur, the son of Geoffrey, who, as the older brother of John, had what appeared to be a better title to succeed their brother, Richard the Lion-Hearted, he unhesitatingly invokes his "strong possession and . . . right for us" (*King John*, I.i.39). However, his own mother, Queen Eleanor, sarcastically voices her doubts about John's entitlement, even though she is a militant supporter of his war:

> Your strong possession much more than your right,
> Or else it must go wrong with you and me:
> So much my conscience whispers in your ear,
> Which none but heaven and you and I shall hear.

> (*King John*, I.i.40–43)

The anti-war message, emphasized in sarcasm and ridicule against both parties to the conflict, is at its strongest at the walls of Angers, a city owing and recognizing allegiance to the King of England. John and Philip and their troops confront each other at Angers. The ritual of claims alleging the justness of the war is followed, with both parties even using some of the same language.

> KING JOHN: Peace be to France, if France in peace permit
>   Our just and lineal entrance to our own.
>   If not, bleed France, and peace ascend to heaven,
>   Whiles we, God's wrathful agent, do correct
>   Their proud contempt that beats his peace to heaven.

> KING PHILIP: Peace be to England, if that war return
>   From France to England, there to live in peace.
>   England we love, and for that England's sake
>   With burden of our armour here we sweat.
>   This toil of ours should be a work of thine;
>   But thou from loving England art so far
>   That thou hast underwrought his lawful king,
>   Cut off the sequence of posterity,
>   Outfacèd infant state, and done a rape
>   Upon the maiden virtue of the crown.

> (*King John*, II.i.84–98)

John then contests Philip's standing to challenge his rights:

KING JOHN: From whom hast thou this great commission, France,
  To draw my answer from thy articles?

KING PHILIP: From that supernal judge that stirs good thoughts
  In any breast of strong authority
  To look into the blots and stains of right.
  That judge hath made me guardian to this boy,
  Under whose warrant I impeach thy wrong,
  And by whose help I mean to chastise it.

KING JOHN: Alack, thou dost usurp authority.

(*King John*, II.i.110–18)

The Anglo-French negotiations having thus reached a deadlock, John and Philip, and then their heralds, try to persuade Angers to surrender, each party threatening destruction if the city refuses.

(*Trumpet sounds. Enter a Citizen upon the walls*)

CITIZEN: Who is it that hath warned us to the walls?

KING PHILIP: 'Tis France for England.

KING JOHN: England for itself.
  You men of Angers and my loving subjects—

KING PHILIP: You loving men of Angers, Arthur's subjects,
  Our trumpet called you to this gentle parle—

KING JOHN: For our advantage; therefore hear us first.

(*King John*, II.i.201–06)

Angers only wants to be left in peace; it admits its allegiance to the King of England and is quite willing to open the city's gates to him. First, however, it seeks assurance regarding who has the right to be considered the King of England.

CITIZEN: In brief, we are the King of England's subjects.
  For him and in his right we hold this town.

KING JOHN: Acknowledge then the King, and let me in.

CITIZEN: That can we not; but he that proves the king,
  To him will we prove loyal; till that time
  Have we rammed up our gates against the world.

KING JOHN: Doth not the crown of England prove the king?
  And if not that, I bring you witnesses:

Twice fifteen thousand hearts of England's breed—

. . .

To verify our title with their lives.

(King John, II.i.267–77)

John's cynical acknowledgement that his title will be proved through physical force belies his prior arguments about just cause. On the other hand, the fact that thirty thousand soldiers loyal to England take part in John's campaign may serve as an argument for some populist legitimacy.

After the heralds present the ultimatums, Angers proposes that the besiegers first fight it out with each other, and then it will cede to the stronger. Until then, the city leaders simply explain that they will accept "the King of England, when we know the King" (King John, II.i.363). The sarcastic Philip the Bastard, Lady Falconbridge's illegitimate son by King Richard I, who is subsequently knighted as Sir Richard Plantagenet, proposes that France and England first join forces to destroy the impudent Angers, and then, after its destruction, defy each other and determine through war who shall be the king of Angers.

Both Kings accept this farcical proposal, and they arrange that John's artillery will attack from the west, the Duke of Austria's from the north, and Philip's from the south. Only the Bastard realizes that "From north to south / Austria and France [will] shoot in each other's mouth" (King John, II.i.414–15). At the last moment, the leaders of Angers cleverly propose that John's niece, Blanche, marry the Dauphin. France and England will be in peace and Angers will open its gates to England. Eleanor elucidates the advantages of this union to her son King John:

"For, by this knot, thou shalt so surely tie
Thy now unsured assurance to the crown
That yon green boy shall have no sun to ripe
The bloom that promiseth a mighty fruit."

(King John, II.i.471–74)

Blanche meekly complies. This pact thus means the abandonment of Arthur, for whose sake the war started in the first place. Only Constance, Arthur's mother, laments the new pact and complains of Philip's breach of oath to support Arthur's claim. The Bastard then makes his famous soliloquy on the opportunism ("commodity") that rules the world:

Mad world, mad kings, mad composition!
John, to stop Arthur's title in the whole,
Hath willingly departed with a part;
And France, whose armour conscience buckled on,
Whom zeal and charity brought to the field

As God's own soldier, rounded in the ear
With that same purpose-changer, that sly devil,
That broker that still breaks the pate of faith,
That daily break-vow, he that wins of all,
Of kings, of beggars, old men, young men, maids,—
   . . .
Commodity, the bias of the world,
The world who of itself is peisèd well,
Made to run even upon even ground,
Till this advantage, this vile-drawing bias,
This sway of motion, this commodity,
Makes it take head from all indifferency,
From all direction, purpose, course, intent;
And this same bias, this commodity,
This bawd, this broker, this all-changing word,
Clapped on the outward eye of fickle France,
Hath drawn him from his own determined aid,
From a resolved and honourable war,
To a most base and vile-concluded peace.
And why rail I on this commodity?
But for because he hath not wooed me yet—
Not that I have the power to clutch my hand
When his fair angels would salute my palm,
   . . .
Since kings break faith upon commodity,
Gain, be my lord, for I will worship thee.

(*King John*, II.i.562–71, 580–91, 598–99)

However, the criticism of war does not end here. Because of the Church's dispute with John, Pandolph, the Pope's envoy, threatens King Philip with excommunication unless he agrees to break the solemn pact he just concluded. After some hesitation, Philip yields and the war with England resumes. The result is that poor Blanche is now married to the enemy of her people, Arthur is captured by England and will soon die, and John is finally reconciled with Rome. Pandolph then persuades the Dauphin to end the war between the two now obedient subjects of Rome, and John dies, poisoned by a monk.

Having started with grandiose claims of dynasty and just cause, the reader is left with only the stupidity and the futility of war, along with an awareness of the hypocrisy and meaninglessness of claims of just war. The play's sarcastic anti-war statement could not have been more effective.

Fighting Wars for Vain Honour and the Futility of War

Renaissance literature on the law of nations taught that war may not be resorted to for a just but minor cause. Alberico Gentili wrote that a just cause should never be "trivial," except that in a war of defence "the distinctions of doubtful, trivial, and obsolete"[54] do not apply. Hugo Grotius similarly insisted on a "most weighty cause"[55] and Suárez and Vitoria agreed. Suárez argued that "it would be contrary to reason to inflict very grave harm because of a slight injustice."[56] Vitoria reached the same conclusion that not every wrong justifies recourse to war; since "the degree of the punishment ought to correspond to the measure of the offence," slight wrongs cannot constitute just causes of war.[57] These writers focused, however, on the causes of war, and did not anticipate the principle of modern international law requiring that a response, especially an armed response to a wrong, must not go beyond a certain reasonable proportionality.[58]

Shakespeare demonstrates that in fact wars are often fought for trivial reasons, for exaggerated notions of honour or to save face. As Charles Wood wrote, honour was all, and even petty or imagined slights led to endless private wars in which the real losers were the peasants, abused by warriors whose code of honour was devoid of concern for the less fortunate.[59] Pursuit of honour was central to the theory and practice of chivalry, and Shakespeare himself is supportive of honour, even when it involves the need to die for a worthy cause. Nonetheless, he is equally aware of the pernicious potential of exaggerated or vain honour, even outside the framework of war, for example, in challenges to a single combat for entirely trivial insults. When Vernon and Basset ask Henry VI to "grant [them] combat" to resolve a completely insignificant quarrel, Shakespeare's King angrily responds:

> Good Lord, what madness rules in brainsick men
> When for so slight and frivolous a cause
> Such factious emulations shall arise?
> . . .
> And you, my lords, remember where we are—
> In France, amongst a fickle wavering nation.
> If they perceive dissension in our looks,
> And that within ourselves we disagree,
> How will their grudging stomachs be provoked
> To wilful disobedience, and rebel!
> Beside, what infamy will there arise
> When foreign princes shall be certified
> That for a toy, a thing of no regard,
> King Henry's peers and chief nobility
> Destroyed themselves and lost the realm of France!

(*1 Henry VI*, IV.i.111–13, 137–47)

Even more than the trivial, the canon censures the invocation of face saving and excessive honour as a justification for war or combat. In *Troilus and Cressida*, for example, Troilus, who later joins the war party, admits to Pandarus that Helen is not worth fighting for, declaring that her beauty is "is too starved a subject for my sword" (*Troilus and Cressida*, I.i.93). In the Trojan council, Hector similarly and persuasively argues not only that fighting for Helen does not constitute a just cause of war, but also that she is not worth so many Trojan lives: "If we have lost so many tenths of ours / To guard a thing not ours—nor worth to us" (*Troilus and Cressida*, II.ii.50–51, 20–21). However, the view that the enemy is dangerous, that being amenable to settlement may send a message of weakness that the enemy will exploit, that Trojan honour is engaged in holding Helen, and that letting her go because of "base compulsion" (*Troilus and Cressida*, II.ii.152) would disgrace Troy ultimately prevails. In this way, face saving leads to the destruction of Troy. But face saving is not the only consideration. Rather, a realist argument powerfully buttresses the face-saving argument, positing that showing weakness and endeavouring to appease the other belligerent may also lead to disaster (*Troilus and Cressida*, II.ii.38–40).

Shakespeare's protagonists attack the futility of war elsewhere in the canon as well. Although the conclusion of the Treaty of Troyes appears to hold the promise of lasting peace and fraternal union between England and France, Shakespeare hastens to disillusion us. *Henry V* ends with the Chorus's admission that the war—even this heroic, patriotic and just war that Shakespeare supported—will prove both bloody and useless because the protector of the infant Henry VI "lost France and made his England bleed" (*Henry V*, Epilogue 12). The ensuing marriage arranged for Henry's son, Henry VI, "as the only means / To stop effusion of our Christian blood," and to stop "immanity and bloody strife / . . . among professors of one faith" (*1 Henry VI*, V.i.8–14), appears as nothing more than a ratification of the loss of France. Shakespeare's Richard Duke of York thus complains of the proposed treaty between Charles VII and Henry VI which would establish against England's interests an "effeminate peace":

> Is all our travail turned to this effect?
> After the slaughter of so many peers,
> So many captains, gentlemen, and soldiers
> That in this quarrel have been overthrown
> And sold their bodies for their country's benefit,
> Shall we at last conclude effeminate peace?
> Have we not lost most part of all the towns
> By treason, falsehood, and by treachery,
> Our great progenitors had conquerèd?
> O Warwick, Warwick, I foresee with grief
> The utter loss of all the realm of France!

> (*1 Henry VI*, V.vi.102–12)

But of all the plays, *Hamlet* unquestionably offers the most powerful statement of the futility of war, against sacrificing thousands of lives for trivial causes, for "a fantasy and trick of fame" (*Hamlet*, Add. Pass. J.52) and for honour. A captain explains to Hamlet the purpose of Fortinbras' military expedition against Poland in this way:

> Truly to speak, and with no addition,
> We go to gain a little patch of ground
> That hath in it no profit but the name.
> To pay five ducats, five, I would not farm it,
> Nor will it yield to Norway or the Pole
> A ranker rate, should it be sold in fee.

> (*Hamlet*, Add. Pass. J.8–13)

Hamlet captures the futility of this war in a few words, realizing that thousands of men will lose their lives for no purpose at all:

> HAMLET: Two thousand souls and twenty thousand ducats
> Will now debate the question of this straw.
> This is th' imposthume of much wealth and peace,
> That inward breaks and shows no cause without
> Why the man dies.

> (*Hamlet*, Add. Pass. J.16–20)

Hamlet is then left alone to his moving soliloquy on war:

> Witness this army of such mass and charge,
> Led by a delicate and tender prince,
> Whose spirit with divine ambition puffed
> Makes mouths at the invisible event,
> Exposing what is mortal and unsure
> To all that fortune, death, and danger dare,
> Even for an eggshell. Rightly to be great
> Is not to stir without great argument,
> But greatly to find quarrel in a straw
> When honour's at the stake. How stand I, then,
> That have a father killed, a mother stained,
> Excitements of my reason and my blood,
> And let all sleep while, to my shame, I see
> The imminent death of twenty thousand men
> That, for a fantasy and trick of fame,
> Go to their graves like beds, fight for a plot
> Whereon the numbers cannot try the cause,
> Which is not tomb enough and continent
> To hide the slain.

> (*Hamlet*, Add. Pass. J.38–56)

Of course, Hamlet here expresses his recognition of the unfavourable reflection of the soldiers' bravery on his own hesitation to avenge his father's murder. He agonizes over his failure to vindicate honour by killing Claudius. Although this, and not the futility of war, is Hamlet's particular concern, he nonetheless fully recognizes the absurdity of the death of twenty thousand men to gain a little patch of land, and therefore simply for honour's sake.

Hamlet's sololiquy can be read on two levels. The first is the recognition of the futility of war driven by honour and fought for a useless piece of land. The second and more equivocal level—which concerns Hamlet's personal dilemma—is about killing for honour's sake. While Hamlet certainly reflects on the absurdity of the death of "twenty thousand men" for nothing more than "to gain a little patch of ground," he remains conscious of how their decisiveness and bravery in such a minor cause reflects poorly on his own hesitation to avenge his father's murder. Hamlet's shame lies in failing to kill Claudius for honour's sake, not in being a part of a world that kills for honour alone. For Shakespeare, it is not clear that Hamlet is wrong about his duty.

Shakespeare does not offer much comfort here. His message is not that peace treaties concluding wars will bring about a lasting serenity, but rather that fighting wars simply in the hope that they will make the world, and us, better off is a worthless pursuit.

The Scourge of War

In advocating the speedy conclusion of the peace negotiations between Henry V and Charles VI, the Duke of Burgundy chillingly demonstrates the devastating effect the war has had on art, agriculture and the education of children, who grow to be savages in wartime:

> What rub or what impediment there is
> Why that the naked, poor, and mangled peace,
> Dear nurse of arts, plenties, and joyful births,
> Should not in this best garden of the world,
> Our fertile France, put up her lovely visage?
> Alas, she hath from France too long been chased,
> And all her husbandry doth lie on heaps,
> Corrupting in its own fertility.
> Her vine, the merry cheerer of the heart,
> Unprunèd dies; her hedges even-plashed
> Like prisoners wildly overgrown with hair
> Put forth disordered twigs;
> . . .
> An all our vineyards, fallows, meads, and hedges,
> Defective in their natures, grow to wildness,
> Even so our houses and ourselves and children
> Have lost, or do not learn for want of time,
> The sciences that should become our country,

But grow like savages—as soldiers will
That nothing do but meditate on blood—
To swearing and stern looks, diffused attire,
And everything that seems unnatural.
Which to reduce into our former favour
You are assembled, and my speech entreats
That I may know the let why gentle peace
Should not expel these inconveniences
And bless us with her former qualities.

(*Henry V*, V.ii.33–44, 54–67)

Shakespeare's plays are replete with references to war, mostly allusions to the negative aspects of war. Thus, the symbols of war for Shakespeare are "famine, sword, and fire" (*Henry V*, Prologue 7), or "blood and sword and fire" (*Henry V*, I.ii.131). War is the "son of hell" (*2 Henry VI*, V.iii.33); it is "fierce and bloody" (*King John*, I.i.17) and "cruel" (*Timon of Athens*, IV.iii.60).

If speaking of the horrors of war discourages war, then Shakespeare does so most effectively, filling his text with moving references to the brutality and bloodiness of war. This remains true even in a just and patriotic war, like that of Henry V against Charles VI, as shown in the ultimatum Exeter delivers to the French King's court:

Deliver up the crown, and to take mercy
On the poor souls for whom this hungry war
Opens his vasty jaws; and on your head
Turns he the widows' tears, the orphans' cries,
The dead men's blood, the pining maidens' groans,
For husbands, fathers, and betrothèd lovers
That shall be swallowed in this controversy.

(*Henry V*, II. iv. 103–109)

Still worse, Henry V offers a disturbing catalogue of horrors in his speech before the walls of Harfleur, threatening retribution if Harfleur refuses to surrender, by denying quarter, resorting to mass slaughter of both civilians and combatants, including women, infants and the aged, and engaging in pillage and rape (*Henry V*, III.iii.84–126). In this episode, Shakespeare's Henry shows little hesitation to shed blood, which appeared to worry him greatly in his legal discussion with the Archbishop. But by now, not only has he obtained the Archbishop's imprimatur; he could also argue that an acceptance of his ultimatum would in fact save lives.

The argument against war is even more effective when it turns from general scenes describing the multitude of victims to individuals and their own special tragedies of war, such as Cassandra prophesying Hector's death:

CASSANDRA: O farewell, dear Hector.
Look how thou diest; look how thy eye turns pale;
Look how thy wounds do bleed at many vents.
Hark how Troy roars, how Hecuba cries out,
How poor Andromache shrills her dolours forth.
Behold: distraction, frenzy, and amazement
Like witless antics one another meet,
And all cry "Hector, Hector's dead, O Hector!"

                          (*Troilus and Cressida*, V.iii.83–90)

Perhaps the most moving passages are those describing a civil, frat-ricidal war in which members of the same family fight on different sides of the conflict. Shakespeare tells of a soldier who, while searching a corpse for gold coins discovers that he has unknowingly killed his father, and of a father who finds that he has unwittingly killed his only son:

(*He removes the dead man's helmet*)
Who's this? O God! It is my father's face
Whom in this conflict I, unwares, have killed.
O, heavy times, begetting such events!
From London by the King was I pressed forth;
My father, being the Earl of Warwick's man,
Came on the part of York, pressed by his master;
And I, who at his hands received my life,
Have by my hands of life bereavèd him.
Pardon me, God, I knew not what I did;
And pardon, father, for I knew not thee.
My tears shall wipe away these bloody marks,
And no more words till they have flowed their fill.
(*He weeps*)
   . . .
(*Enter at another door another Soldier with a dead man in his arms*)

SECOND SOLDIER
(*He removes the dead man's helmet*)
But let me see: is this our foeman's face?
Ah, no, no, no—it is mine only son!
Ah, boy, if any life be left in thee,
Throw up thine eye!
(*Weeping*)   See, see, what showers arise,
Blown with the windy tempest of my heart,
Upon thy wounds, that kills mine eye and heart!
O, pity, God, this miserable age!
What stratagems, how fell, how butcherly,
Erroneous, mutinous, and unnatural,
This deadly quarrel daily doth beget!

O boy, thy father gave thee life too soon,
And hath bereft thee of thy life too late!
. . .

FIRST SOLDIER: How will my mother for a father's death
Take on with me, and ne'er be satisfied!

SECOND SOLDIER: How will my wife for slaughter of my son
Shed seas of tears, and ne'er be satisfied!
. . .

FIRST SOLDIER: Was ever son so rued a father's death?

SECOND SOLDIER: Was ever father so bemoaned his son?

FIRST SOLDIER: (to his father's body)
I'll bear thee hence where I may weep my fill.
(Exit at one door with the body of his father)

SECOND SOLDIER: (to his son's body)
These arms of mine shall be thy winding sheet;
My heart, sweet boy, shall be thy sepulchre,
For from my heart thine image ne'er shall go.
My sighing breast shall be thy funeral bell,
And so obsequious will thy father be,
E'en for the loss of thee, having no more,
As Priam was for all his valiant sons.
I'll bear thee hence, and let them fight that will—
For I have murdered where I should not kill.
(Exit at another door with the body of his son)

(3 Henry VI, II.v.61–72, 82–93, 103–06, 109–22)

Making an Honourable Peace

Medieval and Renaissance writers on the law of nations recognized
the validity of treaties of peace imposed by the victor on the loser.[60]
Indeed, such treaties were binding in international law until the twentieth
century, when, under the aegis of the League of Nations and the United
Nations, international law established important qualifications to the previously almost unlimited power of victors. Shakespeare's plays reflect such
authority to dictate the terms. Alberico Gentili points out that, in reality,
the victor decides which cause is just, that is, that his cause is just,[61] in
order to impose war expenses on the loser.[62] Indeed, "it is the will of the
victor which settles everything . . . [and] it is the part of him who grants
peace, not of him who sues for it, to lay down the conditions."[63]
Shakespeare recognizes that when it comes to peace making, might
is right. When the French implore the English for a general peace in 1
Henry VI, Richard of York warns that after all the losses England has

suffered, peace may lead to the loss of France (*1 Henry VI*, V. vi. 94–112). Warwick assures Richard that

> [i]f we conclude a peace
> It shall be with such strict and severe covenants
> As little shall the Frenchmen gain thereby.

> (*1 Henry VI*, V.vi.114–15)

Charles, the Dauphin, hardly claims to be negotiating as an equal. He comes "to be informèd by yourselves / What the conditions of that league must be" (*1 Henry VI*, V.vi.118–19).

Winchester lays down harsh conditions that are not regarded as negotiable clearly voicing the threat, "[o]r we will plague thee with incessant wars" (*1 Henry VI*, V.vi.154). René and Alençon urge Charles to accept so as to save his subjects from a massacre. But the very harshness of the conditions imposed contains the seeds of the agreement's collapse. Shakespeare's Alençon does not leave much to the imagination:

> And therefore take this compact of a truce,
> Although you break it when your pleasure serves.

> (*1 Henry VI*, V.vi.163–64)

This passage reflects, as Paul Jorgensen observed, a distinctly pessimistic picture of truces. For his dramatic purposes, Shakespeare assumes the superior situation of the English and their power to impose non-negotiable conditions; he thus departs from Holinshed, his source, who reports that the French, apparently not accepting that their condition was so inferior, did present counter-proposals.[64]

In *King John*, the Bastard urges France and England to continue fighting until the outcome "confirm[s] the other's peace" and the possession of Angers.

> Cry havoc, Kings! Back to the stainèd field,
> You equal potents, fiery-kindled spirits!
> Then let confusion of one part confirm
> The other's peace; till then, blows, blood, and death!

> (*King John*, II.i.357–60)

Peace negotiations are particularly detailed in *Henry V*. Responding to Burgundy's description of the war's ravages, Henry's courteous language does not mitigate the nature of his conditions as a brutal ultimatum:

> If, Duke of Burgundy, you would the peace
> Whose want gives growth to th' imperfections

Which you have cited, you must buy that peace
With full accord to all our just demands. . . .

(Henry V, V.ii.68–71)

Despite the self-serving description in Shakespeare as "just," Henry's demands went quite far. His source, Holinshed, is even more explicit, citing Henry V telling Burgundy, during the negotiations at Meulan, that "we will have your kings daughter, and *all* things that we demand with hir, or will drive your king and you out of his realme."[65] The Treaty of Troyes (1420) would describe Henry as Charles's son and the heir of France, thus changing the order of succession; he would marry Catherine, the Valois princess, and secure the inheritance to a Plantagenet-Valois line. The treaty would designate Henry as the regent of France, so as to govern France as of the date of the treaty, but he would refrain from using the title of the King of France until Charles's death.[66] To deter violations, the French lords, communities and subjects were to take an oath to observe the treaty and its provisions for the governance of France. Breaches would be regarded as the supreme crime of *lèse-majesté*. The play describes the situation faithfully:

KING HARRY: Prepare we for our marriage. On which day,
My lord of Burgundy, we'll take your oath,
And all the peers', for surety of our leagues.
Then shall I swear to Kate, and you to me,
And may our oaths well kept and prosp'rous be.

(Henry V, V.ii.365–69)

Of course, the fragility of such oaths is obvious. An excessive and harsh treaty could not survive the pressures of French nationalist sentiments, the rise of Charles VII and Joan of Arc's rallying of the French in 1429.

Gentili wisely alludes to the limitations of oaths and agreements, anticipating the fate of, for example, the Treaty of Versailles:

The worst of all sureties is an oath. Hence it is that Augustus says: 'Things which are done spontaneously are observed without the obligation of an oath; but those which are done unwillingly are not observed though pledged by a thousand oaths.'[67]

A peace treaty that treats both parties honourably has the best prospects of survival. The ill-fated Archbishop of York eloquently states:

A peace is of the nature of a conquest,
For then both parties nobly are subdued,
And neither party loser.

(2 Henry IV, IV.i.315–17)

Concluding Observations

The view that Shakespeare was, or became a pacifist, is contested by some critics, Paul Jorgensen, for example.[68] Although Shakespeare's characters express a wide range of views, in my opinion, the evidence largely supports a pacifist preference. I find persuasive Steven Marx's argument showing an important evolution in Shakespeare's attitude to war and peace from, essentially, the first tetralogy where the heroic depiction of war in the *Henry VI* plays (consider the Talbots, for example) combined with Francophobia to serve the patriotic cause of Tudor (Elizabeth's) wars, to pacifist scepticism of the second tetralogy.[69] Of course, even in the first tetralogy, critical treatments of war can be found. In the second tetralogy, however, they are far more prominent. The *Henry IV* plays (1598–1600), focused on internal wars, present Falstaff's mockery of martial honour, Hotspur's exaggerated sense of it,[70] and highlight the horrors of a fratricidal war which appeared already in *Henry VI* plays (1592–95). Consider also the debunking of the war's justification in *Henry V* (1599), that play's demonstration of the war's cruelty and bloodshed, the sarcastic greed-based description of the quarter for ransom transaction (Pistol), and the showing of the war's eventual futility. *Troilus and Cressida* (1602–1603), a decidedly anti-war play, coincided with the accession to the throne of the pacifist James Stuart.[71] Undoubtedly, the humanist pacifism of Erasmus and More must also have played a role.[72] In *Troilus*, war was reduced from the epic to the satiric, and from chivalric to the simply bloody and chaotic.[73] In *Troilus*, war was no longer a corrective for an imperfect peace. It was a senseless slaughter destined for an annihilation of Troy.

A PAGAN KNIGHT?: SHAKESPEARE'S ANCIENT WARS

hakespeare's ability to extrapolate medieval and Christian concepts of chivalry to Roman, Trojan, early British and mythical wars and yet, at the same time, employ those early wars as a purported source and authority for chivalry should not come as a surprise. In this respect, he follows the tradition of chivalric and English humanist literature. English medieval and humanist writers regarded the Roman and Greek heroes as chivalrous pagan knights and good citizens, similar to those of the Middle Ages, except for their paganism. Shakespeare was apparently familiar with *The Song of Roland*, an eleventh-century epic poem (*1 Henry VI*, I.iii.8–9), which describes the Saracen Blancadrin as "one of the wisest of the pagans [and a] most valiant and worthy knight."[1] As Johan Huizinga wrote, "knightly life is a life without historical dimensions. It makes little difference whether its heroes are those of the Round Table or those of classical antiquity."[2]

Despite the obvious problems of historical incongruity, these writers "medievalized antiquity."[3] The "Nine Worthies" of chivalry thus comprised three Old Testament knights (Joshua, David and Judas Maccabeus), three pagan knights (Hector, Alexander and Julius Caesar), and three Christian knights (Arthur, Charlemagne and Godfrey de Bouillon). According to the chivalric writers, these "worthies" exuded knightly qualities, such as bravery, honour, service to the community and protection of the weak and the defenceless. For the writers of chivalry, biblical and pagan knighthood combined to engender Christian chivalry and its continuing mission, exemplified by the crusades. Seen in this light, ancient chivalry thus constituted a model for the orderly, lawful behaviour of soldiers and citizens[4] at all times.

Shakespeare's treatment of classical and mythical material served his interest in history and chivalry well. Ancient subjects provided a means to circumvent Elizabethan censorship, allowing for greater freedom for the treatment of issues and personalities. Nonetheless, Shakespeare prudently avoided provocative analogies to contemporary figures and was careful to articulate a message of support for the values of monarchy, lineal succession and stability, and reserve towards Roman Republicanism.[5] Shakespeare's *Julius Caesar* reflects the tension between republicanism and tyranny found among Brutus' friends in Plutarch; Cassius was an enemy of tyrants from his very childhood[6] and Faonius insisted that "civill warre was worse then tyrannicall government usurped against the lawe."[7]

In this chapter, I shall illustrate Shakespeare's treatment of chivalric issues in his ancient plays, not only in the more historical Roman plays, *Antony and Cleopatra*, *Coriolanus* and *Julius Caesar*—which are heavily indebted to Plutarch's *Lives of the Noble Greeks and Romans*,[8] but also in the obscenely bloody revenge play *Titus Andronicus*, which draws on Ovid's *Metamorphoses*,[9] the Romano-British play, *Cymbeline*, which borrows some information from Holinshed's *Chronicles*, and *King Lear*, whose story was inspired by several sources.[10] The main issues I will discuss are the treatment of women, prisoners and envoys, and mercy and quarter.

In Shakespeare's pre-Christian world, honour,[11] fame and shame were, of course, central. Shakespeare's ancient heroes speak of knighthood and honour in terms identical to those employed by his medieval knights. Titus Andronicus thus declares:

> Rome, I have been thy soldier forty years,
> And led my country's strength successfully,
> And buried one-and-twenty valiant sons
> Knighted in field, slain manfully in arms
> In right and service of their noble country.

> (*Titus Andronicus*, I.i.193–97)

Similarly, Brutus describes his focus on honour:

> Set honour in one eye and death i' th' other,
> And I will look on both indifferently;
> For let the gods so speed me as I love
> The name of honour more than I fear death.

> (*Julius Caesar*, I.ii.88–91)

Mowbray's medieval tribute to honour is quite comparable:

The purest treasure mortal times afford
Is spotless reputation; that away,
Men are but gilded loam, or painted clay.
A jewel in a ten-times barred-up chest
Is a bold spirit in a loyal breast.
Mine honour is my life. Both grow in one.
Take honour from me, and my life is done.

(*Richard II*, I.i.177–83)

In antiquity, however, these concepts often had a different significance than their medieval counterparts. Most importantly, ancient values
did not require humanitarian action in war and did not command the
application of Roman philosophers' concepts of mercy. In contrast, medieval authors could resort to the guidance of Saint Augustine,[12] Saint
Thomas Aquinas, and religious and ethical standards. Joseph Simmons
writes that Shakespeare represents Rome as a pagan world whose characters operate without any reference outside Rome and thus have no
extra-Roman normative framework.[13]

For example, Shakespeare's Titus summarily rejects Tamora's eloquent claim of mercy ("sweet mercy is nobility's true badge" [*Titus Andronicus*, I.i.119]) and Tamora herself later resorts to barbaric behaviour
to revenge the ritual killing of her son. Similarly, Coriolanus would not
"buy [Sicinius'] mercy at the price of one fair word" (*Coriolanus*, III.iii.94–
95). Of course, Shakespeare's Christian knights did not always accept
pleas of mercy, but the obligation to do so was a major part of the chivalric code.

Nevertheless, certain episodes in these plays resonate with the rules
of chivalry and principles of humanity. Although the rules gained adherence in some instances, the ancient belligerents' license to conquer, kill
and enslave those that escaped the sword underlies the classical plays.
Plutarch, Shakespeare's principal source for several plays, shows that some
military commanders' practices may have been more merciful. In leading
his troops against various Latin cities, Martius (Coriolanus) treated those
that offered resistance harshly, enslaving their inhabitants and plundering
their property. "But he showed great consideration for the cities which
came over to his side of their own accord, and to make sure that his
troops inflicted no damage upon them against his orders, he pitched his
camp at a distance from them and kept away from their territory."[14]

Even when followed, ancient humanitarian rules were soft and mal-
leable and offered little if any expectation of compliance. Like other humanist authors of his period, Shakespeare was fully cognizant of Rome's
great civilization, its philosophers and its poets. He was also aware of the
cruel and inhumane treatment Roman warriors inflicted on their enemies
and rebels, treatment he considered barbaric. As David Bevington points
out, "Shakespeare [in *Titus Andronicus*] presents barbarism and civilization
as polar opposites, but he refuses to equate Rome with civilization, and

he allows Titus at last no escape from the barbarism that he himself set in motion."[15] Awareness of Roman harsh war practices did not detract from the Renaissance authors' admiration both for non-Christian Roman writers such as Cicero and Seneca, and for the noble acts of non-Christian Romans and other classical leaders.

Despite earlier sources, especially Seneca, medieval and chivalric just war doctrine was largely the creation of Christian theologians and scholars. This theory served not only to limit wars but also to set rules concerning their scope, limits and parameters, for example, proportionality, and generated proscriptions of unacceptable behaviour, especially violence towards non-combatants. Earlier discussions of the right to resort to war demonstrated a marked unilateralism and subjectivity. For Joshua's war against the Canaanites, God's authority was sufficient; the Bible was not interested in the Canaanites' perspective. Just as medieval scholars justified the crusades, so they believed that their just war doctrine fully supported Joshua's war. In the same way, the Israeli settlers on the West Bank think that they are accomplishing God's will and disregard Palestinian perspectives. The Athenians justified their resort to constant wars more blatantly, invoking the need to expand their empire;[16] the Romans offered similar reasons.

Nevertheless, the Greeks and the Romans did have some just war doctrines, rudimentary as they were. The Greeks believed that one should not resort to war without a definite and adequate cause, and a previous demand of reparation for injuries done or claims unsatisfied. The Romans took precautions to ensure that any war they were preparing to start was a *justum bellum*, especially with regard to the required formalities. Among the causes the Romans considered as legitimate were violation of a treaty, violation of the sanctity of ambassadors and encroachment on territory.[17] Despite those occasions when some humanitarian principles were applied, both Greek and Roman practices of war were harsh, especially towards those they considered to be barbarians.[18]

With the exception of *Troilus and Cressida*, the focus of the next chapter, Shakespeare's pre-Christian plays do not articulate any doctrine justifying wars, whether internal or foreign. Both Shakespeare's and Homer's discussions of the justness of the Trojan war show, however, that whatever the contours of the doctrine may be, "[f]or as long as men and women have talked about war, they have talked about it in terms of right and wrong."[19] In other places, Shakespeare comes close to a discussion of the justness, if not of war, then of peace. For example, Coriolanus is persuaded to conclude a peace that shows "a noble grace to both parts" (*Coriolanus*, V.iii.122), perhaps reflecting Plutarch's reference to Volumnia's appeal for a peace between the two nations [Volscians and Romans] based upon just and equal rights ("which delivereth equal benefit and safety both to the one and the other").[20] *Cymbeline* ends with an euphoric statement of a peace with Rome, which implies reconciliation and compromise (*Cymbeline*, V.vi.479–86).

Notwithstanding these occasional recognitions of humanitarian behaviour, Shakespeare's description of the harshness that characterized
wars in the ancient environment is quite explicit. Applying chivalric terminology to the pre-chivalric context reinforces his audience's conception
of the superiority of humane behaviour over barbarism, of mercy and
humanity over cruelty.

Prisoners, Quarter, Mercy

In *Coriolanus*, Shakespeare follows Plutarch in describing a distribution of the spoils of war that would comport with later chivalric practices.
The Roman general, Cominius, offers the wounded Martius a far higher
share of the war booty before the rest is distributed to the army, as a
reward for his bravery on the battlefield. Martius rejects the higher share
and, in a manner befitting chivalric modesty and humility, accepts only
a horse, insisting on taking only a common soldier's share (*Coriolanus*,
I.x.20–40).[21] Faithful to Plutarch's text, Shakespeare's Coriolanus asks for
only one favour, that a Volscian whose guest he had been and who had
treated him kindly not be sold into slavery, in accordance with ancient
custom:

> CORIOLANUS: I sometime lay here in Corioles,
>   And at a poor man's house. He used me kindly.
>   He cried to me; I saw him prisoner;
>   But then Aufidius was within my view,
>   And wrath o'erwhelmed my pity. I request you
>   To give my poor host freedom.
>
> COMINIUS: O, well begged!
>   Were he the butcher of my son he should
>   Be free as is the wind. Deliver him, Titus.
>
>   (*Coriolanus*, I.x.81–88)

Plutarch describes the Volscian as one who lived in great wealth, and
who had been a host and a friend of Coriolanus. He recounts how Coriolanus would derive great pleasure from saving the prisoner from the
danger of "being sold as a slave."[22] By referring to the Volscian's poverty
so that ransom was not involved, Shakespeare may have wanted to highlight Coriolanus' altruistic motivation. Although Plutarch tells us nothing
more about the disposition of the case, Shakespeare goes further:

> LARTIUS: Martius, his name?
>
> CORIOLANUS: By Jupiter, forgot!
>   I am weary, yea, my memory is tired.
>
>   (*Coriolanus*, I.x.89–90)

Perhaps satirizing class differences and an aristocrat's attitudes, Shakespeare's Coriolanus can no longer remember the name of the poor captive,
and thus his good intentions cannot be transformed into action.[23]

Titus Andronicus also addresses the distribution of prisoners of war. Titus, a victorious general, presents his prisoners to Saturninus, the eldest son of the late emperor who is about to become an emperor himself (*Titus Andronicus*, I.i.247–52). Among the prisoners is Tamora, the captive queen of the Goths, who later marries Saturninus. Offering the most noble prisoners to the leader corresponded to medieval norms of chivalry, and Tamora thus becomes the emperor's prisoner. Titus promises to treat her well because of her high rank, declaring,

> Now, madam, are you prisoner to an emperor,
> To him that for your honour and your state
> Will use you nobly, and your followers.

> (*Titus Andronicus*, I.i.258–60)

Saturninus is sexually attracted to Tamora and waives his right to parade her as a prisoner in Rome:

> Thou com'st not to be made a scorn in Rome.
> Princely shall be thy usage every way.
> Rest on my word, and let not discontent
> Daunt all your hopes. Madam, he comforts you
> Can make you greater than the Queen of Goths.

> (*Titus Andronicus*, I.i.265–69)

Lavinia, Titus' daughter to whom Saturninus had just promised marriage, describes Saturninus' gesture as "princely courtesy" and "true nobility" (*Titus Andronicus* I.i.271–72). Saturninus' decision to "ransomless . . . set our prisoners free" (*Titus Andronicus*, I.i.274) also demonstrates chivalric generosity.

However, Lucius, Titus' son, had already demolished the chivalric veneer. He asks his father to give him "the proudest prisoner of the Goths" (*Titus Andronicus*, I.i.96) for a religious sacrifice in honour of the Roman victims of the war. Titus delivers the eldest son of the Queen, the "noblest that survives" (*Titus Andronicus*, I.i.102), who is promptly mutilated and burned despite Tamora's moving plea:

> Sufficeth not that we are brought to Rome
> To beautify thy triumphs, and return
> Captive to thee and to thy Roman yoke;
> But must my sons be slaughtered in the streets
> For valiant doings in their country's cause?
> O, if to fight for king and commonweal
> Were piety in thine, it is in these.
> Andronicus, stain not thy tomb with blood.
> Wilt thou draw near the nature of the gods?

Draw near them then in being merciful.
Sweet mercy is nobility's true badge.

(Titus Andronicus, I.i.109–19)

Tamora's response to Titus' rejection of her plea is memorable: "O cruel irreligious piety!" (*Titus Andronicus*, I.i.130). The stage is thus set for the bloody sequence of revenge: Demetrius and Chiron, Tamora's surviving sons, rape Lavinia and mutilate her tongue and hands—so that she cannot reveal the rapists' identity. The rape is primarily an instrument of revenge, not an act of lust (*Titus Andronicus*, II.iii). To complete the circle of revenge, Lavinia participates in her father Titus' revenge on her assailants. Rape, violence, mutilation and revenge are the central elements of the play,[24] and the horror of Lavinia's rape and mutilation conveys the poet's strong condemnation. For our generation, if not for Shakespeare's, the mutilation of Lavinia's tongue and hands adds a denial of freedom of expression to the atrocities of the crime.

In telling this story, Shakespeare drew heavily on Ovid and possibly also on Seneca's *Thyestes*.[25] Ovid told the story of Philomela, who is raped by her brother-in-law, Tereus, who subsequently cuts out her tongue to hide his act. She cleverly depicts the events in a tapestry and sends it to her sister.[26] In revenge, the sisters kill Tereus' son and serve his flesh to Tereus to eat a macabre meal that serves as a model for Shakespeare's story, in which Titus serves Tamora a pie containing the bodies of her sons, Demetrius and Chiron.[27]

In another display of savagery, Saturninus inhumanely subjects Titus' sons, Quintus and Martius, to imprisonment, torture and, finally, execution (*Titus Andronicus*, II.iii.290–99). Saturninus' demand that the ransom Titus must pay for the liberation of his sons be his "chopped hand" (*Titus Andronicus*, III.i.150–56), along with his breach of even this "ransom agreement" by delivering both the chopped hand and the heads of his two sons to Titus, provides still further evidence of this macabre violation of the chivalric rules (*Titus Andronicus*, III.i.233–37). Continuing to violate the rules of chivalry, Saturninus refuses Titus' request to grant his sons a trial by combat with their accusers. To Saturninus, their guilt is clear. Shakespeare drew this refusal to grant trial by combat from one of his sources, *The History of Titus Andronicus*: "they denied [the accusations] and pleaded their Innocence, demanded the Combat against their Accusers, which by the Law of Arms they ought to have been allowed. . . ."[28] After Titus offers Tamora the pie containing the bodies of her sons, the revenge and mutilation continues with an orgy of vengeance in which Tamora, Titus and Saturninus are all killed. These events allow Shakespeare's spectators to indulge in a show of pre-Christian world with its bodily sacrifices, mutilations and unrestricted vengeance against which Shakespeare's Publius warned Titus, "If you will have Revenge from hell, you shall" (*Titus Andronicus* IV.iii.39).

Beyond the specifics, the play raises broader questions about the sort of society Titus' universe represents. Titus' brother, Marcus, pleads with him that he is a Roman and therefore too civilized to behave like a barbarian, a plea that proves effective in persuading Titus to allow an honourable burial for his son Mutius, whom he killed (*Titus Andronicus*, I.i.375). To convince Titus, Shakespeare's Marcus thus invokes the humanity of Roman civilization.

> Thou art a Roman; be not barbarous.
> The Greeks upon advice did bury Ajax,
> That slew himself; and wise Laertes' son
> Did graciously plead for his funerals.
> Let not young Mutius then, that was thy joy,
> Be barred his entrance here.

> (*Titus Andronicus*, I.i.375–80)

Nevertheless, the play as a whole belies any claim of a superior Roman civilization with a high degree of chivalry and humanitarianism. In this sense, I agree with Bevington's observation that "[d]espite the Romans' claim to be superior to the barbarians they fight . . . , their acts too often do not justify that claim to moral superiority."[29]

Cymbeline offers another example of how Shakespeare injects chivalry into the pre-chivalric world. Employing the language of chivalry, Cymbeline, the mythical King of Britain, rewards his brave soldiers by dubbing them as knights (*Cymbeline*, V.v.19–22). *Cymbeline* relates to the reign of a legendary British King, reputed to have reigned from 33 BC until a few years after Christ. In writing this play, Shakespeare drew on Holinshed's discussion of early British and Scottish history and a number of literary sources. Like *Titus Andronicus*, *Cymbeline* also provides an example in which the leader, King Cymbeline, orders prisoners killed in a ritual designed to satisfy the souls of fallen Britons:

> [Britons'] kinsmen have made suit
> That their good souls may be appeased with slaughter
> Of you, their captives, which ourself have granted.

> (*Cymbeline*, V.vi.71–73)

Seeking mercy, Lucius pleads,

> Consider, sir, the chance of war. The day
> Was yours by accident. Had it gone with us,
> We should not, when the blood was cool, have threatened
> Our prisoners with the sword. But since the gods
> Will have it thus, that nothing but our lives

May be called ransom, let it come. Sufficeth
A Roman with a Roman's heart can suffer.

(Cymbeline, V.vi.75–81)

In a reversal of roles, here the Romans plead the cause of humanity against the barbaric Britons.

Even in this sea of brutality, one finds glimpses of chivalrous humanity. His plea to spare the prisoners rebuffed, Lucius asks Cymbeline to ransom Innogen and save his life (Cymbeline, V.vi.83–92). In asking for Innogen's life, Lucius actually invokes arguments of chivalry, arguing that although the boy served a Roman, he did not harm any Briton and should therefore benefit from the presumption of innocence.[30] Cymbeline agrees and pronounces the saving words: "Live, boy" (Cymbeline, V.vi.96).

Shakespeare's classical plays also contain references to the noble status of some prisoners (Cymbeline, V.vi.98–99). In the Middle Ages, the rules of chivalry actually offered noble prisoners greater protection, if not for principles of humanity or the privileges of rank, then to satisfy greed. At Agincourt, Henry V excluded all the dukes, earls and other highly placed leaders from his order to kill the French prisoners, thus saving those whose ransoms would benefit the King himself.[31] In 1 Henry IV, Hotspur agreed to deliver the senior Scots prisoner, Mordake, the Earl of Fife, to the King (1 Henry IV, I.i.91–94). The interest of the captor in munificent ransom for the most senior prisoners enhanced their chances to be spared from death on the battlefield or later. Membership in the highest nobility could also mitigate the severity of one's punishment. While the witches involved in the plot against Henry VI are condemned to be burned or "strangled on the gallows," Dame Eleanor Cobham, the Duchess of Gloucester, is merely dishonoured and banished, apparently a sufficient punishment for one of her noble birth (2 Henry VI, II.iii.7–12). These practices suggest that the nobility devised rules for their own mutual protection.

In contrast, in Shakespeare's pre-Christian plays, rank can actually create greater dangers for the prisoner, especially the possibility of a ritual sacrifice, as in Titus Andronicus. Romans often killed their most senior prisoners on the day of their triumph[32] and, apart from any considerations of ritual, the possibility always existed that the ancient captors would kill the captured enemy leaders in order to punish them for their perceived responsibility for the war or the rebellion.[33] Superimposing medieval-chivalric norms requiring privileged treatment for the most senior prisoners, may have sought, albeit not always successfully, to advocate a pattern of more lenient treatment. When captured, the mad King Lear invokes not only the rules of ransom, but also his royal rank with its implicit suggestion of a claim to privileged treatment and capacity to pay: "Use me well. / You shall have ransom" (King Lear, IV.v.187–88); "Come, come, I am a king. / Masters, know you that?" (King Lear, IV.v.195–96).

In *Julius Caesar*, the captured Lucillus claims to be Brutus and, as in the Middle Ages, the soldiers who captured him realize that this noble prisoner must not be killed but rather delivered to their leader, Antony. Recognizing Lucillus, Antony proclaims that he is "a prize no less in worth," than Brutus, adding,

> "Keep this man safe.
> Give him all kindness. I had rather have
> Such men my friends than enemies."

(Julius Caesar, V.iv.27–29)

Whether the motivation was material gain (the word "prize" may reflect Plutarch's "bootie"),[34] amity, rooted in Antony's desire to acquire Lucillus' friendship, or ambition, aimed at enhancing his military prestige by acquiring famous prisoners, the captive's high rank ensured him quarter and humane treatment.

Shakespeare's text closely follows Plutarch's version, in which Brutus has many chivalric virtues, including honesty, loyalty to his friends and generosity to his troops. Not surprisingly, his officers rally to save him from dangers on the battlefield, and one of them, Lucillus, even claims to be Brutus, risking his life to save Brutus'. Recognizing Lucillus, Plutarch's Antony tells the captors: "I doe assure you, you have taken a better bootie, then that you followed. For, in steade of an enemie, you have brought me a frend. . . . For, I had rather have suche men my frendes, as this man here, then enemies."[35]

Treatment of Women

Aside from times of siege, when troops had a greater license to rape, the chivalric code had norms that protected women from the horrors of war. As a result, knights were obligated to follow these norms in their treatment of women, a practice Shakespeare demonstrates clearly. Rank thus implied obligations in addition to privileges. Of course, even medieval and chivalric principles did not offer absolute protection; protection was conditioned on the principle of innocence, which in the case of women assumed that they did not carry arms. The presumption that women were not strong enough to carry arms and engage in warfare was rebuttable.[36] In contrast, women prisoners were free game in ancient wars and could be enslaved and sexually used. As with his approach to the treatment of prisoners, Shakespeare appears to have applied chivalric values in his pre-Christian plays, emphasizing the stricter, yet frequently violated, medieval requirements for the honourable treatment of women.

Rules are frequently violated in all societies. By invoking them even in the case of violations, by insisting on remedies, and especially by enforcing these rules against violators, we confirm the rules and contribute to their strength. Shakespeare's poem, *The Rape of Lucrece*, with its historical basis in Ovid, provides a useful example. In the poem, a Roman nobleman and tyrant's rape of a noble Roman woman and wife causes an outcry, eventually leading to the establishment of a republic. Of course, this tale involves the crime of rape between Roman nobility rather than a Roman raping a foreign captive. The rules protecting Lucrece would not apply to safeguard women "belonging" to the enemy in foreign wars.

Sextus Tarquinus, a member of the tyrannical family ruling Rome, requests and is granted hospitality in the house of the virtuous Lucrece, wife of the nobleman Collatine who is away on a military compaign. Despite her moving entreaties, Tarquinus rapes Lucrece and returns to Rome. Lucrece commits suicide, but first tells her husband and other Romans of the rape and urges them to revenge the crime. In response, the Romans rise and overthrow the tyrannical leaders. The poem does not mention the establishment of the Republic, but Tarquinus is banished from Rome as a punishment for his crime. From our perspective, Lucrece's invocation of the rules of chivalry is the most interesting aspect of the poem. Although her pleas for the protection of chivalry fail to dissuade Tarquinus, they do galvanize the Romans to unite for the vindication of justice.

In her pleas to Tarquinus, Lucrece invokes "knighthood, gentry, and sweet friendship's oath" (*The Rape of Lucrece*, line 569), and the special responsibility that attaches to kings, reminding her assailant that his crime cannot be covered up:

> O be remembered, no outrageous thing
> From vassal actors can be wiped away;
> Then kings' misdeeds cannot be hid in clay

> (*The Rape of Lucrece*, lines 607–09)

Finally, before taking her life, she emphasizes one of the normative goals of chivalry, the revenge of injustice:

> 'For 'tis a meritorious fair design
> To chase injustice with revengeful arms.
> Knights, by their oaths, should right poor ladies' harms.'
> At this request with noble disposition
> Each present lord began to promise aid,
> As bound in knighthood to her imposition. . . .

> (*The Rape of Lucrece*, lines 1692–97)

Shakespeare's treatment of women demonstrates the contrast between medieval chivalry's respect for women, at least on the rhetorical and theoretical level, and the classical and ancient period's practice according to which captured women, even queens, became the property of the captors. For example, despite Caesar's promises of kindness and friendship, Shakespeare's Cleopatra, the captive queen, has no illusions about what awaits her in captivity, telling her Roman captor Proculeius:

> Sir, I will eat no meat. I'll not drink, sir.
> If idle talk will once be necessary,
> I'll not sleep, neither. This mortal house I'll ruin,
> Do Caesar what he can. Know, sir, that I
> Will not wait pinioned at your master's court,
> Nor once be chastised with the sober eye
> Of dull Octavia. Shall they hoist me up
> And show me to the shouting varletry
> Of censuring Rome? Rather a ditch in Egypt
> Be gentle grave unto me; rather on Nilus' mud
> Lay me stark naked, and let the waterflies
> Blow me into abhorring; rather make
> My country's high pyramides my gibbet,
> And hang me up in chains.

(Antony and Cleopatra, V.ii.48–61)

Rather than face her fate in captivity, Cleopatra ultimately commits suicide.

Apart from the sexual undertones and the strong risk that Octavius will sexually exploit her, Cleopatra faces the same treatment from Caesar as male leaders of defeated countries, such as being paraded in Rome. As Antony's ally and a commander of the Egyptian army, Cleopatra would have found it difficult to claim any kind of immunity even under rules of chivalry. But the rules of chivalry would have protected her from the unlimited indignities to which she would be exposed under customary Roman treatment of captured enemy leaders, especially rape.

Rape involved a double horror in the ancient world. In Shakespeare's pre-Christian plays, rape inflicts an irreparable loss of honour on the victim and her family that can only be remedied through suicide. Lucrece explains:

> The remedy indeed to do me good
> Is to let forth my foul defilèd blood.

> 'Poor hand, why quiver'st thou at this decree?
> Honour thyself to rid me of this shame,
> For if I die, my honour lives in thee,
> But if I live, thou liv'st in my defame. . . . '

(The Rape of Lucrece, lines 1028–33)

> 'My honour I'll bequeath unto the knife
> That wounds my body so dishonourèd.
> 'Tis honour to deprive dishonoured life;

The one will live, the other being dead.
So of shame's ashes shall my fame be bred,
For in my death I murder shameful scorn;
My shame so dead, mine honour is new born. . . . '

(*The Rape of Lucrece*, lines 1184–90)

In *Titus Andronicus*, Lavinia begs Tamora to have her killed rather than raped:

'Tis present death I beg, and one thing more
That womanhood denies my tongue to tell.
O, keep me from their worse-than-killing lust,
And tumble me into some loathsome pit
Where never man's eye may behold my body.
Do this, and be a charitable murderer.

(*Titus Andronicus*, II.iii.173–78)

But Tamora does not relent, because Lavinia's suffering is revenge for Titus' sacrifice of her son. Thus, Lavinia is simply a third-party victim paying for another's deeds. Once she has been raped, Titus must kill her because she brings dishonour upon him as a victim of rape.

TITUS: Was it well done of rash Virginius
    To slay his daughter with his own right hand
    Because she was enforced, stained, and deflowered?

SATURNINUS: It was, Andronicus.

TITUS: Your reason, mighty lord?

SATURNINUS: Because the girl should not survive her shame,
    And by her presence still renew his sorrows.

TITUS: A reason mighty, strong, effectual;
    A pattern, precedent, and lively warrant
    For me, most wretched, to perform the like.
    Die, die, Lavinia, and thy shame with thee,
    And with thy shame thy father's sorrow die.

(*Titus Andronicus*, V.iii.36–46)

Both Lucretia and Lavinia are victims of criminal rape in conflicts which do not rise to the level of war. Ancient rules allowed Romans to enslave and rape captured enemy women, behaviour that the rules of chivalry would have condemned. However, chivalry did not extend to protection for non-Christians, and the crusaders committed untold atrocities, including rape, against the Muslims. Shakespeare's discussion of the stigma of rape, the use of rape as an instrument of policy, and the readiness of a family member to kill the victim of rape to eradicate the dishonour of the family resonates with events in our contemporary society.

Envoys

Shakespeare's historical sources are replete with references to ambassadors, heralds and envoys of all kinds. Customary usage and enlightened and reciprocal interest assured them privileges and immunities throughout both antiquity[37] and the Middle Ages.[38] The *Song of Roland*, which Shakespeare probably read, describes the Saracens' killing of Charles the Great's envoys as one of the reasons for the war: "avenge those whom the traitor put to death."[39] Shakespeare's Antony, following Plutarch, uses ambassadors in his unsuccessful negotiations with Octavius. Shakespeare then describes how Antony, miserable, anxious, full of frustrated anger, aware of his forthcoming end, and jealous of the attention Cleopatra shows to Thidias, Octavius' messenger, orders Thidias whipped. As Plutarch explains, Antony gave this order "when he was easie to be angered, by reason of his present miserie."[40]

> ANTONY: *(calling)*
> Approach, there!—Ah, you kite! Now, gods and devils,
> Authority melts from me of late. When I cried "Ho!",
> Like boys unto a muss kings would start forth,
> And cry "Your will?"—Have you no ears? I am
> Antony yet.
> *(Enter servants)*
>   Take hence this jack, and whip him.
>
> (*Antony and Cleopatra*, III.xiii.89–93)

> ANTONY: Tug him away. Being whipped,
> Bring him again. This jack of Caesar's shall
> Bear us an errand to him.
> *(Exeunt servants with Thidias)*
> *(Enter a Servant with Thidias)*
>
> (*Antony and Cleopatra*, III.xiii.102–04)

> ANTONY: Is he whipped?
>
> SERVANT: Soundly, my lord.
>
> ANTONY: Cried he, and begged a pardon?
>
> (*Antony and Cleopatra*, III.xiii.132–34)

> ANTONY: and be thou sorry
> To follow Caesar in his triumph, since

Thou hast been whipped for following him.

. . .

Get thee back to Caesar[.]

(*Antony and Cleopatra*, III.xiii.137–39, 141)

ANTONY: If he mislike
My speech and what is done, tell him he has
Hipparchus, my enfranchèd bondman, whom
He may at pleasure whip, or hang, or torture,
As he shall like, to quit me. Urge it thou.
Hence, with thy stripes, be gone!
(*Exit Servant with Thidias*)

(*Antony and Cleopatra*, III.xiii.149–54)

Antony vents his pent-up anger at Octavius, his inability to bring
about a revenge, and his own misery and despair by whipping Thidias,
violating all the rules protecting envoys. He is perversely interested in
the details of Thidias's suffering. Even worse, he offers Octavius his freed
slave, Hipparchus, as a scapegoat, in violation of all rules of humanity.
Less chivalrous behaviour is difficult to imagine. Explaining Antony's
state of mind by showing a personality on the verge of a mental break-
down and political ruin[41] does not excuse his behaviour. Shakespeare uses
this scene to show that pressures of this kind often cause respect for norms
and values to collapse. In the same scene, he applies this phenomenon
to the denial of quarter, adding to Plutarch's story:

ANTONY: I will be treble-sinewed, hearted, breathed,
And fight maliciously; for when mine hours
Were nice and lucky, men did ransom lives
Of me for jests; but now I'll set my teeth,
And send to darkness all that stop me.

(*Antony and Cleopatra*, III.xiii.180–84)

Coriolanus offers a similar example. Brutus, a tribune of Rome, insists
on whipping a slave for the sole reason that he delivered the bad news
of a Volscian invasion, and does so despite information confirming the
accuracy of the slave's message:

AEDILE: Worthy tribunes,
There is a slave whom we have put in prison
Reports the Volsces, with two several powers,
Are entered in the Roman territories. . . .

(*Coriolanus*, IV. vi. 39–42)

BRUTUS: (*to the Aedile*) Go see this rumourer whipped. It cannot
be
The Volsces dare break with us.

MENENIUS: Cannot be?
We have record that very well it can,
. . . [R]eason with the fellow,
Before you punish him, where he heard this,
Lest you shall chance to whip your information
And beat the messenger who bids beware
Of what is to be dreaded.

SICINIUS: Tell not me.
I know this cannot be.

BRUTUS: Not possible.
. . .

SICINIUS: (*to the Aedile*)
Go whip him fore the people's eyes.—His raising,
Nothing but his report.   (*Exit Aedile*)

MESSENGER: Yes, worthy sir,
The slave's report is seconded, and more,
More fearful, is delivered.

(*Coriolanus*, IV.vi.49–58, 62–65)

Plutarch's story about the unjust punishment of a slave who had been
flogged through the Forum and afterwards executed may have inspired
Shakespeare. The slave's master, responsible for the abuse, was later penalized.[42] However, Plutarch's version of Coriolanus did not mention the
messenger's whipping. By adding this episode, Shakespeare may have
voiced his concern about the obvious injustice of the slave's treatment
and focused on the rules governing the protection of envoys and their
value.

F O U R

THE HOMERIC WARS THROUGH SHAKESPEARE

M y object in this chapter is to examine how two great poets, in works composed some twenty-three centuries apart, address the humanitarian principles or norms of chivalry supposedly practiced in the Trojan wars. These wars are an established legend with some loose connection to conflicts estimated to have taken place between the fourteenth and twelfth centuries BC. The fall of Troy probably happened in the mid-thirteenth century BC and the *Iliad* was composed a long time thereafter.

Homer and Shakespeare, the authors of the *Iliad* and *Troilus and Cressida*, respectively, address important issues of honour and dishonour, treatment of women, ambassadors, quarter and mercy, treatment of the bodies of defeated enemies, and challenges to single combat. Most important, each author highlights significant questions of *jus ad bellum* and *jus in bello*. In both Homer and Shakespeare, the oath and its sanctity provide the basis of the normative system (*Grundnorm*).

Homer's *Iliad*, probably written down in the eighth century at the latest (some scholars contest the possibility of a single authorship), is a poem of 15,693 lines, divided into twenty-four books, and was originally an oral composition. Part chronicle and part epic poem, the *Iliad* is a story about a few weeks of nearly constant fighting during the tenth year of the siege of Troy. Episodes of courage, honour and occasionally even mercy are almost submerged in the sheer horror of war. Although the *Iliad* primarily describes a mass of people slaughtering each other, there are also

63

scenes of single combat, champions and challenges, somewhat similar to the armed encounters between knights in the Middle Ages. To be sure, chivalric or humanitarian values play a lesser role in the *Iliad* than in Shakespeare, but there are some normative standards nonetheless.[1]

Shakespeare may have read the *Iliad* through George Chapman's partial translation into English that appeared in 1598. He also learned the story of the Trojan wars through important secondary sources, such as William Caxton, John Lydgate and Geoffrey Chaucer,[2] which influenced his play *Troilus and Cressida* (1601–02). *Troilus and Cressida* was written at a time when England feared a Spanish invasion and when a siege atmosphere reigned throughout the country.[3] As Eric Mallin pointed out, "The neurosis of invasion made England something of Troy, a nation ten years at war without strong hope of either victory or truce. Troy, besieged, imaginatively refigures the troubled last years of Tudor rule."[4] He suggested that the Trojans, vaguely antiquated, are guided by medieval chivalry, while the Greeks, modelled on Renaissance, are cynical.[5]

Just War/Unjust War (Jus ad Bellum)

Even in the heroic period of Greece, the Greeks did not resort to war without alleging a definite cause and demanding reparation for injuries done or claims unsatisfied.[6] Both Homer and Shakespeare addressed the importance of a just war. In contrast to Shakespeare's Histories, where neither party will concede that it is in the wrong,[7] in the *Iliad* both parties appear to agree that the Trojan cause is unjust and the Greek cause is just. Paris, also called Alexandros, the son of Priam, was enjoying the hospitality of Menelaos, the king of Sparta, when he carried away Helen, his host's wife, with her full consent. In response, the Greeks united, raised a large armada, and besieged Troy.

Shakespeare offers further recognition that Helen's abduction caused the war, when Lavatch sings, " 'Was this fair face the cause', quoth she, / 'Why the Grecians sacked Troy?' " (*All's Well that Ends Well*, I.iii. 69–70), as does other contemporary literature: "Was this the face that launched a thousand ships / And burnt the topless towers of Ilium?"[8]

According to the then prevailing norms, Helen's consent to her abduction and willing cohabitation with Paris were irrelevant. Helen belonged to her husband, Menelaos, and by taking her without Menelaos' approval, Paris had committed a fundamental breach of existing norms. Furthermore, Troy became an accessory to the crime by supporting his actions. A long and brutal war was therefore inevitable.

Throughout the poem, the Trojans voice their resentment of Paris, the person who brought upon them an unjust and brutal war that endangers their very survival. However, these expressions of anger do not lead to Helen's return, restitution and a peaceful settlement, due to sabotage by gods who seek the destruction of Troy and Trojan indecision and errors.

Homer's Hector states the facts plainly, demonstrating the Trojan recognition of Paris' violation of basic norms and the fact that they must defend nonetheless in an unjust war: Paris

> carried away a fair woman
> from a remote land, . . .
> to your father a big sorrow, and your city, and all your people
> to yourself a thing shameful but bringing joy to the enemy[.]
>
> (3: 48–51)

Anticipating disaster, Hector sends his mother to pray to the pro-Greek goddess, "spoiler Athene," while he searches for Paris, saying, "how I wish at this moment the earth might open beneath him. The Olympian let him live, a great sorrow to the Trojans" (6: 269, 281–83). Addressing Paris, he accuses, "people are dying around the city . . . as they fight hard; and it is for you that this war with its clamour has flared up about our city" (6: 327–29). Many Trojans advocate that Helen be allowed to "go away in the ships, lest she be left behind, a grief to us and our children" (3: 159–60), but no action is taken.

Even the Trojan ambassador, Idaios, in his unsuccessful negotiations with the Achaians, states that Paris is the cause of the strife, explaining that he wishes Paris had died before returning to Troy from his expedition to Greece. Idaios' peace terms were first proposed by the Trojan warrior Antenor, who urged in the Trojan assembly that since the Trojan side was in breach of the agreement to respect the results of the single combat between Menelaos and Paris, and thus clearly at fault, Helen, "the wedded wife of glorious Menelaos" (7: 392), and all her possessions should be returned. Paris agreed to return her possessions and even to add his own goods, but adamantly refused to return Helen. The Greeks reject the Trojan offer, but agree to a short truce that would permit the burning of the bodies (8: 406–20).

Priam is fatalistic, blaming the gods for this "sorrowful war" (3: 164–65), but Hector refuses to shift the onus to the Olympians, even though he is aware of their nefarious, warmongering role, and, for the most part, their pro-Greek bent. Even as he prepares for his final, tragic combat with Achilles, he considers going out to meet "Achilleus the blameless / and promis[ing] to give back Helen, and with her all her possessions, / all those things that once in the hollow ships Alexandros / brought back to Troy, and these were the beginning of the quarrel" (22: 113–116), and even letting the Achaians take anything they can find in Troy (22: 110–22). However, he does not pursue the matter further, fearing that once he is disarmed, Achilles will simply kill him.

The Achaians, of course, regard the Trojans as the wrongdoers. Preparing for single combat with Paris, Menelaos prays to Zeus, "Lord, grant me to punish the man who first did me injury" (3: 351). Nonetheless, Agamemnon, the Greek king, acknowledges that the war could have been settled peacefully and that it continues only because of the Greeks' fear of dishonour if they were to abstain from fighting (2: 115–33).

In Shakespeare's *Troilus and Cressida*, the justness of the war is the central issue, at least to an international lawyer, as it is elsewhere in the canon. Early in the play, Troilus is skeptical about fighting a war for Helen: "I cannot fight upon this argument. It is too starved a subject for my sword" (*Troilus and Cressida*, I.i.92–93). Despite this frustration, the debate that takes place in the Trojan council brings the issue into sharper relief. This discussion of *jus ad bellum* is more significant than any in the *Iliad*, or, for that matter, any other in Shakespeare, including Canterbury's exchange with the king in *Henry V*, I.ii.[9] These deliberations in the Trojan council begin with King Priam's report on the Achaian peace offer, premised on the return of Helen. If Helen is returned, the Achaians as the aggrieved party would waive their legitimate right to war reparations:

> PRIAM: After so many hours, lives, speeches spent,
>   Thus once again says Nestor from the Greeks:
>   'Deliver Helen, and all damage else—
>   As honour, loss of time, travail, expense,
>   Wounds, friends, and what else dear that is consumed
>   In hot digestion of this cormorant war—
>   Shall be struck off.'
>
> (*Troilus and Cressida*, II.ii.1–7)

The Achaian terms, as stated by Shakespeare's Priam, refer not only to Helen's return, but also to damages or war reparations, which they would be prepared to waive. This concept of damages or war reparations— often articulated by Renaissance writers on the law of nations[10]—also appears elsewhere in the canon, most notably in the French demands after Harfleur regarding the magnitude of the future ransom:

> MONTJOY: Thus says my King: "Say thou to Harry of England . . .
>   Bid him therefore consider of his ransom, which must proportion
>   the losses we have borne, the subjects we have lost, the disgrace
>   we have digested—which in weight to re-answer, his pettiness
>   would bow under. For our losses, his exchequer is too poor; for
>   th'effusion of our blood, the muster of his kingdom too faint a
>   number; and for our disgrace, his own person kneeling at our feet
>   but a weak and worthless satisfaction.
>
> (*Henry V*, III.vi.124–32)

In response to the Achaian proposal, Hector declares that although he is not afraid of the Greeks, Helen does not belong to the Trojans and is not worth the Trojan lives already lost.

>   Let Helen go.
> Since the first sword was drawn about this question,

Every tithe-soul, 'mongst many thousand dimes,
Hath been as dear as Helen—I mean, of ours.
If we have lost so many tenths of ours
To guard a thing not ours—nor worth to us,
Had it our name, the value of one ten—
What merit's in that reason which denies
The yielding of her up?

(*Troilus and Cressida*, II.ii.16–24)

Interestingly, in Caxton, this idea that "Helene is nothing of so great price that there behooueth to die for her so many noble men," is attributed to Achilles.[11]

Troilus then challenges Hector's reasoning, arguing that the King's honour, not the material considerations urged by Hector, should prevail.

TROILUS: Fie, fie, my brother!
    Weigh you the worth and honour of a king
    So great as our dread father in a scale
    Of common ounces? . . .
    Fie, for godly shame!

(*Troilus and Cressida*, II.ii.24–31)

When Helenus supports Hector, arguing that Troilus is "empty" of reasons (*Troilus and Cressida*, II.ii.33), Troilus, although otherwise naive or idealistic, invokes realist arguments about dangers presented by the Achaians:

TROILUS: You are for dreams and slumbers, brother priest.
    You fur your gloves with 'reason'. Here are your reasons:
    You know an enemy intends you harm,
    You know a sword employed is perilous,
    And reason flies the object of all harm.

(*Troilus and Cressida*, II.ii.36–40)

Hector insists that Helen is not worth the costs of holding her (*Troilus and Cressida*, II.ii.50–51). Troilus retorts that Priam's sister, Exione, is a captive of the Greeks, who obviously consider that she is worth holding. Paris regards the dispute concerning Exione as the real cause of the war.

As in so many other wars, the parameters of the dispute determine the justness of the cause. If Paris' abduction of Helen is viewed in isolation, the justness of the Greeks' cause is beyond dispute. But if one were to go back to Exione's abduction, the situation would be less clear. Hector, however, does not consider Exione as a critical element to change the justness calculus from being heavily weighted against the Trojans.

Cassandra intervenes in the argument with her prophecy of disaster, warning that unless Helen is released, Troy and her people will be destroyed. However, Troilus calls her mad and tells her that she cannot understand that the quarrel engages honour, thus making it "gracious" (*Troilus and Cressida*, II.ii.124). Joining the debate, Paris argues that returning Helen would constitute a treason to her; yielding to compulsion by delivering her would be dishonourable.

In a remarkable statement, Hector replies that these arguments are flawed, that the moral laws of nature and of nations require that Helen be returned:

> HECTOR: Paris and Troilus, you have both said well,
>   But on the cause and question now in hand
>   Have glossed but superficially—not much
>   Unlike young men, whom Aristotle thought
>   Unfit to hear moral philosophy.
>   The reasons you allege do more conduce
>   To the hot passion of distempered blood
>   Than to make up a free determination
>   'Twixt right and wrong; for pleasure and revenge
>   Have ears more deaf than adders to the voice
>   Of any true decision. Nature craves
>   All dues be rendered to their owners. Now,
>   What nearer debt in all humanity
>   Than wife is to the husband?
>   . . .
>   If Helen then be wife to Sparta's king,
>   As it is known she is, these moral laws
>   Of nature and of nations speak aloud
>   To have her back returned. Thus to persist
>   In doing wrong extenuates not wrong,
>   But makes it much more heavy.

(Troilus and Cressida, II.ii.162–75, 182–87)

The moral laws of nature and of nations are, of course, medieval concepts which Shakespeare extrapolates to Hector. Having pled a just war position effectively and movingly, Hector inconsistently turns into a supporter of resuming the war. Although unpersuaded by the arguments advanced in favour of holding Helen, Hector decides to yield to the majority. Joining the hawks on grounds of dignity and solidarity, he promises to issue a challenge to the Greeks, a challenge that is, in a way, a reversal of his position against keeping Helen:[12]

> Hector's opinion
> Is this in way of truth—yet ne'ertheless,
> My sprightly brethren, I propend to you
> In resolution to keep Helen still;

For 'tis a cause that hath no mean dependence
Upon our joint and several dignities.

(Troilus and Cressida, II.ii.187–92)

With Hector's decision, the war debate ends and the hawks win. Although in both versions the war will go on until Cassandra's prophecy of destruction is fulfilled, the reason for the failure of peace is different. In Homer, the malice of the gods frustrates the settlement; in Shakespeare, it is the foolishness of men.

Shakespeare's treatment of *jus ad bellum* conforms to medieval concepts of just war doctrine. His "moral laws of nature and of nations" are extrapolated from the medieval to the mythological wars. In the Middle Ages, war to regain property lost to the enemy, including persons so lost, and to obtain restitution, damages and reimbursement of the war's expenses, like that against Troy, was considered a just war.[13] Shakespeare's fascinating discussion of *jus ad bellum* must have stemmed from reading Caxton's much paler account of the deliberations that took place in Priam's council before the war broke out. The question debated was whether Troy should send an expedition to Greece to revenge the killing of Priam's father and the abduction of Priam's sister, Exione. The context of the discussion was different, but some of the arguments and the protagonists were the same as in Shakespeare's story.[14]

Honour and Dishonour

Issues of vain honour clearly played a critical role in preventing a peaceful resolution of the conflict. As in medieval chivalry and Shakespeare's plays, including *Troilus and Cressida*, honour and dishonour occupy an important, even critical, place in Homer's poem. For example, Agamemnon "dishonoured" Achilles when he took Briseis away from him, thus causing the wrath of Achilles and many of the events described in the *Iliad* (1:355–56). Since dying was not particularly honourable for Homeric heroes, Hector had to appeal to the patriotism of the Trojans to assure them that making the supreme sacrifice in defence of Troy was not dishonorable:

> He who among you
> finds by spear thrown or spear thrust his death and destiny,
> let him die. He has no dishonour when he dies defending
> his country, for then his wife shall be saved and his children afterwards,
> and his house and property shall not be damaged. . . .

(15:494–98)

As Moses Finley noted, prowess and honour were the defining qualities for the Homeric heroes. Even life may not stand in the way. Dying was thus less of an evil than being shamed and losing face.[15] Once the war begins, if the Greeks were to return home before victory it would be a "dishonour" (2:115–24), even though an agreement between the parties may have been possible and the war had, so far, proved useless, with no accomplishments to show for the effort. Achilles' decision to stay demonstrates this focus on honor. He knows from his mother, the goddess Thetis, that his destiny is either to die in everlasting glory fighting Troy or to return home to a long life without glory. He chooses to stay (9: 410–16).

Answering the moving pleas of his wife, Andromache, against the war, which must lead to disastrous results, Hector argues that to agree with her would mean shame and cowardice, while fighting will win him glory:

> 'All these
> things are in my mind also, lady; yet I would feel deep shame
> before the Trojans, and the Trojan women with trailing garments,
> if like a coward I were to shrink aside from the fighting;
> and the spirit will not let me, since I have learned to be valiant
> and to fight always among the foremost ranks of the Trojans,
> winning for my own self great glory, and for my father.
> For I know this thing well in my heart, and my mind knows it:
> there will come a day when sacred Ilion shall perish. . . .

(6:440–48)

Troilus and Cressida's discussion of honour is somewhat different in that it does not focus on the Homeric notion of shame. The arguments for a more reasonable approach, even in the face of sacred vows, are stronger. Nevertheless, Shakespeare's Hector, too, is concerned about shame. As Hector's final confrontation with Achilles approaches, Andromache, aided by Cassandra, begs him not "to stop his ears against admonishment" and not to fight that day (*Troilus and Cressida*, V.iii.2– 3). Hector pleads that honour and the sanctity of his vows (see Chapter 9) to fight compel him to return to the battlefield. Cassandra and Andromache assert that these vows are not binding:

HECTOR: Begone, I say. The gods have heard me swear.

CASSANDRA: The gods are deaf to hot and peevish vows.

 . . .

It is the purpose that makes strong the vow,
But vows to every purpose must not hold.

 . . .

HECTOR:
Mine honour keeps the weather of my fate.

Life every man holds dear, but the dear man
Holds honour far more precious-dear than life.

(*Troilus and Cressida*, V.iii.15–16, 23–24, 26–28)[16]

And I do stand engaged to many Greeks,
Even in the faith of valour, to appear
This morning to them.
. . .
I must not break my faith.
. . .
Let me not shame respect, but give me leave
To take that course, by your [Priam's] consent and voice. . . .

(*Troilus and Cressida*, V.iii.70–77)

Much has already been written about the distinctions between medieval and Greek concepts of honour. Homeric heroes are informed by a
culture of shame and honour, in which one avoids actions that will shame
one before one's peers and selects those others will respect.[17] In contrast
to the guilt culture of the Elizabethan heroes, in which the individual
answers to God and normative systems, the Greek heroes' culture of
shame considered life as a completion of personal destiny, with the dominant factors being the pursuit of honour and public approbation.[18]
    In the Homeric culture of shame,[19] failure, in peace and especially in
war, is decried as shameful. Intentions are unimportant, as is the difference
between a moral error and a mistake. Rather, it is defeat in war that is
shameful. Skill and courage, the qualities that secure survival, are most
highly regarded[20] and public perceptions are the most important. The
cruel war practices that stem from these attitudes continued from the
Homeric legend to the historical wars between the Greek cities, the *poleis*.
The recognition that defeat in war would result in killing, torture or
slavery was a powerful motivation.[21]
    At the risk of oversimplification, it is common to contrast the Ho-
meric heroes' conceptions of honour, dishonour and shame with the chivalric notion of honour, purity, guilt. The latter was, of course, a Christian
idea different from earlier notions of honour developed without references
to Christianity. Still, the dishonour-shame concept played a role in the
chansons de geste as well, as in Roland's refusal to call for help, which
resulted in the sacrifice of his entire force (see Chapter 5). In reality,
dishonour often meant nothing more than shame for medieval knights,
but medieval dishonour, more the result of normative considerations than
Homeric dishonour, often triggered merciful and socially beneficial behaviour. In the medieval legends of the quest for the Holy Grail, the cup
of life and eucharistic sustenance, there is a mix of religious allegory and

martial adventures. In the Arthurian legend, the stories of the romance of Lancelot, and the story of Perceval, it is the perfect, pure and unblemished knight who is given the privilege of finding the Grail.[22]

Honour and dishonour perform useful social functions in Shakespeare. They lead, in most cases, to mercy, quarter and other positive chivalric acts. In contrast, honour in the *Iliad* generally means arid pride. While for Shakespeare's knights it is dishonourable not to show mercy, for the Homeric warrior, it is dishonourable to lose face.

Treatment of Women

Strictly speaking, the rules of chivalry were limited to the battlefield. As a result, medieval norms did not protect the population of besieged cities that refused to surrender.[23] Such cities could be sacked, women raped[24] and men massacred or ransomed, but, in contrast to antiquity, Christian captives could not be enslaved. Despite these permissive rules, Shakespeare's Henry V does not justify rape at the walls of Harfleur; rather, he argues that rape might happen because he will lose control over his soldiers, perhaps suggesting his distaste for allowing rape. To avoid this result, he urges surrender (*Henry V*, III.iii.84–124).

Aside from the issue of siege, the chivalric code had norms that protected women from the horrors of war. As a result, knights were obligated to follow these norms in their treatment of women, a practice Shakespeare demonstrates clearly. For example, when Margaret, the daughter of the King of Naples and the future wife of Henry VI, is taken prisoner by Suffolk in *1 Henry VI*, her first reaction, like that of women prisoners throughout the centuries, is to fear rape. But she quickly realizes that Suffolk is a knight and therefore considers herself secure.

> MARGARET: (*aside*) he seems a knight
> And will not any way dishonour me.

> (*1 Henry VI*, V. v. 57–58)

In *Henry VIII*, martial sounds interrupt a banquet, frightening the ladies. However, Cardinal Wolsey reassures them, saying, "Nay, ladies, fear not. By all the laws of war you're privileged" (*Henry VIII*, I. iv. 52–53).

Throughout Shakespeare's Histories, adversaries arouse their troops by warning them that their enemies will ravish their wives and daughters. Henry of Richmond thus urges his soldiers to fight against Richard III:

> If you do fight in safeguard of your wives,
> Your wives shall welcome home the conquerors.

> (*Richard III*, V. v. 213–14)

Richard III, his enemy, is even more explicit:

Shall these enjoy our lands? Lie with our wives?
Ravish our daughters?

(Richard III, V. vi. 66–67)

By attributing any violations to the enemy, and implicitly asserting their own respect for the rule, Shakespeare's heroes thus reaffirmed the existence of a firm proscription against the violation of women.[25]

Homeric heroes also fear that their wives will be raped and enslaved. Sarpedon mocks Hector for his passivity, declaring that he should be urging the Trojans to "fight in defence of their own wives"(5:486). Hector does worry about attacks on the women and asks his mother to pray to Athene to have pity on "the Trojan wives, and their innocent children" (6:276). He also reveals to his wife, Andromache, that what really troubles him is

"the thought of you, when some bronze-armoured Achaian leads you off, taking away your day of liberty, in tears; and in Argos you must work at the loom of another, and carry water from the spring, . . . all unwilling, but strong will be the necessity upon you."

(6:454–58)

In contrast to the obligations of the chivalric code, however, the Homeric warriors had no rules for the protection of women, despite these concerns. Like other non-combatants, including infants, women enjoyed no immunity from acts of war and could be killed, or, more typically, carried off as slaves.

Agamemnon incurs the wrath of Achilles by taking away his war prize, the beautiful Briseis. Berating Agamemnon for taking Briseis from Achilles, the Achaians remind him "that there are plenty of the choicest women for you within your shelter, whom we Achaians give to you first of all whenever we capture some stronghold" (2:226–28). Furthermore, Agamemnon attempts to entice Achilles to resume fighting in the Greek cause by promising to "let him choose for himself twenty of the Trojan women who are the loveliest of all after Helen of Argos" (9:139–40). These statements demonstrate that the Homerics asserted their right to enslave women, unlike the knights of the Middle Ages.

Shakespeare's *Troilus and Cressida* addresses the treatment of women primarily through the character of Cressida, a person in the *Iliad* (Chryseis, later Criseyde, Cressida, the captive mistress of Agamemnon, was released by him to her father, Chryses, priest of Apollo) borrowed from Chaucer's love poem, *Troilus and Criseyde*. Troilus, the knight, is also prominently mentioned in Caxton and Lydgate. In contrast, Homer devotes only one line of the *Iliad* to someone named Troilus, describing him as a person "whose delight was in horses" (24:257).

In Shakespeare's play, the Trojan council of war and King Priam decide to accept the Achaian offer to exchange the Trojan warrior Antenor, who has been captured by the Greeks, for Cressida, without consulting her. The deal is engineered by Calchas, Cressida's father, who defected to the Achaians and seeks to be reunited with his daughter. Although Cressida does not agree to the exchange, she has no choice (*Troilus and Cressida*, IV.iii.16–27, 35). James O'Rourke suggests that Cressida demonstrates how women were denied the ability to make important choices about their lives; she is reduced to the status of a commodity to be traded or exchanged.[26]

Shakespeare highlights Cressida's parting from Troilus, even portraying its poignancy in the otherwise comic scene in the *Merchant of Venice*, when Lorenzo says to Jessica:

> in such a night
> Troilus, methinks, mounted the Trojan walls,
> And sighed his soul toward the Grecian tents
> Where Cressid lay that night.

> (*Merchant of Venice*, V.i.3–6)

The Achaians kiss Cressida one after the other upon her arrival in their camp (*Troilus and Cressida*, IV.vi), behaviour that resonates, for the modern reader, with the bitter analogy to women sex slaves in an enemy camp. O'Rourke believes that in her first appearance in the Greek camp, Cressida employs her wit to avoid a gang rape[27] and that she realizes that she needs Diomedes to serve as her protector from sexual assaults, calling him "my sweet guardian" (*Troilus and Cressida*, V.ii.8). One production of *Troilus and Cressida* showed Cressida carried away from one war camp to another in her nightdress, emphasizing her sexual vulnerability.[28] Stephen Wall speaks of the ugly suggestiveness of the scene in which Cressida is gang-kissed by the Greek commanders; she needs Diomedes to "protect her from worse things."[29] For Mallin, the scene is "evocative of a group rape."[30]

However, Caxton's treatment of Cressida's arrival in the Achaian camp has none of the lusty elements of Shakespeare's play. According to Caxton, the Greeks treat Cressida courteously, feast her, give her presents, promise to regard her as a daughter, and then leave for their tents.[31] Shakespeare may have departed from Caxton deliberately in order to highlight the tragic aspects of Cressida's treatment.

Shakespeare does not challenge directly the legality of trading a woman non-combatant for a prisoner of war. There was, of course, an important difference between the Trojan norms and the medieval-chivalric standards. Even in *1 Henry VI*, V.v., however, Suffolk's capture of Margaret was not questioned. It is unfortunate that Shakespeare did not follow Chaucer's *Troilus and Criseyde* for this aspect of the episode. Chaucer, in Knapp's modern English rendering, writes:

> Now Hector, who had heard the Greeks' demand,
> For Cressida Antenor to restore,

Against this spoke and firmly took his stand:
"Sirs, she is not a prisoner of war!
I know not what you want this lady for,
But for my part, you can go back and tell
Your friends, we have no women here to sell![32]

Certainly Shakespeare could have emphasized more effectively how
women should be treated in wartime by drawing on Chaucer's version of
the events. It is not clear that he was aware of this normative issue, but
Troilus's admonitions and warnings to Diomedes to treat Cressida fairly
demonstrate his awareness of the importance of Cressida receiving chivalrous treatment from the Greeks (*Troilus and Cressida*, IV.v.113,126–29).
Eric Mallin suggested that Troilus raised no objection to the exchange
because he was conditioned to think that exchanging a woman for a man
was a good trade.[33]

Treatment of Bodies

In antiquity, in the Middle Ages, but even in our times in Vietnam,
Cambodia, Korea, the Middle-East, the former Yugoslavia and elsewhere,
sworn enemies desecrate their enemies' bodies in violation of international humanitarian law.[34] Often, return of the bodies for an honorable
burial is treated as a bargaining chip, as shameful leverage for what is in
effect ransom. Faced with this situation, Shakespeare's plays contain many
strong chivalric appeals for dignified treatment of the dead. These appeals
extend beyond the Histories. Even Shakespeare's ancient warriors sometimes respect these norms. After Antony and Cleopatra die, Octavius, the
victor, decides to grant them an honourable burial, to be attended by the
army in "great solemnity" (*Antony and Cleopatra*, V.ii.360). In *Julius Caesar*, Brutus resists calls to dismember Caesar's body:

Let's be sacrificers, but not butchers . . .
And not dismember Caesar!
Let's kill him boldly, but not wrathfully.
Let's carve him as a dish fit for the gods.
Not hew him as a carcass fit for hounds.

(II.i.166–74)

Later in this play, Octavius orders a respectful funeral for Brutus (in Plutarch's version it is Marc Antony who orders the burial):[35]

OCTAVIUS: According to his virtue let us use him,
With all respect and rites of burial.
Within my tent his bones tonight shall lie,
Most like a soldier, ordered honourably.

(*Julius Caesar*, V.v.75–78)

In *Coriolanus*, Aufidius and the conspirators decide to treat honourably Martius' body:

FIRST LORD: Bear from hence his body,
And mourn you for him. Let him be regarded
As the most noble corpse that ever herald
Did follow to his urn.

(V.vi.143–45)

In *Henry V*, the French herald at Agincourt, Montjoy, pleads with Henry
for permission to collect and bury the bodies of the dead French nobles
in a statement that highlights class differences between the nobles and
the commoners. Henry chivalrously gives his consent:

MONTJOY: I come to thee for charitable licence,
That we may wander o'er this bloody field
To book our dead and then to bury them,
To sort our nobles from our common men—
For many of our princes, woe the while,
Lie drowned and soaked in mercenary blood.
So do our vulgar drench their peasant limbs
In blood of princes, and our wounded steeds
Fret fetlock-deep in gore, and with wild rage
Jerk out their armèd heels at their dead masters,
Killing them twice. O give us leave, great King,
To view the field in safety, and dispose
Of their dead bodies.

(*Henry V*, IV.vii.69–81)

When the Bastard of Orléans wants to have the bodies of John Talbot
and his son, two magnificent English warriors, mutilated, Charles, the
Dauphin of France, retorts that such an act would be wrong, clearly addressing the rules of chivalry in his response.

BASTARD: Hew them to pieces, hack their bones asunder,
Whose life was England's glory, Gallia's wonder.

CHARLES: O no, forbear; for that which we have fled
During the life, let us not wrong it dead.

(*1 Henry VI*, IV.vii.47–50)

After his victory over Richard III, Henry the Earl of Richmond and
the future Henry VII, orders honourable burial for his enemies: "Inter
their bodies as becomes their births" (*Richard III*, V.viii.15). Alberico
Gentili's writings also reflect these norms requiring humane treatment of
defeated enemies' bodies. Warning against venting one's anger against
corpses or preventing their burial, a base and impious act, Gentili argued
that the right to injure ceases with death.[36]

Violations of these rules requiring respectful treatment of bodies, such as the Welsh committed during a rebellion in *1 Henry IV*, draw a devastating rebuke, in this case from Westmoreland:

> A thousand of his people butcherèd,
> Upon whose dead corpse' there was such misuse,
> Such beastly shameless transformation,
> By those Welshwomen done as may not be
> Without much shame retold or spoken of.

> (*1 Henry IV*, I.i.42–46)

Shakespeare's choice of women for this atrocity attracted the criticism of such feminist writers as Jean Howard and Phyllis Rackin. The respect chivalry required for the treatment of the bodies of warriors applied only in a just war or international war. It did not apply to the punishment of rebels or traitors in civil wars, whose bodies were not protected by the rules of chivalry. For example, rebels' heads, like York's, could be displayed as a lesson or a warning to potential traitors: "Off with his head and set it on York gates" (*3 Henry VI*, I.iv. 180), stated Queen Margaret. Shakespeare also knew that traitors would be "drawn and quartered" (*King John*, II.i.509).

In the Homeric wars, in which honour and fame were central, the fear of a body's desecration by the enemy was extremely important. Honour required that external form, physical appearance and social decorum be maintained and respected. To mutilate a dead body meant to make it unseemly and therefore dishonoured.[37] Not surprisingly, the *Iliad* is replete with examples of people closing ranks to protect the body of a fallen companion from being stripped of its armour, and even worse, mutilated.

Shakespeare reserves his most serious condemnation of the violation of these norms in the Homeric wars for Achilles' desecration of Hector's body in *Troilus and Cressida*. After killing Hector, the Trojan chivalric hero, Achilles orders his men to "tie his body to my horse's tail. Along the field I will the Trojan trail" (*Troilus and Cressida*, V.ix.21–22). Troilus fills in the morbid picture, pleading with the gods to speed up the inevitable destruction of his native Troy:

TROILUS: Hector is slain.

ALL THE OTHERS: Hector? The gods forbid.

TROILUS: He's dead, and at the murderer's horse's tail
  In beastly sort dragged through the shameful field.
  Frown on, you heavens; effect your rage with speed;
  Sit, gods, upon your thrones, and smite at Troy.

> I say, at once: let your brief plagues be mercy,
> And linger not our sure destructions on.

(Troilus and Cressida, V.xi.3–9)

The cruel image of horses dragging the bodies of defeated enemies appears in an earlier play, when Jack Cade orders that the bodies of the Stafford brothers from the King's army "be dragged at my horse heels till I do come to London" (2 Henry VI, IV.iii.11–12).

Homer shocks us with constant references to the practice of combatants stripping the armour from the bodies of their vanquished enemies and letting dogs devour the remains. The Trojans' fear that vultures and dogs will feed on their comrades' bodies is constantly raised as a motivation for continuing to fight (18:271–72). Even though Shakespeare presents Hector in a more favourable light than Achilles, Homer's Hector is far from the knight he appears to be in Shakespeare. He says,

> That man I see in the other direction apart from the vessels, I will
> take care that he gets his death, and that man's relations nei-
> ther men nor women shall give his body the rite of burning. In
> the space before our city the dogs shall tear him to pieces.

(15:347–51)

After killing Patroclus, Hector strips off his armour and tries to cut off his head and give his body to the dogs, but Ajax, other Achaians and the gods prevent this desecration (17: 125–30). A tremendous battle subsequently rages over the possession of Patroclus's body. This type of behaviour would surely violate medieval norms of chivalry.

Even without automatically binding rules, the fate of the body and the right of an honourable burial assumed an important place in the negotiations, agreements and ransom. In his famous challenge to the Greeks, Homer's Hector proposes that, should he die, the Greeks may strip his armour but should return his body, so the "Trojans . . . may give me in death my rite of burning" (7:78–80). Should he win, he would strip his opponent's armour but return the body so that the Greeks could give it "due burial" (7:84–85). As the final combat between Achilles and Hector is about to begin, Hector proposes an agreement on honourable burial, one that anticipates the rules of modern humanitarian law:

> 'I must take you now, or I must be taken. Come then, shall we
> swear before the gods? For these are the highest who shall be
> witnesses and watch over our agreements. Brutal as you are I
> will not defile you. . . . But after I have stripped your glorious
> armour, Achilleus, I will give your corpse back to the Achai-
> ans. Do you do likewise.'

(22:253–59)

But Achilles rejects any notion of civilized warfare. He is against rules and favors a mortal, or total combat:

Then looking darkly at him swift-footed Achilleus answered: 'Hektor, argue me no agreements. I cannot forgive you [for the killing of Patroclus]. As there are no trustworthy oaths between men and lions, nor wolves and lambs have spirit that can be brought to agreement but forever these hold feelings of hate for each other, so there can be no love between you and me, nor shall there be oaths between us, but one or the other must fall before then.

(22:260–66)[38]

After he is wounded, the dying Hector appeals once more to Achilles to agree to ransom his body:

'I entreat you, by your life, by your knees, by your parents, do not let the dogs feed on me . . . , but take yourself the bronze and gold that are there in abundance, those gifts that my father and the lady my mother will give you, and give my body to be taken home again, so that the Trojans . . . may give me in death my rite of burning.'

(22: 338–43)

Despite this appeal, Achilles is merciless. He wants his spirit to drive him to hack away Hector's meat and eat it raw, and hopes the dogs and the birds will have Hector's body for feasting, even if the ransom offered were twenty times greater, and Hector's bulk were weighed out in gold. As Hector is about to die, he warns Achilles that his heart is made of iron, and the gods may yet destroy him for his cruelty. Hector is then repeatedly stabbed, fastened to a chariot, dragged and given to the dogs, but despite all these indignities inflicted on him, the gods protect him from desecration. Eventually, Zeus arranges for Priam to offer a ransom for the body, and for Achilles to accept it. Thus, in one of the rare displays of humanity between enemies, in this case Priam and Achilles, Hector's body is returned intact for an honourable burial and a general truce is declared for a period that will allow the besieged Trojans to burn the bodies of their dead (24:485–670).

In the end, although the practice of war in the Trojan wars is extremely cruel, the reaction of Homer's gods to Achilles' treatment of Hector reveals the more humane normative principles. Phoibos Apollo, Hector's divine protector, blames the other gods for being hard and destructive and eventually persuades them to protect Hector's body:

Now you cannot bring yourselves to save him, though he is only a corpse, for his wife to look upon, his child and his mother and Priam his father, and his people, who presently thereafter would burn his body in the fire and give him his rites of burial. No, you gods; your desire is to help this cursed Achilleus within whose breast there are no feelings of justice, nor can his

mind be bent, but his purposes are fierce, like a lion who when
he has given way to his own great strength and his haughty
spirit, goes among the flocks of men, to devour them. So
Achilleus has destroyed pity, and there is not in him any
shame. . . . But this man, now he has torn the heart of life from
great Hektor, ties him to his horses and drags him around . . . ;
and nothing is gained thereby for his good, or his honour.

(24:35–52)

The *Iliad* thus hints at supporting respect for the bodies of the enemy
through its condemnation of Achilles' brutal conduct and its portrayal of
the gods' protection of Hector's body.

Mercy and Ransom: the End of Chivalry?

In the final confrontation between Achilles and Hector, mercy and
ransom were denied and bestiality prevailed, as was often the case in the
Trojan wars. Although the concept of ransom for a captive's life or the
release of his body for an honourable burial must have been known and
occasionally practised, in contrast to the norms of chivalry[39] there was no
expectation that ransom be granted regularly. The principles may have
been known, but their acceptance was discretionary.

Throughout the *Iliad*, ransom is often offered and rejected together
with pleadings for mercy. In Book 1, Agamemnon rejects ransom from
Chryses the priest for his daughter Chryseis. However, Apollo punishes
the Achaians with a plague and they force their king to return Chryseis
to her father. In another example, Menelaos is about to kill Adrestos
when he pleads for mercy and promises an enormous ransom for his life.
Menelaos is moved to mercy, but Agamemnon censures him severely,
saying,

[A]re you concerned so tenderly with these people. . . . No, let not
one of them go free of sudden death and our hands; not the
young man child that the mother carries still in her body, not
even he, but let all of Ilion's people perish, utterly blotted out
and unmourned for.

(6:55–60)

Achilles also disdains granting mercy to his opponents. He denies quarter
to Peisandros and Hippolochos, killing and mutilating them. At least in
this case, however, there is an element of vengeance. Their father, An-
timachos, not only had opposed the return of Helen to Menelaos, but
had also advised the Trojans to murder Menelaos when he came to Troy
as an envoy with Odysseus (11:122–42), thus disregarding equally important norms protecting ambassadors.

Achilles then captures and rejects ransom from Lykaon, a son of
Priam whom he had previously captured and liberated for ransom. He

claims that while in the past he had practised mercy for the vanquished
Trojans, now he is angry at the killing of Patroclus and rejects the notion
of mercy altogether:

> 'Poor fool, no longer speak to me of ransom, nor argue it. In the
> time before Patroklos came to the day of his destiny then it
> was the way of my heart's choice to be sparing of the Trojans,
> and many I took alive and disposed of them. Now there is not
> one who can escape death.'
>
> (21:99–103)

Achilles here demonstrates the weakness and malleability of the ancient
norms pertaining to quarter and ransom, showing that their application
will yield to anger, vengeance or necessity. Although not intentionally,
Shakespeare's Antony resonates with Homer's Achilles in one instance
(*Antony and Cleopatra*, III.xiii.180–84).

Even Shakespeare's medieval heroes occasionally echo this softness
inherent in the rules regarding the granting of mercy, such as Shakespeare's Henry V at Agincourt when he threatens that unless the French
either retreat or fight, he will "cut the throats of those we have,/ And
not a man of them that we shall take/ Shall taste our mercy" (*Henry V*,
IV.vii.61–63). An interesting aspect of the killing of Lykaon, one that
resembles Shakespeare's setting for the killing of Hector by Achilles' Myrmidons in *Troilus and Cressida*, is that Achilles suddenly saw Lykaon "naked and without helm or shield, and he had no spear left but had thrown
all these things on the ground, being weary and sweating" (21:50–51).
To Shakespeare, and modern scholars as well, these words suggest a time
for mercy, but Homer presents these facts in a value-neutral way. He
makes no allusion to the possibility that it may be wrong to kill a disarmed
warrior.

If not inspired by this episode of Lykaon in writing his tale of Hector's
death, Shakespeare certainly must have drawn on Caxton and Lydgate.
Caxton writes that Hector had captured a noble and richly armed Greek
baron and, leading him away from the battlefield, "had cast his shielde
behinde him at his backe, and had left his breast discouered: and as hee
was in this point, and tooke none heede of Achilles, he came priuily vnto
him, and thrust his speare within his bodie, and Hector fell downe dead
to the grounde."[40] Lydgate speaks of the same episode in greater detail,
explaining that Hector, "this floure of knighthood of manhode pereles"[41]
was riding with the captured knight, in whose armour he was interested.
His breast was not armed and he was bare except for plates that could
not resist weapons. When Achilles, "cruell and venymous, . . . sawe Hector disarmed ryde," he attacked and killed him.[42]

According to both Lydgate and Caxton, Hector's body was then carried away to Troy lamenting his death.[43] Neither writer describes any
desecration of his body. As a result, Shakespeare probably borrowed the
story of Achilles' instructions to his Myrmidons and of Hector's killing

from Lydgate's account of Troilus' death at the hands of Achilles and his Myrmidons,[44] including the idea that Achilles should attack Hector unawares.[45] According to Lydgate, Achilles ordered his Myrmidons to entrap Troilus, surround him, and hold him until Achilles could come to kill him.[46] Following these orders, the Myrmidons destroyed Troilus' armour, leaving him disarmed and naked, when Achilles came riding over. The cruel Achilles came behind Troilus and slew him, and then tied the body to his horse's tail. Lydgate comments that this treachery unworthy of a knight was a foul and unknightly act and resulted in the killing of the best and most worthy knight.[47] He adds that Homer should be ashamed of glorifying Achilles for his chivalry, since he cheated and was cruel to his enemies. Most significant for Shakespeare's inspiration, Lydgate then writes that Achilles slew two Hectors, that is, Hector and his brother Troilus, both of whom, Lydgate emphasizes, were unarmed at the time of their death.[48]

But Lydgate's setting for Hector's death is less than heroic. He describes the encounter between Hector and the Greek king, Agamemnon, who wore an armour laden with precious stones, recounting that Hector killed the Greek and, guided by a covetousness unworthy of a knight, carried him away to strip the armour and spoil his body. At this point, when Hector bares his chest while riding with the body of the Greek, Achilles kills him. He is thus brought "to his endynge only for spoillynge of his riche kyng."[49] Lydgate censures Hector's greed, a characteristic not befitting a knight, just as he criticizes Achilles' cruelty.[50]

This story from Lydgate inspired Shakespeare's tale of the knight in sumptuous armour,[51] the one episode in *Troilus and Cressida* in which Shakespeare censures Hector's behaviour as not meeting knightly standards. Encountering the knight in sumptuous armour, Hector expresses his intent to capture the armour and dehumanizes the Greek, calling him a "beast" to be hunted down for his armour, shouting, "I'll hunt thee for thy hide" (*Troilus and Cressida*, V. vi. 27–31). He captures the Greek, kills him and strips his body, and then, adding insult to injury, states: "[M]ost putrefièd core, so fair without, thy goodly armour thus hath cost thy life" (*Troilus and Cressida*, V.ix.1–2). His day's work finished, he decides to rest, removes his armour and is then attacked by the Myrmidons and killed. Despite Shakespeare's suggestion that Hector was entitled to rely on the protection chivalry granted to unarmed knights, he nevertheless connects Hector's end with the one incident in the play where Hector's behaviour was less than honourable, although to a lesser degree than Lydgate does.

In Shakespeare's *Troilus and Cressida*, Hector's death at the hands of those who not only violate the rules of chivalry, but reject them altogether, is particularly poignant. Throughout most of the play, Hector epitomizes the knight who will not resort to foul play, who is honourable, merciful and gives quarter to the fallen. Even his Greek enemies recognize his merciful qualities:

NESTOR: I have, thou gallant Trojan, seen thee oft,

   ...

When thou hast hung th'advancèd sword i' th' air,
Not letting it decline on the declined,
That I have said unto my standers-by,
'Lo, Jupiter is yonder, dealing life'.

(Troilus and Cressida, IV.vii.67–75)

Nonetheless, Hector is still a warrior and his mission is killing and winning. The same Nestor, after the killing of Patroclus, thus describes Hector's martial role:

There is a thousand Hectors in the field.

   ...

And there they fly or die, like scalèd schools
Before the belching whale. Then is he yonder,
And there the strawy Greeks, ripe for his edge,
Fall down before him like the mower's swath.

(Troilus and Cressida, V.v.19, 22–25)

Hector's Trojan comrades consider his mercy to be a foolish characteristic. But for Hector, giving quarter to his foes is an elementary matter of fairness and civilized behaviour. The alternative, foul play and cruel murder, would be savagery:

TROILUS: Brother, you have a vice of mercy in you,
   Which better fits a lion than a man.

HECTOR: What vice is that? Good Troilus, chide me for it.

TROILUS: When many times the captive Grecian falls
   Even in the fan and wind of your fair sword,
   You bid them rise and live.

HECTOR: O 'tis fair play.

TROILUS: Fool's play, by heaven, Hector.

HECTOR: How now! How now!

TROILUS: For th' love of all the gods,
   Let's leave the hermit pity with our mother
   And, when we have our armours buckled on,
   The venomed vengeance ride upon our swords,
   Spur them to ruthful work, rein them from ruth.

HECTOR: Fie, savage, fie!

(Troilus and Cressida, V.iii.37–51)

This exchange between Hector and Troilus resonates with similar themes in the literature of chivalry, especially Sir Thomas Malory's Le

Morte d'Arthur (1469–70). Sir Lancelot thus tells Sir Gawayne, "I woll never smyte a felde [fallen] knyght. . . . For whan I se you on foote I woll do batayle uppon you all the whyle I se you stande uppon youre feete; but to smyte a wounded man that may not stonde, God defende me from such a shame!"[52]

Troilus's reference to the vice of mercy that befits a lion may reflect the tradition that regarded lions as clement because of their inherent nobility.[53] Hector even spares the life of his arch-enemy, Achilles. In contrast to this chivalric action, Achilles disdains Hector's gesture even while accepting quarter from him, because gratitude would make him subject to the same rules of fair play.

> HECTOR: Pause, if thou wilt.
>
> ACHILLES: I do disdain thy courtesy, proud Trojan.
>   Be happy that my arms are out of use.
>   My rest and negligence befriends thee now;
>   But thou anon shalt here of me again.
>   Till when, go seek thy fortune.
>
> (*Troilus and Cressida*, V.vi.14–19)

Since Hector, the lone chivalric hero, cannot prevail against the law of the jungle, he is therefore doomed. His noble, anachronistic chivalry is no match for Achilles' total war. Shakespeare's Achilles prepares the attack on Hector as if it were a gang-execution, as seen in his advance instructions to the Myrmidons:

> (*Enter Achilles with Myrmidons*)
>
> ACHILLES: Come here about me, you my Myrmidons.
>   Mark what I say. Attend me where I wheel;
>   Strike not a stroke, but keep yourselves in breath,
>   And when I have the bloody Hector found,
>   Empale him with your weapons round about.
>   In fellest manner execute your arms.
>   Follow me, sirs, and my proceedings eye.
>   It is decreed Hector the great must die.
>   (*Exeunt*)
>
> (*Troilus and Cressdia*, V.vii.1–8)

Although Hector himself spared Achilles' life earlier in the play, Achilles denies Hector's plea for quarter and orders his Myrmidons to attack and murder the Trojan hero. Not just one, but the entire group of Myrmidons attacks Hector, taking advantage of the fact that he is resting unarmed, having removed his armour moments earlier. The unarmed knight is thus killed in violation of the chivalric principles to which Hector appeals in vain.

HECTOR: I am unarmed. Forgo this vantage, Greek.

ACHILLES: Strike, fellows, strike! This is the man I seek.

(*Troilus and Cressida*, V.ix.9–10)

Chivalry has fallen. In *Troilus and Cressida*, and more importantly, in the world around Shakespeare, in the religious wars, in the Saint Bartholomew's Day massacre, in the war between England and Spain, chivalry is nowhere to be found. Under these circumstances, nothing could constitute a better appeal for the revival of chivalric rules than a dramatic showing of the horrors that await us when there is no chivalry, no code of humanity, and no law. The *Iliad* not only offers examples of such brutality, but also provides a taste of the benefits of some adherence to normative principles. Homer's Hector censured the rejection of mercy and quarter and Apollo has condemned Achilles' behaviour.

Furthermore, the *Iliad* offers a positive description of those cases in which mercy actually prevails. For example, Diomedes, a Greek, stops fighting and embraces Glaukos, a Trojan, on the battlefield after discovering that their fathers were friends. They even exchange armour as a gesture of friendship (6:215–33). In addition, although Achilles killed Aetion, he "did not strip his armour, for his heart respected the dead man, but burned the body in all its elaborate war-gear and piled a gravemound over it" (6:417–19). Similarly, even though Achilles slaughtered Andromache's seven brothers, he granted ransom to her mother (6:421–27). In a scene reminiscent of the encounter between Glaukos and Diomedes, Caxton tells of an encounter between Hector and his cousin Germain. Realizing that he is fighting his own cousin, Hector embraces him and agrees to interrupt the battle for that day, even though the Trojans were winning.[54]

Although frequently violated, the theoretical assumption in the Middle Ages was that both adversaries would fight by the same rules of chivalry. As a result, they would be equal in status and their conduct would be governed by the same norms. Shakespeare knew that this "level playing field" did not exist in the Trojan wars, raising the question of whether a belligerent following the rules of chivalry can have a chance against an enemy challenging those same rules. While he does not address this question expressly, Caxton, whom he read, does:

This was the cause wherefore the Troyans missed to haue the victorie, to the which they might neuer after attaine, nor come: for fortune was to them contrary: and therefore Virgile saith: *Non est misericordia in bello*, that is to say, that there is no mercy in battaile.

A man ought not to be too mercifull, but take the victory when he may get it.[55]

Ambassadors and Spies

Homer's treatment of Idaios, the Trojan ambassador who went to the Achaians' camp to negotiate the Trojan proposal for the ending of the war without Helen's return, demonstrates that norms protecting ambassadors were observed in the Trojan wars. Although his proposal was rejected, Idaios was well treated and also managed to conclude a truce agreement allowing for the burning of bodies (7:381–420). Caxton also shows the respect given these rules when he reports on the unsuccessful peace mission Ulysses and Diadem made to Priam. The envoys asked for Helen's return and for reparation for the damage Paris caused to the Greeks. Priam contemptuously rejected the offer, but he protected the envoys from the angry Trojans, proclaiming that "if it were not that ye be messengers, I shoulde make you die an euill death."[56]

Herodotus beautifully illustrates the immunity provided for heralds in the Greek world. To pay for the murder of Xerxes' heralds in Sparta, the Lacedaemonians sent a group of persons to the court of Xerxes to be killed in revenge, that is, "to pay the penalty."[57] Xerxes' refusal to resort to savage reciprocity is moving and enlightened:

> Xerxes with magnanimity said that he would not be like the Lacedaemonians, 'for they,' he said, 'have broken what is customary usage among all mankind by killing the heralds; but I will not myself do what I rebuke them for, nor by counterkilling will I release the Lacedaemonians from their guilt.[58]

In contrast, spies receive quite different treatment.[59] When the Achaians capture Dolon, the Trojan spy, he pleads for his life in exchange for ransom. Odysseus implies that he will be merciful if Dolon reveals Troy's secrets: " 'Do not fear, and let no thought of death be upon you. But come, tell me this thing and recite to me accurately' " (10:383–84). Dolon complies with his captors' demands, but is killed and mutilated anyway, because the Achaians' security interests cannot allow him to live. The Achaians explain the justification for their lack of mercy clearly: "[L]ater you will come back again . . . either to spy on us once more, or to fight strongly with us. But if, beaten down under my hands, you lose your life now, then you will nevermore be an affliction upon the Argives" (10:449–53).

Challenges to Single Combat

In antiquity as well as in the Middle Ages, agreements pertaining to challenges and single combats between champions were important and complied with by all concerned, as were, in the *Iliad*, truce agreements designed to enable the adversaries to burn the bodies of their fallen men.[60] Titus Livius and Plutarch show us that challenges between champions were an ancient institution, practised in Roman times; Homer demonstrates in the *Iliad* that it was practised in the Trojan wars; and the Bible gives us the example of the single combat between David and Goliath as well. The literature and chronicles of the Middle Ages are replete with stories of single combats, and Shakespeare's plays reflect the fact that, at least on the rhetorical plane, single combats between leaders flourished in the Middle Ages, the time of chivalry. However, reality did not comport with the tales of chroniclers and dramatists. Thus, as Johan Huizinga asserts, the princely duel was "a very special form of knightly fiction used as political propaganda . . . but never accomplished."[61]

Soon after conquering Harfleur, in an episode not reported by Holinshed and therefore unknown to Shakespeare, Henry V made an offer to the Dauphin "to . . . end th[e] controversy respecting the right and dominion over the kingdom, . . . without any other shedding of fraternal blood, . . . by a duel between them, man to man."[62] Because of King Charles's madness or mental disorder, Henry challenged the French King's first-born son, the Dauphin, instead. The purpose of such a challenge was to put the quarrel in the hands of God.[63] Since Henry V was a mature man and an experienced warrior and the Dauphin was still in his teens and was physically weak and sick, the challenge required little courage. Not surprisingly, the challenge was not even answered. Like Caesar in *Antony and Cleopatra*, the Dauphin had no interest in accepting the challenge. His army was strong and he could lose everything in a combat with a strong and experienced fighter.

Shakespeare's plays, as well as the literature and history of chivalry, contain several examples of such events.[64] One of the more celebrated episodes occurs when Antony challenges Octavius Caesar to a single combat that, if accepted, would end the war and determine the victor:

CLEOPATRA: He goes forth gallantly. That he and Caesar might
    Determine this great war in single fight!

(*Antony and Cleopatra*, IV.iv.36–37)

Despite the chivalric nature of Antony's conduct, Caesar sarcastically rejects Antony's challenge:

CAESAR: He calls me boy, and chides as he had power
To beat me out of Egypt. My messenger
He hath whipped with rods, dares me to personal combat,
Caesar to Antony. Let the old ruffian know

I have many other ways to die; meantime,
Laugh at his challenge.

(*Antony and Cleopatra*, IV.i.1–6)

Shakespeare draws here on Plutarch's *Parallel Lives*, which was written sometime in the late first century AD. As a result, Caesar's response in *Antony and Cleopatra* mirrors the corresponding response in Plutarch: "Antonius sent again to challenge Caesar to fight with him hand to hand. Caesar answered him, 'That he had many other ways to die than so.' "[65]

Shakespeare speaks of challenges to a single combat by the leaders or by their champions in other plays as well. In 3 *Henry VI*, Montgomery, as champion for King Edward, challenges anyone who disputes Edward's title to the crown (3 *Henry VI*, IV.viii.71–74). In 1 *Henry IV*, Prince Harry challenges Hotspur declaring that he "will, to save the blood on either side, / Try fortune with him in a single fight" (1 *Henry IV*, V.i.99–100).

He thus invokes the classic chivalric justification for combat between leaders: to save the blood of soldiers and end the war. While there was a significant difference in the Middle Ages between single combats between leaders as champions for their nations and judicial duels, both were supposedly based on assigning to God the arbiter's role.[66] In preparing for the judicial duel between Mowbray and Bolingbroke, Richard II states that "we shall see justice design the victor's chivalry" (*Richard II*, I.i.202–03).

Peter, surprised by his victory over Horner, proclaims that he has "prevailed in right" (2 *Henry VI*, II.iii.103) and the King confirms

Go, take hence that traitor [Horner] from our sight,
For by his death we do perceive his guilt.
And God in justice hath revealed to us
The truth and innocence of this poor fellow. . . .

(2 *Henry VI*, II.iii.104–07)

In the *Iliad* (Book 3), Paris challenges Menelaos to a single combat for Helen, following Hector's prompting. His terms are akin to a negotiation: whoever wins will "take the possessions fairly and the woman, and lead her homeward. But the rest of you, having cut your oaths of faith and friendship, dwell, you in Troy where the soil is rich, while those others return home to horse-pasturing Argos, and Achaia the land of fair women" (3:72–75). Thus, much like medieval combats between leaders or their champions, this combat will determine the outcome of the war, bring peace, and prevent further shedding of blood. Scholars have demonstrated that such combats were in fact practised in ancient Greece.[67]

Agamemnon accepts the challenge on behalf of the Achaians but his terms differ somewhat from Paris', including the element of war reparations, perhaps as an assertion that the Greek cause was just and the Trojan cause unjust:

> If it should be that Alexandros [Paris] slays Menelaos, let him
> keep Helen for himself, and all her possessions, and we in our
> seafaring ships shall take our way homeward. But if the fair-
> haired Menelaos kills Alexandros, then let Trojans give back
> Helen and all her possessions, and pay also a price to the Ar-
> gives which will be fitting, which among people yet to come
> shall be as a standard.

> (3:281–87)

Furthermore, Agamemnon addresses the possibility of default on the
agreement. If Priam and his sons fail, after Paris' defeat "to pay me the
penalty, I myself shall fight hereafter for the sake of the ransom, here
remaining, until I have won to the end of my quarrel" (3:289–91). Then,
appealing to Zeus as the ultimate guarantor of the agreement, the Trojans
and the Achaians pour wine ritually and swear that those "whichever side
they may be, who do wrong to the oaths sworn first[,] let their brains be
spilled on the ground as this wine is spilled now, theirs and their sons',
and let their wives be the spoil of others" (3:299–301). Thus, both sides
recognize the importance of adherence to the normative rules surrounding
challenges and single combat.

Menelaos prevails in the combat, at which point Agamemnon declares that the Trojans should return Helen with all her possessions, as
restitution, and pay war reparations as well (3:456–60). The war would
thus have ended here had it not been for the malevolent Olympians, the
goddesses Athene and Hera, who were "devising evil for the Trojans" (4:
21). They persuade Zeus to "give orders to Athene to visit horrible war
again on Achaians and Trojans, and try to make it so that the Trojans
are first offenders to do injury against the oaths to the far-famed Achaians" (4:64–67). Athene persuades the Trojan Lykaon to shoot an arrow
at Menalaos, breaking the solemn pact and sparking further hostilities (4:
93–94). After this foul killing of Menelaos, Agamemnon addresses the
dead Menelaos and proclaims that the Trojans violated the sacred agreement, vowing that they will pay dearly for this violation:

> 'Dear brother, it was your death I sealed in the oaths of friendship,
> setting you alone before the Achaians to fight with the Tro-
> jans. So, the Trojans have struck you down and trampled on
> the oaths sworn. Still the oaths and the blood of the lambs
> shall not be called in vain. . . . They must pay a great penalty,
> with their own heads, and with their women, and with their
> children.'

> (4:155–62)

The collapse of the agreement to have the results of the combat
between Paris and Menelaos dictate the outcome of the war, illustrates
the problems of enforcing agreements in the Trojan wars. The natural

quest for something beyond self-help to redress violations is apparent when Achaians and Trojans implore Zeus and other immortals to punish those who would violate their oaths (3:296–301). As a hint of normative rules this is interesting despite the fact that Zeus is hardly an objective and neutral third-party guarantor. He thus yields to Hera's pleas to provoke the Trojans to appear to be the first to violate their oaths.

The second challenge to single combat in the *Iliad*, Hector's combat with Ajax after his challenge the Achaians in Book 7, involves the less appealing side of chivalry, a form of vain or frivolous chivalry. Hector's challenge appears to suggest a test of courage and of strength rather than a means of saving lives and ending the war. The only condition Hector requires is that while the victor may strip the armour of the vanquished, he must return the body for the rites of burning (7:66–90). As a result, this combat involves nothing more valuable than honour and glory and serves no useful purpose.[68]

In *Troilus and Cressida*, Shakespeare presents Hector's challenge as a useless one inspired by vain and frivolous reasons. Restless from the ten-year siege, Hector seeks a way to enliven his boredom, a challenge directed solely at determining whose lady is more beautiful and more virtuous. To emphasize the futility and vainness of this behaviour, Shakespeare does not even name Hector's lady. Rather than a challenge between champions aimed at the conclusion of the conflict, or a challenge to resolve a point of law, this is a classic example of the socially useless and vain chivalric challenge that Shakespeare ridicules in several of his plays. Aeneas' proclamation to the Achaians enunciates Shakespeare's distaste clearly:

> (*The trumpet sounds*)
> We have, great Agamemnon, here in Troy
> A prince called Hector—Priam is his father—
> Who in this dull and long-continued truce
> Is resty grown. He bade me take a trumpet
> And to this purpose speak: 'Kings, princes, lords,
> If there be one among the fair'st of Greece
> That holds his honour higher than his ease,
> That seeks his praise more than he fears his peril,
> That knows his valour and knows not his fear,
> That loves his mistress more than in confession
> With truant vows to her own lips he loves,
> And dare avow her beauty and her worth
> In other arms than hers—to him this challenge.
> Hector in view of Trojans and of Greeks
> Shall make it good, or do his best to do it:
> He hath a lady wiser, fairer, truer,
> Than ever Greek did compass in his arms,
> And will tomorrow with his trumpet call

Midway between your tents and walls of Troy
To rouse a Grecian that is true in love.
If any come, Hector shall honour him.
If none, he'll say in Troy when he retires
The Grecian dames are sunburnt and not worth
The splinter of a lance.'

(*Troilus and Cressida*, I.iii.257–80)[69]

In the *Iliad*, sunset suspends the single combat between Hector and Ajax without a conclusion, and the two combatants exchange courtesies more characteristic of a chivalric war than of a Homeric war. They exchange presents and Hector states, "any of the Achaians or Trojans may say of us: / 'These two fought each other in heart-consuming hate, then / joined with each other in close friendship, before they were parted' " (7:300–302). The one positive result of the single combat is that the Greeks and the Trojans proclaim a truce for the burning of the bodies, providing an opportunity for Antenor's futile peace proposal (3:347–53).

The encounter between Hector and Thersites is another satirical episode in *Troilus and Cressida* that mocks chivalric rules concerning resort to single combat. Hector questions Thersites to ascertain whether he is worthy to confront Hector in combat, and Thersites, to save his life, is only too happy to proclaim his unworthiness:

HECTOR: What art thou, Greek? Art thou for Hector's match?
Art thou of blood and honour?

THERSITES: No, no, I am a rascal, a scurvy railing knave, a very filthy rogue.

HECTOR: I do believe thee: live.

THERSITES: God-a-mercy, that thou wilt believe me. . . .

(*Troilus and Cressida*, V.iv.24–29)

Hector spares Thersites' life because he is not of Hector's rank and level of accomplishment. Separate from the question of mercy, this episode involves the rule of chivalry requiring that combatants have a certain measure of equality of status and adhere to established procedures.[70] Artificial as this may be, both the *Iliad* and *Troilus and Cressida* regard the giant struggle between thousands of soldiers as a series of single combats in which Shakespeare's Hector, if no one else, attempts to apply rules of chivalry.

Gods

Homer's gods play a central role in the Trojan wars. Immortal, omnipotent and capable of human emotions, they manipulate the humans, supporting one side or another at any given time. At times they play a beneficial role, such as when Achilles' mother, the goddess Thetis, protects the body of Patroclus from flies and worms (19:29–33). Similarly, Aphrodite and Phoibos Apollo defend Hector's body from desecration (23:182–91, 24:18–21), so that it remains immune from mutilation and decay despite Achilles' efforts (24:411–23).

However, aside from these occasional gestures of mercy, the Olympians play a nefarious role, making them responsible for the continuation of the war and the fall of Troy. For example, Athene and Hera persuade Zeus to order Athene to engineer, through Lykaon, the violation of the truce agreement and doom the prospects for ending the war (4:20–140). Hera also schemes, causing Hector to kill Patroclus and thus ensuring that Achilles, in angry reprisal, will kill Hector (15:34–68).

In addition, the gods also interfere with combats between the protagonists, often cheating the mortals' efforts. As Hector threw his spear against Achilles, "Athene blew against it and turned it back . . . with an easy blast" (20:438–40). When Achilles turns against Hector, Phoibos Apollo saves Hector by wrapping him in mist (20:444). Ultimately, in the final confrontation, Achilles warns Hector that Pallas Athene will kill him with his spear. Achilles' spear misses its target, but "Athene snatched it, and gave it back to Achilleus, unseen by Hector" (22:276–77). Hector finally understands that he is doomed, because "it was Athene cheating me, and now evil death is close to me" (22:299–300).

In Homer, the gods can help, they can destroy, and they can manipulate events. As a result, humans are often pawns in the hands of the Olympians, who intervene against the winning party, prolonging the agony of the war. This behaviour allows the mortals to impute responsibility for their misfortune to the gods. The *Iliad* is replete with complaints of men and women against the unfairness of the gods. For example, despite Paris' culpability, Priam asserts that "the gods are blameworthy who drove upon me this sorrowful war against the Achaians" (3:164–65). While focusing on Paris and his role in causing the war, Homer nonetheless suggests that this war is a situation where responsibility is shared between the mortals and the immortals. The great Irish poet Seamus Heaney makes Philoctetes indict the gods alone:

NEOTOLEMUS: Philoctetes. Let me educate you
In one short sentence. War has an appetite
For Human goodness but it won't touch the bad.
. . .

PHILOCTETES: The gods do grant immunity, you see,
To everybody except the true and the just.
The more of a plague you are, and the crueller,
The better your chances of being turned away
From the doors of death. Whose side are gods on?
What are human beings to make of them?

> How am I to keep on praising gods
> If they keep disappointing me, and never
> Match the good on my side with their good?[71]

In contrast, respect for the rules and consequences of violations are solely the responsibility of men and women in Shakespeare, as he emphasizes throughout the canon, especially in *King John*, *Richard II* and *Richard III*. Although *Troilus and Cressida* mentions the gods on a number of occasions, the invocation of God is quite modern, as in "God [be with] you" (*Troilus and Cressida*, III.iii.283). Departing from his sources, Shakespeare neutralizes the gods as actors. As a result, the heroes of *Troilus and Cressida* cannot take cover behind the gods. Rather, they live in a world in which the gods do not appear to be active participants, whether for good or for evil. Humans are therefore wholly responsible for their conduct, stripped of the convenient option of blaming the gods for their misfortune and their behaviour.

Horrors of War

The *Iliad*, a story of an almost endless slaughter, brings to mind another great epic war poem, also first composed for oral presentation: *The Song of Roland*, the oldest *chanson de geste* in the French language. Describing events that were likely part of the eighth-century war in Spain between Charles the Great and the Saracens, *The Song of Roland* (*La Chanson de Roland*) was probably recorded in the eleventh century.

In contrast to Shakespeare, who usually spares us the most gory details in describing the brutality of war, *The Song of Roland*, like the *Iliad*, recounts the horrors of war in a painfully realistic, even macabre manner. Thus, Charles the Great, with the help of Saint Gabriel, "strikes the emir with his sword from France; / He breaks his helmet glittering with gems, / Slicing through his head and spilling out his brains."[72]

The *Iliad* provides similar anatomical detail: "He hit him at the joining place of head and neck, at the last vertebra, and cut through both of the tendons, so that the man's head and mouth and nose hit the ground far sooner than did the front of his legs and knees as he fell" (14:465–68). In another example, "Hector saw Polidoros, his own brother, going limp to the ground and catching his bowels in his hands" (20:419–20). Yet again, "Achilleus took his life with the sword from close up for he struck him in the belly next the navel, and all his guts poured out on the ground" (21:179–81). Finally, after Achilles' victory over Hector, not a single Achaian standing nearby refrained from stabbing the body. No less, Achilles "now thought of shameful treatment for glorious Hektor. In both of his feet at the back he made holes by the tendons in the space between ankle and heel, and drew thongs of ox-hide through them, and fastened them to the chariot so as to let the head drag" (22:395–98).

However the *Iliad* also contains more subtle, yet equally moving descriptions of war, such as those by Andromache, Cassandra and others. Priam, the king of Troy, characterizes the image of the war as his country falls to the Greeks:

> Oh, take pity on me, the unfortunate still alive, still sentient but
> ill-starred, . . . after I have looked upon evils and seen my sons
> destroyed and my daughters dragged away captive and the
> chambers of marriage wrecked and the innocent children taken
> and dashed to the ground in the hatefulness of war, and the
> wives of my sons dragged off. . . . And myself last of all, my
> dogs in front of my doorway will rip me raw, after some man
> with stroke of the sharp bronze spear . . . has torn the life out of
> my body; those dogs I raised in my halls to be at my table, to
> guard my gates, who will lap my blood in the savagery of their
> anger. . . . [W]hen an old man is dead and down, and the dogs
> mutilate the grey head and the grey beard and the parts that
> are secret, this, for all sad mortality, is the sight most pitiful.

(22:58–76)

This damning statement bears some similarity to the catalogue of the horrors of war that Shakespeare's Henry V voices at the walls of Harfleur, but Priam's is even more brutal and sickening. For both poets, the dramatic effect of their texts was critically important. The immediate and intimate nature of the combat conducted by sword and spear in the Homeric wars led to a style that described the anatomical havoc wreaked on the bodies of the combatants in graphic terms and thus lent itself better to poetry than to the stage. In the medieval wars on which Shakespeare focused in his Histories, however, bows, cross-bows and, increasingly, firearms, and especially artillery, reduced the physical proximity of the adversaries and, as a consequence, the need for anatomical particulars. Shakespeare nonetheless sought to discourage war by depicting the horrors of war in great detail and moving language.

In Shakespeare's *Troilus and Cressida*, Cassandra (*Troilus and Cressida*, II.ii.100–11) and, ironically, the once pro-war Troilus articulate the evils of war. Although the rest of the Trojans disdain Cassandra's warning of a total disaster, Hector tries to convince them of the importance of her pleas.

> Now, youthful Troilus, do not these high strains
> Of divination in our sister work
> Some touches of remorse? Or is your blood
> So madly hot that no discourse of reason,

Nor fear of bad success in a bad cause,
Can qualify the same?

(Troilus and Cressida, II.ii.112–17)

At the end of the play, Troilus is even more poignant in bemoaning the horrors of the war and the inevitable destruction of Troy (*Troilus and Cressida*, V.xi.3–9). When Aeneas rebukes Troilus for demoralizing the troops, saying, "My lord, you do discomfort all the host" (*Troilus and Cressida*, V.xi.10), the very same Troilus who had once urged war in the Trojan council now recognizes the tragedy of war and the approaching destruction of Troy:

You understand me not that tell me so.
I do not speak of flight, of fear of death,
But dare all imminence that gods and men
Address their dangers in. Hector is gone.
Who shall tell Priam so, or Hecuba
Let him that will a screech-owl aye be called
Go into Troy and say their Hector's dead.
There is a word will Priam turn to stone,
Make wells and Niobes of the maids and wives,
Cold statues of the youth, and in a word
Scare Troy out of itself. But march away.
Hector is dead; there is no more to say.

(Troilus and Cressida, V.xi.11–22)

Ultimately, however, Troilus never learns his own bitter lesson, still claiming that sorrow will yield to a "hope of revenge" (*Troilus and Cressida*, V.xi.31). Unlike *Romeo and Juliet*, where the deadly feud between the Capulets and the Montagues triggers reconciliation, in *Troilus and Cressida* the parties are destined to revisit the horrors of war.[73]

Concluding Observations

Hector is less than a perfect knight in Homer's *Iliad*. In contrast to *Troilus and Cressida*, the *Iliad* contains no opportunities for Hector to spare the life of Achilles and the vanquished Greeks. Homer's Hector is brutal and unrelenting, planning to give the bodies of defeated enemies, including Patroclus, to the dogs. Achilles kills Hector when his body is not covered by armour, but the killing takes place in an one-on-one situation; there is no mass attack by the Myrmidons, and thus less of a violation of any normative principles. In addition, Shakespeare must have known from Lydgate that Hector was only too happy to "spoil" or try to spoil the bodies of vanquished Greeks, including Patroclus.[74]

Thus, Shakespeare departs from his sources in order to make Hector more chivalrous and Achilles more brutal, just as in *Richard III* and *Henry V*, for example, the good become very good, and the bad, evil. He could find support for his glorification of Hector as the perfect knight in chivalric literature and its mythology. As early as 1312, Jacques de Longuyon included Hector as the first of the "Nine Worthies" (*les neufs preux*), the nine heroes of chivalry.[75]

Beyond dramatic considerations, by sharpening the differences between Hector and Achilles, Shakespeare may have tried to send a message about the inherent superiority of the rules of chivalry. In describing Hector's acceptance of his Achaian cousin's request for a truce, even though the Trojans were winning and could have succeeded in burning the Achaians' ships, Caxton comments that there should be no mercy in battle, that a man should take victory when he can get it, and that this display of mercy caused the Trojans to be defeated. This episode in not reflected in *Troilus and Cressida*, perhaps because Shakespeare may have preferred not to ask whether humanitarian limitations on the conduct of war doom the party complying with the rules, hoping instead to encourage a reinvigoration of the chivalric principles exalted earlier in the Middle Ages.

Perhaps the play symbolizes the decline, even the demise of chivalry, with the necessities of war gaining the upper hand over humanitarian principles. The one chivalrous person dies defeated, while his enemy survives victorious.

FIVE

THE BRAVE OR THE WISE?:
TWO CONFLICTING CONCEPTIONS
OF CHIVALRIC HONOUR

Shakespeare's abiding interest in chivalry[1]—William Henry Schofield remarked that Shakespeare's "whole face was tanned by the sun of chivalry"[2]—is reflected in his writings. In this chapter, I would like to demonstrate by a number of texts how deeply Shakespeare's work is rooted in the literature, norms and myths of chivalry.

The first text is one of Henry V's famous heroic statements. Rebuking Warwick for wishing that thousands of men then in England could have reinforced the beleaguered English at Agincourt, Henry replies with an oration intended to raise the morale of his troops. His speech not only rallies the troops, it also highlights several important chivalric values: honour, refraining from material pursuits, generosity and tolerance for the weak:

> If we are marked to die, we are enough
> To do our country loss; and if to live,
> The fewer men, the greater share of honour.
> God's will, I pray thee wish not one man more.
> By Jove, I am not covetous for gold,
> Nor care I who doth feed upon my cost;
> It ernes me not if men my garments wear;
> Such outward things dwell not in my desires.
> But if it be a sin to covet honour
> I am the most offending soul alive.

No, faith, my coz, wish not a man from England.

. . .

Rather proclaim it presently through my host
That he which hath no stomach to this fight,
Let him depart. His passport shall be made
And crowns for convoy put into his purse.
We would not die in that man's company
That fears his fellowship to die with us.

(*Henry V*, IV.iii. 20–30, 33–39)

It is hard to imagine a modern military leader giving his troops the option to leave just before the start of a critical battle. However, perhaps the same idea survives in modern military practice whereby certain duties regarded as especially hazardous need only be performed by volunteers. For the great chivalric heroes, however, the pursuit of honour and glory and the idealization of prowess, courage and magnanimity made the offer to leave the battlefield less fantastic.

In Henry's oration, Shakespeare drew heavily on Holinshed (who attributed Warwick's statement to "one of the host").[3] Although Holinshed does not mention Henry V's offer to those fearing the battle to depart, he tells of King Edward granting his troops this option. Shakespeare must have come across this reference to Edward's offer on the battlefield, a possibility strengthened by the fact that the *Henry VI* trilogy was written before *Henry V*. Holinshed thus writes that

King Edward . . . made proclamation that all men which were afraid to fight should depart; and to all those that tarried the battle he promised great rewards; with addition, that any soldier which voluntarily would abide and afterward, either in or before the fight, should seem to flee or turn his back, then he that could kill him should have a great reward and double wages.[4]

However, the idea of allowing those that feared the battle to depart had already appeared half a millenium earlier, in *The Song of Roland*, the famous epic poem, originally oral (*chanson de geste*), probably composed towards the end of the eleventh century, the time of the First Crusade. *Chansons de geste* are among the earliest chivalric sources.[5] Several factors suggest Shakespeare's familiarity with *The Song of Roland*. First, Roland and Oliver are mentioned in Holinshed.[6] Second, they appear in *1 Henry VI*, when René, the duke of Anjou and King of Naples, refers to the military prowess of the English, stating: "Froissart, a countryman of ours, records England all Olivers and Rolands bred" (*1 Henry VI*, I.iii.8–9, composed perhaps by Thomas Nashe). No less important, Roland the Brave and Oliver the Wise have entered the "private pantheon of heroes"[7] from which Shakespeare must have drawn some of his characters. Thus, to describe a man as Roland or Oliver was to praise him for great valour.[8]

Set in northern Spain during Charles the Great's eighth-century campaign, the poem tells of Charles's attempts to subjugate the major remaining Muslim city, Saragossa, held by King Marsile. During the Franks' retreat to France, they were ambushed in the pass of Roncesvalles in the Pyrenees, and the members of the rearguard were slaughtered.[9] Roland and Oliver, who were in the rearguard with twenty thousand men, were ambushed and massacred. When Charles eventually returns to battle, he realizes that the odds are against him. His oration to the Franks before his victorious battle could be a model for Shakespeare's Henry at Agincourt:

> The King of France shouts out loud and clear:
> 'Frankish barons, you are fine vassals,
> You have fought on so many battlefields.
> See the pagans; they are villains and cowards;
> Their entire faith is not worth a penny.
> If they have a huge army, what matter, my lords?
> Let anyone who does not wish to come with me depart!'

(*The Song of Roland*, lines 3334–40)

As at Agincourt, no soldier takes up the King's offer:

> The Franks say: 'This king is valiant;
> Ride, baron, none of us will fail you."

(*The Song of Roland*, lines 3343–44)

The second text involves the beautiful exchange in Shakespeare between Sir John Talbot,[10] the paradigm of chivalry, and his son John when facing the battle against an overwhelming French army, with Talbot senior advancing a utilitarian argument and John one of vain honour:

> TALBOT: O young John Talbot, I did send for thee
> To tutor thee in stratagems of war,
>
> . . .
>
> Now thou art come unto a feast of death,
> A terrible and unavoided danger.
> Therefore, dear boy, mount on my swiftest horse,
> And I'll direct thee how thou shalt escape
> By sudden flight. Come, dally not, be gone.
>
> JOHN: Is my name Talbot, and am I your son,
> And shall I fly? O, if you love my mother,
> Dishonour not her honourable name
> To make a bastard and a slave of me.
> The world will say he is not Talbot's blood
> That basely fled when noble Talbot stood.

TALBOT: Fly to revenge my death if I be slain.

JOHN: He that flies so will ne'er return again.

TALBOT: If we both stay, we both are sure to die.

JOHN: Then let me stay and, father, do you fly.
　　Your loss is great; so your regard should be.
　　My worth unknown, no loss is known in me.
　　Upon my death the French can little boast;
　　In yours they will: in you all hopes are lost.
　　Flight cannot stain the honour you have won,
　　But mine it will, that no exploit have done.
　　You fled for vantage, everyone will swear,
　　But if I bow, they'll say it was for fear.
　　　　. . .

TALBOT: Shall all thy mother's hopes lie in one tomb?

JOHN: Ay, rather than I'll shame my mother's womb.

TALBOT: Upon my blessing I command thee go.

JOHN: To fight I will, but not to fly the foe.

TALBOT: Part of thy father may be saved in thee.

JOHN: No part of him but will be shamed in me.

TALBOT: Thou never hadst renown, nor canst not lose it.

JOHN: Yes, your renownèd name—shall flight abuse it?

TALBOT: Thy father's charge shall clear thee from that stain.

JOHN: You cannot witness for me, being slain.
　　If death be so apparent, then both fly.

TALBOT: And leave my followers here to fight and die?
　　My age was never tainted with such shame.

JOHN: And shall my youth be guilty of such blame?

(*1 Henry VI*, IV.v.1–2, 7–29, 34–47)

Once the battle has started, Talbot again tries to convince John to leave the battle and escape death.

　　Art thou not weary, John? How dost thou fare?
　　Wilt thou yet leave the battle, boy, and fly,
　　Now thou art sealed the son of chivalry?

Fly to revenge my death when I am dead;
The help of one stands me in little stead.

(1 Henry VI, IV.vi.27–31)

But John refuses to flee, and the two Talbots resolve to die together with honour and glory (1 Henry VI, IV.vi.49–57).

Holinshed contains a short text that likely inspired Shakespeare:

> It was said that after he perceived there was no remedy but present loss of battle, he counseled his son the Lord Lisle to save himself by flight, sith the same could not redound to any great reproach in him, this being the first journey in which he had been present. Many words he used to persuade him to have saved his life; but nature so wrought in the son that neither desire of life nor fear of death could cause him to shrink or convey himself out of the danger, and so there manfully ended his life with his said father.[11]

Hall is more explicit and may have had a greater influence on Shakespeare's version: Talbot argues that since this is his son's first military mission, fleeing would not be shameful, just as dying would not contribute to his glory. A "hardy" man can wisely flee, Talbot explains. By escaping and surviving, the young Talbot would one day be able to revenge his father's death and help the kingdom.[12]

Phyllis Rackin, citing Michel Foucault, writes that a hero's death represents the trade-off between the hero and his story: dying young ensures that life, magnified by death, might pass into immortality. Talbot and his son's paternal and filial devotions combine with their mutual commitment to honour to ensure that, although no survivor will carry their name, it will survive, recorded by history and celebrated by Shakespeare.[13] Comparing the Talbots' end to that of Joan of Arc in 1 Henry VI, V.iv, where she rejects her father and claims pregnancy, Rackin suggests that the Talbots chose historical glory over their lives, while Joan placed life above historical glory.[14] This is reminiscent of Achilles's decision to die young in battle and gain immortal glory rather than die old in obscurity. Similarly, in Scandinavian and Germanic mythology only warriors killed in battle were admitted to Walhalla.

The Talbots' exchange contains an echo of the dispute between Roland and Oliver about whether to sound the horn and alert Charles the Great to aid their besieged Frank troops. As the Franks are about to be attacked, Roland actually prays for the battle in such a just war, saying, "May God grant it to us"; "[t]he pagans are wrong and the Christians are right" (The Song of Roland, lines 1008, 1015). Realizing the enormity of the odds they face, Oliver the Wise asks Roland the Brave to blow his horn, but Roland refuses, because blowing the horn would be dishonourable. Eventually, Roland changes his mind and blows his oliphant. By now, however, the roles are reversed. Oliver argues that once it is too late to save the troops, sounding the horn would be shameful. Thus, as in *1 Henry VI*, Roland's extreme notions of honour prevail over Oliver's advocacy of the need for a knight to avoid folly and excessive zeal and unnecessary casualties.

The dialogue between Roland and Oliver, two friends and brothers-in-law, resonates with the tension between honour and shame. It is another example of vain glory versus utilitarianism; of prowess versus wisdom ("Roland est preux et Olivier est sage").

> Oliver said: 'There is a huge army of pagans
> But mighty few of our Franks, it seems to me.
> Companion Roland, blow your horn;
> Charles will hear it and the army will turn back.'
> Roland replies: 'That would be an act of folly;
> Throughout the fair land of France I should lose my good name.
>
> (*The Song of Roland*, lines 1049–54)

> 'Companion Roland, blow your horn;
> Charles will hear it and turn the army round.
> With his barons the king will come to our aid.'
> Roland replies: 'God forbid that
> My kinsmen should incur reproach because of me
> Or that the fair land of France should fall into disrepute.'
>
> (*The Song of Roland*, lines 1059–64)

> Oliver said: 'I see no blame in this.
> I have seen the Saracens from Spain;
> The valleys and the mountains are covered with them. . . .
> But we have a tiny company of men.'
> Roland replies . . .
> 'I prefer to die than to suffer such shame.'
> . . .
> Roland is brave [preux] and Oliver is wise [sage].
>
> (*The Song of Roland*, lines 1082–93)

> Roland said: 'I shall sound the oliphant
> And Charles, who is going through the pass, will hear it.
> I pledge to you, the Franks will soon return.'
> Oliver said: 'That would be most shameful
> And all your kinsmen would then be blamed;
> Such shame would endure as long as they live.
> When I spoke to you of this, you did nothing.
> But you will not now act so on my advice.
> If you sound the horn, there will be no valour in it.
>
> (*The Song of Roland*, lines 1702–10)

Roland said: 'Why do you bear a grudge?'
And he replies: 'Companion, you have been the cause of it.
For a true vassal's act, in its wisdom, avoids folly;
Caution is better than great zeal.'

(*The Song of Roland*, lines 1722–25)

The fighting Archbishop, Turpin, finally resolves the controversy. Although blowing the horn would be of no avail for the saving of the troops, he counsels, it would at least allow Charlemagne to avenge their deaths defeating the enemy.

The basic question *The Song of Roland* poses also appeared in the twelfth-century *Romance of Alexander*, in which the companions of Eumenides of Arcady, suprised by the enemy in overwhelming numbers, refuse to call Alexander for aid. Although the story is reminscent of Roland's refusal to sound his horn, Alexander, when finally summoned, arrives in time to save his troops.[15]

There is thus a certain parallelism between the epic poem, *Chanson de Roland*, and *1 Henry VI*. In both, the heroes confront impossible odds, the spirit of chivalry dominates, and honour prevails over common sense and utilitarian logic. The *Chanson* offers the two sides of chivalry: Roland's vain prowess, which proves not only useless but counterproductive, and true chivalry, exemplified by Oliver, which in its wisdom, avoids folly. Talbot's English forces disintegrated upon the death of their commander.[16] In *The Song of Roland*, the decision to not call for help meant sacrificing the protagonists and their twenty thousand troops.

Shakespeare's text parallels the ideas expressed by the fourteenth century's principal authors on the norms of chivalry, Honoré Bouvet and Giovanni da Legnano. Bouvet starts from the premise that to flee from battle is better than to stay and await a certain death. Nevertheless, after referring to Aristotle's admonition that to "flee is wicked, and brings great reproach and shame,"[17] Bouvet lends his support to staying and fighting. Facing battle makes life "everlasting" and is preferable to saving the mortal body, "which is but meat for worms."[18] But Bouvet is not a fanatic: when not engaged in battle against the Saracens or to defend the faith, a man should flee if escape is possible and staying would not prevent a defeat.[19]

Giovanni da Legnano's discussion is similar, emphasizing not only immortality, but nobility:

[B]y fleeing he wins his bodily life, whereas by waiting and meeting the death of the body, he wins the life of the soul, which is without comparison nobler, and therefore to be chosen. . . . [I]f a man dies, he wins an act of fortitude, which is most noble.[20]

The exchange between the Talbots articulates these chivalric values. When the father urges the son to flee, his son's response is, in the vein of Honoré Bouvet and Giovanni da Legnano that "the world will say he is not Talbot's blood that basely fled when noble Talbot stood" (*1 Henry VI*, IV.v.16–17). The father then echoes the same idea of nobility and immortality: "side by side together live and die, and soul with soul from France to heaven fly" (*1 Henry IV*, IV.v.54–55).

I turn now to two episodes concerning the chivalric norm condemning retreat on the battlefield. Shakespeare used the first to ridicule Charles, the Dauphin of France, and the second to elevate Bedford, England's Regent of France, to even greater glory. In the first episode, seeking to encourage the French to assault the English besieged in Orléans, Charles promises not to retreat under any circumstances, inviting anyone to kill him should he breach this promise: "Him I forgive my death that killeth me / When he sees me go back one foot or flee" (*1 Henry VI*, I.ii.20–21).[21] Beaten back by the English, the French flee with Charles blaming his troops for abandoning him: "Who ever saw the like? What men have I? / Dogs, cowards, dastards! I would ne'er have fled, / But that they left me 'midst my enemies" (*1 Henry VI*, I.iii.1–3).

The chroniclers do not mention this episode. Nevertheless, Shakespeare may have wanted to reflect the normative sources of his era and enunciate the chivalric rule allowing punishment by death for a knight who abandons the battlefield. Honoré Bouvet rather inconsistently supports killing a man "who is the first to flee from the battle while the others stand their ground."[22] Shakespeare's Charles effectively gives any man that sees him violate his chivalric obligations the authority to inflict this punishment. Anyone who kills him under these circumstances would not be liable because he would be carrying out the legal rules of chivalry. In reality, of course, no one would dare touch the Dauphin of France.

At a time when kings were actually expected to fight at the head of their troops, disaster followed when they were killed or captured. Christine de Pisan, the one major female compiler of rules of chivalry, sensibly urged that kings should stay away from battle. Even though a king's presence on the battlefield raises the morale of his men and sets an example, his death or capture is a catastrophe, not only for the king and his family, but for the entire realm.[23]

The second episode concerning the obligation not to leave the battle is the story of the old and dying Bedford, the Regent of France, at the siege of Rouen. Bedford bravely refuses Talbot's offer to be repatriated to a safer place, arguing that doing so would dishonour him, while his presence at the battle would raise the soldiers' morale and "revive the soldiers' hearts" (*1 Henry VI*, III.v.56). Again, the chroniclers do not describe this episode, but Shakespeare's treatment of Bedford is fully in accordance with the mores of chivalry. For Bedford, like the Talbots, retreat would be shameful.

Shakespeare's text also implicates the issue of the treatment of the old and sick in time of war. By suggesting that Bedford should allow them to "bestow [him] in some better place, fitter for sickness and for crazy age"

(*1 Henry VI*, III.v.47–48), Talbot demonstrates that the chivalric rules prohibiting retreat did not apply to the old and the infirm. Bouvet teaches that the elderly are privileged and cannot be compelled to go to war.[24] In fact, by addressing the old warrior as "courageous Bedford," Burgundy reinforces the notion that Bedford will lose none of his honour by leaving the scene of the siege. Upon learning that Bedford has died, Talbot declares: "A braver soldier never couchèd lance; / A gentler heart did never sway in court" (*1 Henry VI*, III.vi.20–21).

The obligation not to retreat was deeply rooted in the mores of chivalry. Although from a military perspective, sacrificing military strategy to romantic principles of chivalry was certainly senseless,[25] for a time this obligation was taken quite seriously. The knights of the French King John's Order of the Star (founded 1351) were required to take an oath that they would not retreat in battle more than a certain specified distance, failing which they promised to die or surrender.[26] However, this policy cost so many lives that it was abandoned before long. Henry V's experience on the eve of Agincourt offers another example of adherence to such foolish rules. In moving towards the enemy, he mistakenly advanced too far and found himself in an area where he was unprotected and could be attacked and captured by the French. However, he was in battle dress and had issued an order that his knights on reconnaisance missions should take off their armour to spare them the shame of retreating on their way back to the English camp. He thus had to spend the night at the place he had reached, in order to await his troops.[27]

Punishment by death was not the usual sanction for retreating from the battlefield, despite Bouvet's recommendation. There were various gradations of dishonour. Reversal upside down of a knight's coat of arms (*subversio armorum*) was a common sanction.[28] Thus, Sir John Fastolf was suspended from the Order of the Garter for displaying cowardice at the battle of Patay.[29] Shakespeare devotes considerable attention to this incident in *1 Henry VI*, changing some historical data in the process. His treatment of Fastolf's flight from the battle of Patay and his subsequent dishonour is both interesting and eloquent.

CAPTAIN: Whither away, Sir John Fastolf in such haste?

FASTOLF: Whither away? To save myself by flight.
 We are like to have the overthrow again.

CAPTAIN: What, will you fly, and leave Lord Talbot?

FASTOLF: Ay, all the Talbots in the world, to save my life.
 (*Exit*)

CAPTAIN: Cowardly knight, ill fortune follow thee!

(*1 Henry VI*, III.v.63–68)

When Shakespeare's Fastolf delivers a letter to Talbot from the Duke of Burgundy, who has been persuaded by Joan of Arc to join the French side, Talbot impulsively rips off Fastolf's Garter, without awaiting the approval of his peers. He beautifully articulates the virtues expected of a knight, especially one endowed with the Order of the Garter.

> I vowed, base knight, when I did meet thee next,
> To tear the Garter from thy craven's leg,
> (*He tears it off*)
> Which I have done because unworthily
> Thou wast installèd in that high degree.—
> Pardon me, princely Henry and the rest.
> This dastard at the battle of Patay
> When but in all I was six thousand strong,
> And that the French were almost ten to one,
> Before we met, or that a stroke was given,
> Like to a trusty squire did run away;
> In which assault we lost twelve hundred men.
> Myself and divers gentlemen beside
> Were there surprised and taken prisoners.
> Then judge, great lords, if I have done amiss,
> Or whether that such cowards ought to wear
> This ornament of knighthood: yea or no?
>
> GLOUCESTER: To say the truth, this fact was infamous
>   And ill beseeming any common man,
>   Much more a knight, a captain and a leader.
>
> TALBOT: When first this order was ordained, my lords,
>   Knights of the Garter were of noble birth,
>   Valiant and virtuous, full of haughty courage,
>   Such as were grown to credit by the wars;
>   Not fearing death nor shrinking for distress,
>   But always resolute in most extremes.
>   He then that is not furnished in this sort
>   Doth but usurp the sacred name of knight,
>   Profaning this most honourable order,
>   And should—if I were worthy to be judge—
>   Be quite degraded, like a hedge-born swain
>   That doth presume to boast of gentle blood.
>
> KING HENRY: (*to Fastolf*)
>   Stain to thy countrymen, thou hear'st thy doom.
>   Be packing, therefore, thou that wast a knight.
>   Henceforth we banish thee on pain of death.

(*1 Henry VI*, IV.i.14–47)

Here, Shakespeare departs from his sources in several respects. While in the chroniclers, the Duke of Bedford, heroic Regent of France, removes the garter, in Shakespeare it is Talbot who enforces the chivalric code. In the chroniclers, the garter is eventually returned, but no further mention of the garter is made in Shakespeare. Hall wrote that Bedford also restored the garter despite Talbot's opposition.[30] Furthermore, Shakespeare adds banishment pronounced by the King to the sanction of dishonour. In this way, he uses a historical episode to emphasize the importance of adhering to the chivalric code.

CHIVALRY AS A
NORMATIVE IDEAL

The literature of chivalry paints a noble and idealistic picture of the perfect knight. For the modern reader, that image is unrealistic and unachievable, a beautiful fiction. Nevertheless, as a catalogue of virtues and values, it remains an enviable model for honourable conduct in peace and in war. Divorced from its aristocratic and martial aspects, chivalry's pertinence persists, not only for honourable and therefore humanitarian behaviour in war, but also as a model of responsible conduct in the civil society. Commands to spare the enemy who asks for mercy, to aid women in distress, to keep one's promise, to act charitably and to be magnanimous transcend any one particular historical period or sociopolitical context. Malcolm Vale suggests that chivalric ideals such as honour, loyalty, courage and generosity fulfilled a fundamental human need, especially among the warrior elites. Chivalry was thus "the sentiment of honour in its medieval guise . . . [, which] among warrior classes . . . possesses a universal and, perhaps, an eternal validity."[1] By creating a culture in which honour and shame are cardinal, chivalry sends a lasting message.

In his classical *Libre del ordre de cavayleria*, translated into English by William Caxton in the fifteenth century, Ramon Llull writes that the duties of the *chevalier sans reproche* are to defend the faith against unbelievers, to defend the temporal lord and to protect the weak, women, widows and orphans. He must pursue robbers and malefactors, uphold justice and train to acquire the virtues necessary to perform these duties: wisdom, charity, loyalty and courage. He must strive to achieve honour and avoid pride, false-swearing, idleness, lechery and treason. Within the limits of his means, he should practise generosity. He should possess loyalty, truth, hardiness, largesse, humility,[2] independent spirit (franchise), courtesy and prowess.[3]

In theory, honour prevailed over military strategy, requiring that both parties should enjoy an even playing field, or equality in their battlefield positions. Thus, although often ignored, chivalric custom encouraged the belligerents to stipulate a time and a place for battle.[4] Loyalty not only meant fidelity to one's lord and the Church, but also observance of the mutual obligations that bound the order of chivalry and chivalric customs.[5]

Of course, Shakespeare was a Renaissance humanist writer, far removed from the medieval era on which he focused in his Kings. The radical individualism of the Middle Ages and the emphasis on individual prowess, courage, justice and honour[6] over collective achievement, values exemplified by Shakespeare's Hotspur, had to cede to considerations of public power, the cardinal role of the king, citizenship,[7] nationalism and patriotism. Justice became a function of the state.[8] The vision of a knight as an individualistic "protector of the community" had to succumb to considerations of national policy.[9]

Seeking to increase their prestige and promote public relations, Renaissance kings tried to identify themselves with the traditions and trappings of chivalry, and to appear as repositories of chivalric honour.[10] Earlier times demonstrated similar concerns. Lydgate began his Troy book in response to Henry V's desire to remember better "the prowess of old chivalry."[11] In emulating chivalric values such as the insistence on clarifying the justness of war before resorting to it,[12] piety and humility at Agincourt, Henry himself may have deliberately played to a chivalric gallery.[13] Reviving the tradition of chivalry, at least rhetorically, and finding chivalric heroes in England's kings, especially Henry V, English writers and historians in the fifteenth and sixteenth centuries used chivalry to advance patriotic foreign policy.

In Shakespeare's own times, the Tudors (Henry Tudor of Richmond—Henry VII—was the first Tudor monarch) turned chivalry to the service of the state and the dynasty, and claimed a monopoly on the validation of knightly honour, including the use of violence to assert such honour.[14]

By the later Middle Ages, grafting of personal honour onto the requirement of loyalty to the prince—often regarded as an aspect of loyalty to God—helped create a more national and patriotic chivalry.[15] In return, meritorious service to the Crown could be rewarded with titles of nobility. By exalting chivalry in his plays, Shakespeare may have served the interests of the Crown. He accepts the chroniclers' vision applying the chivalric tradition to kings, but his recognition that the kings' public interests are paramount makes his kings different from the medieval model of super-knights.[16]

Shakespeare's belief in social mobility, his insistence that "virtue may highly ennoble a peasant, as vice may deeply degrade a lord,"[17] gave the message of chivalry a broader relevance. One who acts chivalrously deserves elevation to knighthood and merits chivalric status. Thus, despite the importance of noble birth, knighthood was not hereditary. The Renaissance humanists' view that education and learning were of paramount importance and that nobility of mind was superior to that of blood probably inspired Shakespeare's attitudes. As Joan Simon explained, the tradition that honour rested on long lineage appeared out of date at the time Shakespeare wrote.[18] As a result, nobility of merit was more important than nobility of birth.

Petruccio underlines the importance of merit:

> For 'tis the mind that makes the body rich,
> And as the sun breaks through the darkest clouds,
> So honour peereth in the meanest habit.

(The Taming of the Shrew, IV.iii.170–72)

King Simonides makes the same point: "Opinion's but a fool, that makes us scan the outward habit for the inward man" (*Pericles, Prince of Tyre*, sc. 6, 59–60). Similarly, Thaisa describes the basis of nobility:

> (*kneeling*) Suppose his birth were base, when that his life
> Shows that he is not so, yet he hath virtue,
> The very ground of all nobility,
> Enough to make him noble.

(Pericles, Prince of Tyre, sc. 9, 77–80)

The King in *All's Well That Ends Well* makes an eloquent statement for equality of merit:

> Strange is it that our bloods,
> Of colour, weight, and heat, poured all together,
> Would quite confound distinction, yet stands off
> In differences so mighty. . . .
> From lowest place when virtuous things proceed,
> The place is dignified by th' doer's deed.
> Where great additions swell's, and virtue none,
> It is a dropsied honour. Good alone
> Is good without a name, vileness is so:
> The property by what it is should go,
> Not by the title . . .
>   . . .
>   . . . honours thrive

When rather from our acts we them derive
Than our foregoers.

(*All's Well That Ends Well*, II.iii.119–32, 136–38)

Aragon, in *The Merchant of Venice*, makes a powerful plea for the superiority of those whose rank was gained through and reflects merit:

for who shall go about
To cozen fortune, and be honourable
Without the stamp of merit? Let none presume
To wear an undeservèd dignity.
O, that estates, degrees, and offices
Were not derived corruptly, and that clear honour
Were purchased by the merit of the wearer!
How many then should cover that stand bare,
How many be commanded that command?
How much low peasantry would then be gleaned
From the true seed of honour. . . .

(*The Merchant of Venice*, II.ix.36–46)

Finally, before the walls of Harfleur, Henry alludes to the inherent nobility of his yeomen:

For there is none of you so mean and base
That hath not noble lustre in your eyes.

(*Henry V*, III.i.29–30)

In his oration to his outnumbered soldiers at Agincourt, Henry V mentions elevation to knighthood as a reward for bravery, refering to his brotherhood with his soldiers:

For he today that sheds his blood with me
Shall be my brother; be he ne'er so vile,
This day shall gentle his condition.

(*Henry V*, IV.iii.61–63)

In thus espousing social mobility, Shakespeare remains faithful to the chivalric tradition that actually enabled commoners and others to attain knighthood and noble status through chivalric service. Indeed, Shakespeare lived in a period of English social history "unprecedented in its degree of social mobility."[19]

As Maurice Keen demonstrates, material gain was not war's sole attraction. In addition to the glamour associated with the knightly profession and status, many took its ethical principles seriously. For those who started from lower social status and those "whose gentle or near gentle birth was put at risk by social and economic pressures,"[20] chivalry was thus a calling and a profession. Dubbings, ceremonial knightings before battles, the prospect of ennoblement for common men who distinguished themselves through courage, and the fact that proven service in arms could support a claim to noble status all helped explain the broader allure of chivalry.

Shakespeare refers to such knightings on several occasions, particularly when characters are dubbed knights in return for their courage on the battlefield. Titus recalls his many "valiant" sons:

> Knighted in field, slain manfully in arms
> In right and service of their noble country.

> (Titus Andronicus, I.i.196–97)

Henry VI, "in reguerdon of that duty done," dubs Richard Plantagenet and creates him Duke of York (1 Henry VI, III.i.174). Alexander Iden, a poor esquire of Kent who kills the rebel Jack Cade, is "created knight for his good service" (2 Henry VI, V.i.77).

The Bastard refers to his mother's husband, Robert Falconbridge, as "a soldier, by the honour-giving hand of Coeur-de-lion knighted in the field" (King John, I.i.53–54). In knighting him, King John states: "Kneel thou down Philip, but arise more great" (King John, I.i.161). Heroes and leaders are rewarded with higher titles of nobility. Thus Henry VI dubs John Talbot the Earl of Shrewsbury in return for his courage (1 Henry VI, III.viii.16–27). After the young Talbot has fought bravely against the French and thus proven himself, his father tells him "now thou art sealed the son of chivalry" (1 Henry VI, IV.vi.29).

The chivalric notion of justice as the righting of wrongs by individuals applied through an extension of the idea of just war.[21] According to just war theory, knights should not fight in unjust wars, or for booty, because honour and fame can only be gained in a just war.[22] Their primary duty is to protect others through the exercise of arms. Thus, in dubbing his son, Henry VI proclaims, "Edward Plantagenet, arise a knight—and learn this lesson: draw thy sword in right" (3 Henry VI, II.ii.61–62). Despite the fact that his war is a rebellion against the monarch, Hotspur declares:

> Now for our consciences: the arms are fair
> when the intent of bearing them is just.

> (1 Henry IV, V.ii.87–88)

Shakespeare's Suffolk, captured at sea by pirates, refuses to plead for his life, because a true knight prefers death to shame and dishonour.[23] He says proudly, "True nobility is exempt from fear" (2 Henry VI, IV.i.131). In the same vein, Shakespeare's Julius Caesar, one of chivalry's nine worthies, declares that "cowards die many times before their deaths; / the valiant never taste of death but once" (*Julius Caesar*, II.ii.32–33).

Furthermore, "a true knight" (*Richard II*, I.iii.34) has an obligation to respect his oath. Thomas Mowbray declares that he comes "engagèd by my oath—which God defend a knight should violate" (*Richard II*, I.iii.17–18). He has come to "defend [his] loyalty and truth to God, my king, and my succeeding issue" (*Richard II*, I.iii.19–20). After his defeat, Charles the Dauphin is made "to swear allegiance to his majesty [Henry VI], as thou art knight, never to disobey nor be rebellious to the crown of England" (*1 Henry VI*, V.vi.169–71). As King John dies, poisoned by a monk, the Bastard swears knightly allegiance to the new king, Henry III:

> To whom with all submission, on my knee,
> I do bequeath my faithful services
> And true subjection everlastingly.
>
> (*King John*, V.vii.103–5)

Finally, as he lies dying at Agincourt, the Earl of Suffolk's last words to Exeter are to "commend my service to my sovereign" (*Henry V*, IV.vi.23).

The Rape of Lucrece highlights the duty to protect women. Thus Lucrece says to the assembled knights:

> ['T]is a meritorious fair design
> To chase injustice with revengeful arms.
> Knights, by their oaths, should right poor ladies' harms.
>
> (*The Rape of Lucrece*, lines 1692–94)

Although Tarquinus breaches these rules, Lucrece pleads with him not to violate her by reference to "knighthood," and he himself recognizes in his soliloquies that his deed was "shame to knighthood and to shining arms" (*The Rape of Lucrece*, line 197). In fact, a man's knightly status should make a woman feel safe, not threatened by the prospect of rape (*1 Henry VI*, V.v.57–58).

Courtesy is also an important knightly virtue and knights are a model of "courage, courtship, and proportion" (*2 Henry VI*, I.iii.57). By giving a disadvantaged Achilles a pause from fighting, Hector treats him courteously, and Achilles "disdain[s] [Hector's] courtesy" (*Troilus and Cressida*, V.vi.13–15) because he does not want to be subjected to the same fair rules of the game that chivalry provides. This courtesy can, however, reach vain proportions. In responding to the invitation of the Countess of Auvergne, Sir John Talbot explains that he does so for the sake of "courtesy" (*1 Henry VI*, II.ii.58), even though he suspects she is trying to capture him.

Despite these excessive aspects, courtesy can lead to honorable and generous acts not required by the rules. When, after his victory in Shrewsbury, Henry IV chivalrously decides to liberate his enemy Douglas "ran-somless" in recognition of his great bravery on the battlefield, admired even by his "adversaries," John of Lancaster describes Henry's gesture as "high courtesy" (1 Henry IV, V.v.29–33). Promising to treat the captive queen of the Goths, Tamora, respectfully, the new emperor Saturninus consults Lavinia, whom he claims as his bride, and Lavinia responds: "sith true nobility warrants these words in princely courtesy" (Titus Andronicus, I.i.271–72). When the "First Knight" in Pericles, Prince of Tyre says that he and his peers as "gentlemen have neither in our hearts nor outward eyes envied the great, nor shall the low despise" (Pericles, Prince of Tyre, sc. 7, 22–24), Pericles replies: "You are right courteous knights" (Pericles, Prince of Tyre, sc. 7, 25).

Piety is a paramount knightly virtue and service to God trumps even service to the king. In recounting to Henry VI his conquests in France, Talbot presents his victory as a tribute to God.

> TALBOT: Lets fall [my] sword before your highness' feet,
> And with submissive loyalty of heart
> Ascribes the glory of his conquest got
> First to my God, and next unto your grace.
> (He kneels)
>
> (1 Henry VI, III.viii.9–12)

With the humility of a prince who recognizes God's hand in his victory, Henry V commands his troops to acknowledge that "God fought for us" and orders the singing of Non nobis, Domine, non nobis, sed nomini tuo do gloriam and Te Deum (Henry V, IV.viii.119–23). "Take it God for it [the victory] is none but thine" (Henry V, IV.viii.111–12). Even Richard III recognizes that piety is necessary to mobilize popular support and cynically stages a farce showing him praying between two bishops, emphasizing his modesty and piety.

> MAYOR: See where his grace stands 'tween two clergymen.
>
> BUCKINGHAM: Two props of virtue for a Christian prince,
> To stay him from the fall of vanity;
> And see, a book of prayer in his hand—
> True ornaments to know a holy man.
>
> (Richard III, III.vii.95–99)

Respect for the Church is thus a fundamental part of knighthood. Even a knight as bloody as Clifford, who does not hesitate to kill a young boy, Rutland, in vengeance, would not kill a priest: "Chaplain, away— thy priesthood saves thy life" (3 Henry VI, I.iii.3). However, this mercy towards the clergy does not save Clifford when King Edward quickly yields to Richard's insistence to kill Clifford in revenge for York and Rutland, even after articulating chivalry's rule for the protection of non-combatants: "And now the battle's ended, / If friend or foe, let him be gently used" (3 *Henry VI*, II.vi.44–45).

Although yielding to vengeance in some cases, pity is an important knightly attribute. Accused of various offences, Humphrey, Duke of Gloucester, asserts that he had practised pity (2 *Henry VI*, III.i.125) and the King recognizes that that he is endowed with the principal chivalric virtues of "honour, truth, and loyalty" (2 *Henry VI*, III.i.203).

Edward's statement also demonstrates the obligation of respectful treatment for the bodies of the dead. Mutilating vanquished bodies and denying the right of honourable burial and return to the families remains a major problem even in modern wars, despite clear rules of modern humanitarian law requiring respectful treatment of the dead and a search for the missing.[24] As I show in Chapter 4, chivalry condemned such excesses, especially between knights, who are bound to act honourably on the battlefield.

Henry of Richmond's decision to pardon the soldiers that fled during the battle against Richard III raises interesting questions about the true motivations for this magnanimity. Shakespeare describes the pardon as triggered by utilitarian considerations: "Proclaim a pardon to the soldiers fled that in submission will return to us" (*Richard III*, V.viii.16–17). This mixture of humanitarianism and utilitarianism is equally apparent in the reasons behind Henry V's decision to set an example by ordering Bardolph's execution for robbing a French church:

> KING HARRY: We would have all such offenders so cut off, and we
> here give express charge that in our marches through the coun-
> try there be nothing compelled from the villages, nothing
> taken but paid for, none of the French upbraided or abused in
> disdainful language. For when lenity and cruelty play for a
> kingdom, the gentler gamester is the soonest winner.
>
> (*Henry V*, III.vi.108–14)

Shakespeare explains this proclamation, which anticipates the modern law of war, on grounds of effectiveness rather than abstract humanity, the same way humanitarian principles are taught in modern military academies.

Knights had religious duties in addition to secular obligations. Throughout the canon, kings and leaders articulate their wish for Christian unity against the "pagans," glorify crusaders and pay lip service to the idea of leaving on a crusade, if only peace at home would allow them to go. Soldiers of Christ, they are obligated to liberate the holy places from Islamic rule. Salisbury states eloquently the chivalric dream:

> O nation,
>
> . . .
>
> . . . gripple thee unto a pagan shore,
> Where these two Christian armies might combine

The blood of malice in a vein of league,
And not to spend it so unneighbourly.

(*King John*, V.ii.34, 36–39)

Prince Arthur is praised for the very fact that he is a descendant of "Richard that robbed the lion of his heart / And fought the holy wars in Palestine" (*King John*, II.i.3–4). In his famous eulogy to England, the dying John of Gaunt praises her kings for the "Christian service and true chivalry" of their crusaders (*Richard II*, II.i.54). Similarly, the Bishop of Carlisle, in lamenting Norfolk's death in Italy, praises him for the service in the crusades:

Many a time hath banished Norfolk fought
For Jesu Christ in glorious Christian field,
Streaming the ensign of the Christian cross
Against black pagans, Turks, and Saracens[.]

(*Richard II*, IV.i.83–86)

Mistakenly believing that peace at home has finally arrived, Henry IV pledges, as a priority, to leave on a crusade:

As far as to the sepulchre of Christ—
Whose soldier now, under whose blessèd cross
We are impressèd and engaged to fight—
Forthwith a power of English shall we levy,
Whose arms were moulded in their mothers' womb
To chase these pagans in those holy fields
Over whose acres walked those blessèd feet
Which fourteen hundred years ago were nailed,
For our advantage, on the bitter cross.

(*1 Henry IV*, I.i.19–27)

Once informed by Westmoreland of the fighting in Wales, however, Henry IV resignedly concludes that

It seems then that the tidings of this broil
Brake off our business for the Holy Land.

(*1 Henry IV*, I.i.47–48)

The hope and the quest remain, nonetheless, even as Henry IV's death is approaching, he states: "were these inward wars once out of hand, we would, dear lords, unto the Holy Land" (*2 Henry IV*, III.i.102–03).

Although Henry IV's dream of fighting in the crusades, of "draw[ing] no swords, but what are sanctified" (*2 Henry IV*, IV.iii.3–4), seems to be motivated by religious and chivalric fervor, he finally reveals other, more self-serving motivations on his deathbed. He thus tells the future Henry V that a crusade would distract his detractors from the memory of his usurpation of Richard II's crown. To avoid being overthrown, Henry IV intended "to lead out many to the Holy Land lest rest and lying still might make them look too near into my state" (*2 Henry IV*, IV.iii.339–41). He therefore counsels his son "to busy giddy minds with foreign quarrels, that action hence borne out may waste the memory of the former days" (*2 Henry IV*, IV.iii.342–43). This "cynical, self-protective strategy"[25] may well reflect Henry's guilt and malaise about Richard II's death. However, his repeated wishes to fight in the crusades may be more than lip-service and hypocrisy. The King's exchange with Warwick contains a real poignancy. Upon discovering that the room in which he fell sick is called Jerusalem, Henry declares:

Laud be to God! Even there my life must end.
It hath been prophesied to me many years
I should not die but in Jerusalem,
Which vainly I supposed the Holy Land;
But bear me to that chamber; there I'll lie;
In that Jerusalem shall Harry die.

(*2 Henry IV*, IV.iii.364–69)

The most heroic of Shakespeare's princely knights is of course Henry V. Although he was "a truant . . . to chivalry" (*1 Henry IV*, V.i.94) in his youth as Prince Hal, he recognizes the "majesty and power of law and justice" (*2 Henry IV*, V.ii.77) on his accession to the throne as Henry V. He is ready to submit "his greatness . . . into the hands of justice" (*2 Henry IV*, V.ii.110–11). Shakespeare reserves the most flattering picture of the perfect knight for Henry V at Agincourt, one that emphasizes honour, courage, lack of material pursuits and generosity, which includes allowing those that fear the fighting to depart. Clarence describes him as one who is "as full of valour as of kindness, princely in both" (*Henry V*, IV.iii.15–16). Henry's oration to his soldiers on the eve of the battle of Agincourt (Chapter 5) is a masterpiece of chivalric principles (*Henry V*, IV.iii.20–39).

This image of the perfect knight was quite unreal, even for medieval knights, but it had a powerful role as an ideal. In his critique of chivalry, Huizinga writes that when viewed with a sober realism, the highly praised chivalry was merely "a fabricated, ridiculously anachronistic comedy."[26] However, he admits that dreams and illusions are important in the history of culture, and that the desire to imitate chivalric life was great among the medievals.[27]

The rules of chivalry can rightly be criticized as artificial, with higher and lower nobility engaging in wars and plundering the countryside largely for ransom and booty. Chivalry's mystique likely contributed to the endemic nature of medieval wars, as Keen has suggested.[28] Nevertheless, chivalry tried to contain and control the endemic violence of the Middle Ages, albeit ineffectively. An element of glory, "the tinsel glint of chivalry,"[29] tended to promote more honourable behaviour. In medieval wars, honour, chivalry and knighthood enhanced any existing compliance with humanitarian norms and strengthened protection for non-combatants. The idea that chivalry requires soldiers to act in a civilized manner is one of its most enduring legacies.

SEVEN

DEBUNKING CHIVALRY'S MYTH: COMMONERS, FOOLS, CYNICS

Although chivalry was a normative system only applicable to knights and nobility, it radiated values for the lower classes. Commoners thus could and did aspire to be elevated to knighthood. Huizinga demonstrated that "the knightly ideal, artificial and worn-out as it may have been,"[1] exercised a powerful influence on the political history of the Middle Ages. The bourgeoisie's tendency to imitate chivalry was a major factor in the spread of its norms and values.

However, the chivalric ideal excluded the lower classes. Knights mistreated and ridiculed the commoners; the commoners, including those in Shakespeare, reciprocated by deprecating chivalry. Shakespeare used commoners to poke fun at chivalry and demystify it, primarily by showing its limitations and the artificiality of its rites.

Despite its power within the noble class, the chivalric code offered no guidance for interclass relations. I have already explained that there was little sense of community cutting across class lines. The chivalric class affinity extended across national boundaries and loyalties, but not to the lower classes, including commoners and mercenaries. As a result, knights were careful to avoid being captured by commoners during battle, because there was no expectation that quarter and mercy would be granted. Similarly, commoners would not expect mercy from knights.[2] Mercy was also not expected in battles between communal troops. When Henry V ordered the killing of the French prisoners at Agincourt, the English captors, who were knights themselves, were reluctant to carry out the order. Not only did they expect ransoms, but they also had scruples about killing members of their own class, behaviour that ran contrary to the mores of the Anglo-French wars in which chivalric norms were respected and ransom normally granted.[3] The King, not surprisingly, ultimately had to use his archers to carry out the massacre.

Shakespeare's commoners are not the only voices of sarcasm. Just as important are the knights he presents as either paradigms of excess and vanity or cynics who take advantage of the system. In either case, the myth implodes. While debunking some aspects of chivalry, Shakespeare still takes care not to denigrate its positive qualities as a code for honourable behaviour. Certainly the perfect knight provides the role model. Shakespeare is nonetheless a dramatist who observes human nature with a shrewd eye and rejects the utopian and romantic picture of what Huizinga sarcastically called the "beautiful life." In this chapter, I focus on Shakespeare's attempt to debunk some aspects of the chivalric myth.

Despite Shakespeare's acknowledgement and advocacy of the honourable commoner's potential for upward mobility, his attitude towards commoners is far from sympathetic. In his discussion with the gamekeepers, Shakespeare's Henry VI voices his famous complaint about the common men whose loyalties sway with the political wind, not knowing to whom their conflicting promises must be kept:

> Ah, simple men, you know not what you swear.
> . . .
> Commanded always by the greater gust—
> Such is the lightness of you common men.
>
> (3 *Henry VI*, III.i.82, 87–88)

Clifford similarly complains of the role of common people who abandon Henry VI to side with Edward:

> The common people swarm like summer flies,
> And whither fly the gnats but to the sun?
> And who shines now but Henry's enemies?
>
> (3 *Henry VI*, II.vi.8–10)

This theme of the crowd of commoners attracted to a demagogue is an important one throughout the canon. The citizens of Rome are easily manipulated through the oratory of Brutus and of Antony in *Julius Caesar*, just as Buckingham sways the Londoners in *Richard III*.

For the hanging in *Henry V*, Shakespeare chose Bardolph, a rather disreputable commoner, not a knight, as an example of the punishment due a violation of the sanctity of churches and the robbing of a pyx. Interestingly, a knight who committed the same crime would be beheaded, not hanged.

Commoners, for their part, often ridicule knighthood. The rebel Jack Cade pokes fun at its sacred rites, such as the ceremony of dubbing. Informed that the King's forces led by Sir Humphrey Stafford are approaching, Cade insists that Stafford will be met by an equal:

> He is
> but a knight. . . .
> To equal him I will make myself a knight presently.
> (*He kneels and knights himself*)
> Rise up, Sir John Mortimer.

(2 Henry VI, IV.ii.115–19)

Mistress Quickly and First Beadle play games with words: "arrant knave" and "knight-errant" (2 Henry IV, V.iv.1, 22).

The most effective use of a commoner to deflate some sacred principles of chivalry appears in the episode in which Pistol captures a knight in Henry V. The doctrine of chivalry disguised the granting of quarter for ransom as an act of mercy and honour, hiding the ugly greed. The transaction was limited, in theory, to knights. Pistol the commoner mocks the status of knights and reduces the transaction to its crude essentials:

FRENCH SOLDIER: : O Seigneur Dieu!

PISTOL: (*aside*) O Seigneur Dew should be a gentleman.—

 . . .

> O Seigneur Dew, thou diest, on point of fox,
> Except, O Seigneur, thou do give to me
> Egregious ransom.

FRENCH SOLDIER: O prenez misericorde! Ayez pitie de moi!

PISTOL: 'Moy' shall not serve, I will have forty 'moys',
> Or I will fetch thy rim out at thy throat
> In drops of crimson blood.
> . . .

FRENCH SOLDIER: O je vous supplie, pour l'amour de Dieu, me pardonner. Je suis le gentilhomme de bonne maison. Gardez ma vie, et je vous donnerai deux cents ecus.

PISTOL: What are his words?

BOY: He prays you to save his life. He is a gentleman of a good house, and for his ransom he will give you two hundred crowns.

PISTOL: Tell him, my fury shall abate, and I the crowns will take.
 . . .

BOY: He gives you upon his knees a thousand thanks, and he esteems himself happy that he hath fallen into the hands of one, as he thinks, the most brave, valorous, and thrice-worthy seigneur of England.

PISTOL: As I suck blood, I will some mercy show.

(*Henry V*, IV.iv.6, 9–15, 37–46, 57–61)

Shakespeare also uses knights to debunk the pomp and circumstance of chivalry's rites. In *Henry V*, he ridicules knights' passion for their armour and horses, and, at the same time, the traditional praise of ladies in chivalric literature by making fun of a French nobleman, Bourbon, who, with bawdy overtones, extols the virtues of his horse in the emphatic terms he would use for a lady, saying that he even wrote a sonnet in his praise and concluding, "I had rather have my horse to my mistress" (*Henry V*, III.vii.11–14, 20–25, 39–43).

Even Shakespeare's most noble protagonists are not immune from vanity generated by inflated chivalric honour. Shakespeare does not spare even them from his sarcasm. Talbot's heroic image yields to ridicule when he proclaims that he would have preferred to die rather than be exchanged for a prisoner from a lower class:

TALBOT: The Duke of Bedford had a prisoner,
Called the brave Lord Ponton de Santrailles;
For him was I exchanged and ransomèd.
But with a baser man-of-arms by far
Once in contempt they would have bartered me—
Which I, disdaining, scorned, and cravèd death
Rather than I would be so pilled esteemed.
In fine, redeemed I was, as I desired.

(*1 Henry VI*, I.vi.5–12)

Talbot soon provides another striking illustration of silly chivalrous games. As he marches through France with his troops, a messenger from the Countess of Auvergne stops him with an invitation to visit her at her castle:

The virtuous lady, Countess of Auvergne,
With modesty admiring thy renown,
By me entreats, great lord, thou wouldst vouchsafe
To visit her poor castle where she lies,
That she may boast she hath beheld the man
Whose glory fills the world with loud report.

(*1 Henry VI*, II.ii.38–43)

Shakespeare's Burgundy sarcastically observes:

Is it even so? Nay, then I see our wars
Will turn unto a peaceful comic sport,

When ladies crave to be encountered with.
You may not, my lord, despise her gentle suit.

(1 Henry VI, II.ii.44–47)

Talbot, the great military leader, appears to feel that the chivalric principles of service and courtesy to women, especially those belonging to high nobility, require that he should abandon his martial duties and attend to the Countess:

> for when a world of men
> Could not prevail with all their oratory,
> Yet hath a woman's kindness overruled.—
> And therefore tell her I return great thanks,
> And in submission will attend on her.

(1 Henry VI, II.ii.48–52)

However, Talbot's excessive adherence to the shallower rites of chivalry does not dull his military senses; his test of the countess' "courtesy" (*1 Henry VI*, II.ii.58) is only for appearances. When the Countess tries to imprison the "bloodthirsty lord" (*1 Henry VI*, II.iii.33), and, patriotically but unchivalrously, "chain these legs and arms of thine that hast by tyranny these many years wasted our country, slain our citizens, and sent our sons and husbands captivate" (*1 Henry VI*, II.iii.38–41), Talbot sounds his horn and his hidden soldiers come to his rescue. Chivalric niceties resume once the Countess realizes she has been outsmarted, and Talbot does not claim any satisfaction for the wrong he has suffered. All he asks for is food and wine for his troops, and the Countess is "honoured to feast so great a warrior in [her] house" (*1 Henry VI*, II.iii.81–82).

In the case of the Countess of Auvergne, Shakespeare depicts courtly love and the service of women (*Frauendienst*) as but a veneer and a façade. Antiquated rules yield to reality and military necessity and shrewdness is the order of the day. This episode is not mentioned in Shakespeare's chroniclers or his other sources and is thus more significant as a demonstration of Shakespeare's own attitudes.[4] It is a work of fiction, regardless of whether it reflects actual examples of English officers visiting French noble ladies.[5] Phyllis Rackin suggests that Shakespeare included the Countess of Auvergne episode to define the conflict between England and France as one between masculine and feminine values and between chivalric virtue and pragmatic craft.[6] For me, it illustrates Shakespeare's scepticism about the frivolous aspects of chivalry.

In some cases, leaders and even kings exposed themselves to the dangers of romantic war adventure, with strategy yielding to the chivalric ideal.[7] The French chronicler Jean Froissart recorded cases where the overarching interest in gaining glory through prowess and courage preempted all practical and military considerations.[8] The famous Elizabethan knight and poet Sir Philip Sidney (1554–86) thus demonstrated utterly foolish courtesy by chivalrously casting off his own thigh armour because his leader, Sir William Pelham, did not have time to find his own. As a result, Sidney was wounded in the leg and the wound led to his death.[9]

Talbot provides fuel for Shakespeare's protagonists to mock chivalry's vanity even after his death. When Lucy comes to the French camp after the battle to inquire about the prisoners ("I come to know what prisoners thou hast ta'en, and to survey the bodies of the dead" (1 Henry VI, IV.vii.56–57)), he recites all of Talbot's titles, creating a ridiculous image:

> But where's the great Alcides of the field,
> Valiant Lord Talbot, Earl of Shrewsbury,
> Created for his rare success in arms
> Great Earl of Wexford, Waterford, and Valence,
> Lord Talbot of Goodrich and Urchinfield,
> Lord Strange of Blackmere, Lord Verdun of Alton,
> Lord Cromwell of Wingfield, Lord Furnival of Sheffield,
> The thrice victorious lord of Falconbridge,
> Knight of the noble order of Saint George,
> Worthy Saint Michael and the Golden Fleece,
> Great Marechal to Henry the Sixth
> Of all his wars within the realm of France?

> (1 Henry VI, IV.vii.60–71)

Joan of Arc's sarcastic response seems particularly apt:

> Here's a silly, stately style indeed.
> The Turk, that two-and-fifty kingdoms hath,
> Writes not so tedious a style as this.

> (1 Henry VI, IV.iii.72–74)

Shakespeare did not actually invent these titles but borrowed them almost literally from an epitaph for Talbot in Richard Crompton's *Mansion of Magnamitie* (1599), in turn based on the epitaph found on Talbot's tombstone in Roane.[10] Richard Hardin comments that this scene serves to "demythologize aristocracy."[11] Even Talbot's heroic death is deprived of its glory. When the Bastard of Orléans wants to mutilate the bodies of the father and the son, to "hew them to pieces, hack their bodies asunder" (1 Henry VI, IV.vii.47), the Dauphin Charles chivalrously saves them from this outrage. However, after Lucy's arrival, Joan manages to bring their death from the pantheon of heroic glory to morbid reality:

> Him that thou magnifi'st with all these titles
> Stinking and flyblown lies here at our feet.
> . . .

For God's sake let him have them. To keep them here
They would but stink and putrefy the air.

(1 Henry VI, IV.vii.75–76, 89–90)

Even Lucy's threat that "from their ashes shall be reared a phoenix that shall make all France afeard" (1 *Henry VI*, IV.vii.92–93) does not relieve the sense of nausea. Perhaps Shakespeare wanted to communicate that Talbot's death was in vain, since it did not prevent the loss of France. He may also have been influenced by the traditional contrast in medieval and sixteenth-century literature between the glory of this world and the horror of death—where all, kings and beggars alike, are equal and are eaten up by worms.

Shakespeare distinguished judicial duels (trials by battle) and single combats between leaders designed to determine the outcome of a war from duels over trivial points of honour. Chivalric literature is replete with duels over points of honour, which represented the exhibitionist and the extravagant in chivalric culture.[12] For Shakespeare, such duels were yet another chivalric rite that deserved his ridicule. The quarrel between Basset and Vernon, who asked Henry VI to grant them a right to combat, provides a quintessential example. King Henry's angry denunciation is admirably rational (1 *Henry VI*, IV.i.111–13, 137–47, 166–68).

I have already discussed Hector's challenge to the Greeks to determine whose lady is more beautiful as an example of vain chivalry, a socially useless rite. Since Shakespeare's Aeneas does not even name Hector's lady, the stupidity of that exercise is obvious (*Troilus and Cressida*, I.iii.257–80). Nestor the Greek regards the challenge for what it is, "a sportful combat" (*Troilus and Cressida*, I.iii.329), using the term "sport," like Burgundy, in the classical chivalric sense.

The desire to honour a lady was a fashionable motive for fighting for medieval and even Renaissance knights.[13] Arthur Ferguson describes Essex's ridiculous posturing before the walls of Lisbon, challenging any Spaniard of rank to meet him in single combat to fight for the honour of his mistress.[14] In a bid for personal glory at the siege of Rouen, Essex challenged Rouen's Governor to meet him to resolve a question of politics and personal honour; whether his King's cause was more just and his "mistress . . . more beautiful than yours."[15] The French just shook their heads in disbelief.

As Ferguson reports, Elizabeth's courtiers went to war as they entered the lists: "[S]o ended that day's sport" wrote a contemporary knight after an engagement with the enemy.[16]

Shakespeare understates the inherent ridiculousness of the challenge. The scene calls for the bluntness and deceiving simplicity of Cervantes's Sancho Panza and other commoners whom Don Quixote meets on his travels through the countryside. Having just encountered a group of merchants and muleteers, the errant knight Don Quixote cries: "Let everyone . . . stand where he is, unless everyone will confess that there is not in all the world a more beauteous damsel than the Empress of La Mancha, the peerless Dulcinea del Toboso."[17] Realizing that they are doing business with a madman, one of the merchants responds:

> 'Sir Knight,' he said, 'we do not know who this beautous lady is of whom you speak. Show her to us, and if she is as beautiful as you say, then we will right willingly and without any compulsion confess the truth as you have asked of us.'
>
> 'If I were to show her to you,' replied Don Quixote, "what merit would there be in you confessing a truth so self-evident? The important thing is for you, without seeing her, to believe, confess, affirm, swear, and defend that truth. Otherwise, monstrous and arrogant creatures that you are, you shall do battle with me. Come on, then, one by one, as the order of knighthood prescribes; or all of you together, if you will have it so, as is the sorry custom with those of your breed. Come on, and I will await you here, for I am confident that my cause is just.'[18]

Not surprisingly, the encounter ends with Don Quixote being beaten by the muleteers.

Shakespeare's Hotspur is the paradigm of the excessive, self-centered and egomaniacal knight. He is the fearless combatant for whom honour is the main if not the exclusive consideration; if seeking honour brings disaster on himself, his family, his followers and his country, so be it. The good of the country and the goals of governance are at best secondary. His selfish honour thus reflects medieval "knight errantry": he is vain and his rhetoric is inflated, making him almost a caricature.[19] Medieval honour always involved tension between individual honour and the duty of loyalty and obedience to the prince, but for Hotspur, the latter is not a major consideration. Shakespeare demonstrates that Hotspur's excesses prevent him from being a perfect knight.

Nevertheless, Shakespeare's Henry IV recognizes Hotspur's chivalric attributes: Hotspur gained "never-dying honour" (1 Henry IV, III.ii.106) against the renowned Douglas, and his "great name in arms" (1 Henry IV, III.ii.108) gained him "military title capital" (1 Henry IV, III.ii.110). The King favourably compares Hotspur's model to his own son, who is still the irresponsible juvenile and truant Prince Hal, whom he calls "the shadow of succession" (1 Henry IV, III.ii.99), and a "degenerate" (1 Henry IV, III.ii.128). Even Hal admits that Hotspur is a "child of honour and renown, . . . gallant . . . , [an] all-praisèd knight . . . [with] every honour sitting on his helm" (1 Henry IV, III.ii.139–42). In challenging Hotspur to single combat, Prince Hal is even more effusive in his praise of the knight:

> I do not think a braver gentleman,
> More active-valiant or more valiant-young,

More daring, or more bold, is now alive
To grace this latter age with noble deeds.

(1 Henry IV, V.i.89–92)

Again emphasizing the central place of honour in the world of chivalry, Douglas calls Hotspur "the king of honour" (1 Henry IV, IV.i.10). Lady Percy, his widow, remembers him as a model of chivalry:

For his [honour] stuck upon him as the sun
In the grey vault of heaven, and by his light
Did all the chivalry of England move
To do brave acts. He was indeed the glass
Wherein the noble youth did dress themselves.

. . .

So that in speech, in gait,
In diet, in affections of delight,
In military rules, humours of blood,
He was the mark and glass, copy and book,
That fashioned others. And him—O wondrous him!
O miracle of men!

(2 Henry IV, II.iii.18–22, 28–33)

But when these noble qualities are taken to the extreme, they become destructive and negative. Hotspur's pride is excessive, his anger extreme and impetuous, his sensitivity acute and his insistence on "rights" absolute and uncompromising. Overreacting to real or imagined indignities, he thus becomes a raving madman, reminiscent of Horatius' ira brevis furor est (anger is a short madness). The fact that Hotspur may have a legal case against the King's demand to deliver all the prisoners is of no consequence.[20] Although a more reasonable person, balancing honour with wisdom, would realize that he could not prevail against the King, Hotspur views insisting on his rights as the ultimate value, notwithstanding the inevitable consequences of this attitude. As Shakespeare shows, this extreme upholding of honour, so characteristic of proud, vain and excessive chivalry, is utter madness, not a model of honourable behaviour.

When the King's elegant and perfumed messenger demands on the battlefield that the tired Hotspur hand over the prisoners, not surprisingly, he makes Hotspur "mad" (1 Henry IV, I.iii.52). Later, practically suicidal, Hotspur tells the King:

An if the devil come and roar for them
I will not send them. I will after straight
And tell him so, for I will ease my heart,
Although it be with hazard of my head.

(1 Henry IV, I.iii.123–26)

Northumberland rebukes Hotspur for this display of disrespect, in vain urging restraint: "What, drunk with choler? Stay and pause awhile"

(*1 Henry IV*, I.iii.127). He continues scolding, saying, "Why, what a wasp-stung and impatient fool art thou to break into this woman's mood" (*1 Henry IV*, I.iii.234–35). Hotspur's own wife, Lady Percy, calls him mad: "Out, you mad-headed ape! A weasel hath not such a deal of spleen as you are tossed with" (*1 Henry IV*, II.iv.75–77).

Both parts of *Henry IV* highlight this tension between excessive pride and reason. Urging caution in his discussion with Hotspur's father, Northumberland, Lord Bardolph pleads: "Sweet Earl, divorce not wisdom from your honour" (*2 Henry IV*, I.i.161). Worcester then paints a picture that balances Hotspur's positive and negative qualities in advocating restraint and pleading against further antagonizing the King.

> In faith, my lord, you are too wilful-blame,
> And since your coming hither have done enough
> To put him quite besides his patience.
> You must needs learn, lord, to amend this fault.
> Though sometimes it show greatness, courage, blood—
> And that's the dearest grace it renders you—
> Yet oftentimes it doth present harsh rage,
> Defect of manners, want of government,
> Pride, haughtiness, opinion, and disdain,
> The least of which haunting a nobleman
> Loseth men's hearts, and leaves behind a stain. . . .

> (*1 Henry IV*, III.i.173–83)

A passage in Edmund Spenser's poem, the *Faerie Queene*, which spoke of another intemperate, "wilful blame"[21] knight, Blandamour, may have inspired this image of the "wilful-blame" Hotspur. By rejecting all compromise, Hotspur brings inevitable disaster upon himself and his followers. Lord Bardolph starkly explains Hotspur's end at Shrewsbury:

> Flatt'ring himself with project of a power
> Much smaller than the smallest of his thoughts;
> And so, with great imagination
> Proper to madmen, led his powers to death,
> And winking leapt into destruction.

> (*2 Henry IV*, I.iii.29–33)

One is reminded of a warning given by Shakespeare's contemporary Montaigne, that valour "once transgressed . . . may very easily unawares run into temerity, obstinacy and folly."[22]

In contrast to Hotspur, whose tragedy is caused by his excessive sense of honour, Sir John Oldcastle (Falstaff in *Henry IV*), Fastolf in *1 Henry VI* is a delinquent, a robber, a thief, a liar and a clown. He is the "cowardly knight" (*1 Henry VI*, III.v.68) who faces dishonour and the deprivation of his garter as punishment for his cowardice and flight from the battle of Patay. Above all, however, he is a cynic, deliberately offending chivalry's most sacred principles and bringing harsh reality and materialism to the fore. While a solemn promise meant everything for most knights, to Sir John Falstaff, a promise means nothing, even though he invokes his knightly status ("as I am a true knight, and he sends me 'security'!" (2 *Henry IV*, I.ii.43–44)) against a merchant's demand for a credible security for payment. He thus raises the same cynical questions that *Don Quixote's* Sancho Panza does in his deceptive symplicity. Shakespeare uses a reference in a letter to "John Falstaff, knight" to ridicule the obsession with distinguished titles of nobility:

> 'John Falstaff, knight'.—Every man must know that, as oft as he has occasion to name himself; even like those that are kin to the King, for they never prick their finger but they say 'There's some of the King's blood spilt.' 'How comes that?" says he that takes upon him not to conceive. The answer is as ready as a borrower's cap: 'I am the King's poor cousin, sir.'

> (2 *Henry IV*, II.ii.102–08)

More importantly, Fastaff-Oldcastle launches a frontal attack on honour, which for him is devoid of any utility:

> Well, 'tis no matter; honour pricks me on. Yea, but how if honour prick me off when I come on? How then? Can honour set-to a leg? No. Or an arm? No. Or take away the grief of a wound? No. Honour hath no skill in surgery, then? No. What is honour? A word. What is in that word "honour"? What is that "honour"? Air. A trim reckoning! Who hath it? He that died o' Wednesday. Doth he feel it? No. Doth he hear it? No. 'Tis insensible then? Yea, to the dead. But will it not live with the living? No.Why? Detraction will not suffer it. Therefore I'll none of it. Honour is a mere scutcheon. And so ends my catechism.

> (1 *Henry IV*, V.i.129–40)[23]

Driven by the primary instinct of self-preservation, Falstaff is both a critic of chivalric and martial activity, realistic and rational in his understanding of danger, and a coward. For him, life is more precious than anything else. Since death brings nothing, there is nothing that merits a sacrifice of one's life. He rejects the Christian ideal of immortality after death and thus represents the antithesis of chivalry.

Humanists, especially More and Erasmus, satirized the degenerate aspects of romantic chivalry. Erasmus's would-be-knight, Harpalus, asks how he could get as quickly and as cheaply as possible the reputation of nobility. His conversations may well have inspired Shakespeare's epitome of fake chivalry, Falstaff.[24]

For Shakespeare's chivalric protagonists, honour must be respected even at the risk of death. When challenged by Bolingbroke, Mowbray proclaims:

> Take but my shame,
> And I resign my gage.
> My dear dear lord,
> The purest treasure mortal times afford
> Is spotless reputation; that away,
> Men are but gilded loam, or painted clay.
> . . .
> Mine honour is my life. Both grow in one.
> Take honour from me, and my life is done.

> (*Richard II*, I.i.175–79, 182–83)

Brutus declares "I love the name of honour more than I fear death" (*Julius Caesar*, I.ii.90–91). Falstaff, who places himself outside the chivalric tradition, advocates a contrary approach. When the "gallant knight" Sir Walter Blunt, disguised as Henry IV, is killed in Shrewsbury by the "great Douglas," Falstaff-Oldcastle says that he himself would always choose life over glory in death:

> I like not
> such grinning honour as Sir Walter hath. Give me life,
> which if I can save, so; if not, honour comes unlooked
> for, and there's an end.

> (*1 Henry IV*, V.iii.58–61)

Falstaff unchivalrously fakes death on the battlefield at Shrewsbury to save himself from Douglas's sword (*1 Henry IV*, V.iv.75, 141). He plays the chivalric game by cheating, more than willing to claim honour he does not deserve. He thus pretends to have vanquished Hotspur, who was actually killed by Shakespeare's Prince Harry, in order to be rewarded with an earldom or a dukeship. To claim reward on the ground that he inflicted the wound, he stabs Hotspur's corpse before carrying it from the battlefield as his precious prize (*1 Henry IV*, V.iv.159) and promises to stop drinking and live decently should he be rewarded with a high title of nobility for his "courage." In his memorable soliloquy on lying, Falstaff rationalizes lying, cheating and saving his life. Before the body of Hotspur, he declares:

> Counterfeit? I lie, I am no counterfeit. To die is to be a counter-
> feit, for he is but the counterfeit of a man who hath not the
> life of a man. But to counterfeit dying when a man thereby liv-
> eth is to be no counterfeit, but the true and perfect image of

life indeed. The better part of valour is discretion, in the which
better part I have saved my life.

(1 Henry IV, V.iv.113–20)

In the tension between the romantic ideal and harsh reality, Falstaff
exemplifies the latter and Hotspur characterizes the former, an honourable
but extreme and egomaniacal knight. The two characters explain the
clash between the realistic demands of life and the chivalric ideal that
led to romantic and adventurous choices to the detriment of considerations of warfare and tactics.[25] Shakespeare is critical of both Hotspur and
Falstaff, but does not challenge the normative core of chivalry and its
ideals. Once stripped of its extreme and artificial rituals, Shakespeare's
normative chivalry represents a noble and honourable code of behaviour
that controls manifestations of violence through civilized behaviour. It is
therefore as pertinent to our times as to the Middle Ages.

Although Cervantes is considered the greatest literary critic of chivalry, he nonetheless respects the core chivalric principles.[26] Like Shakespeare, Cervantes mercilessly ridicules the excesses of the knight errantry.
However, Shakespeare and Cervantes part company in their assessment
of the present and future potential of chivalry. Cervantes considers Don
Quixote's efforts to "restore to the world the forgotten order of chivalry"[27]
a useless attempt to revive an anachronism that has no role in the post-
medieval world. He thus censures an artificial revival of the romantic tale
of a knight errant.[28] For him, the institution of chivalry died in the Middle
Ages and is incongruous in peaceful Spain. The traveller Vivaldo makes
this point when he asks Don Quixote what led him "to go armed in that
manner in a land that was so peaceful."[29]

In contrast, Shakespeare does not regard chivalry as an anachronism,
even while debunking its artificial aspects. The different political environment in which he wrote is one likely explanation for this contrast. I
have already referred to the interest of the royal court in a renewed focus
on chivalry. Moreover, Shakespeare was trying to ensure the survival of
the humanitarian core of chivalry at the time he was writing, some two
hundred years after Agincourt, when Western Europe was no longer solely
Catholic and the religious wars brought almost unprecedented savagery
to the fore.

EIGHT

PRINCIPLE UNDER STRESS

In this chapter, I address Shakespeare's discussion of how the principles of chivalry fare under the stress of factors such as necessity, reprisal, vengeance, anger and *Staatsraison*. I focus on mercy and quarter, treatment of women and oaths. Although I concentrate on the violations, I do not intend to imply that the rules were "[m]ore honoured in the breach than the observance" (*Hamlet*, I.iv.18). Actually, principles of chivalry were generally respected in medieval warfare. However, the violations, especially those on a large scale or with regard to prominent persons, the conflicts and the behaviour under pressure naturally attracted chroniclers, poets and dramatists.

Mercy and Quarter

Chivalric rules required that defeated knights be granted quarter on the battlefield, except in siege situations.[1] Given the promise of ransom for prisoners captured, granting quarter served the financial interests of the captor. However, beyond these material interests, quarter was a manifestation of mercy, a cardinal principle emphasized not only by medieval philosophers and writers on chivalry, but also throughout Shakespeare's canon. Mercy was the secular counterpart and reflection of the Christian concept of charity or *caritas*.[2] Saint Thomas Aquinas articulated the medieval convention that justice and mercy are the twin attributes of kingship and, indeed, of God himself.[3] Some situations called for the exercise of clemency; others for the full rigour of the law. The ideal king knew which was appropriate in any situation.

Shakespeare's treatment of mercy remained true to these medieval conceptions. In his plays, replete with references to mercy, Shakespeare accords mercy his highest and most poetic support. As the ultimate value, mercy is a quality of God, as well as that of kings, the brave and the noble. Consider Portia's incomparable eulogy to mercy:

> The quality of mercy is not strained.
> It droppeth as the gentle rain from heaven
> Upon the place beneath. It is twice blest:
> It blesseth him that gives, and him that takes.
> 'Tis mightiest in the mightiest. It becomes
> The thronèd monarch better than his crown.
> His sceptre shows the force of temporal power,
> The attribute to awe and majesty,
> Wherein doth sit the dread and fear of kings;
> But mercy is above this sceptred sway.
> It is enthronèd in the hearts of kings;
> It is an attribute to God himself,
> And earthly power doth then show likest God's
> When mercy seasons justice.

(*The Merchant of Venice*, IV.i.181–94)

Malcolm, son of the murdered King Duncan and poised to be the next king of Scotland, lists mercy among several chivalric "king-becoming graces" (*Macbeth*, IV.iii.92–95). Tamora's moving but futile invocation of mercy offers another example of this chivalric principle. Trying to spare her prisoner son from mutilation and death as a religious sacrifice, the captive Queen of the Goths pleads for mercy with the Roman rulers (*Titus Andronicus*, I.i.109–20).

The medieval laws of war distinguished between the treatment of combatants on the battlefield, who were entitled to quarter, and the treatment of combatants and civilians in a besieged city or fortress. If a city was taken by assault rather than by agreed terms that guaranteed protection for its inhabitants, the conquerors could kill the men and, in the view of some authors, rape the women, on the theory that the population's contumacious disregard for a prince's summons to surrender merited punishment.[4] Michel Eyquem de Montaigne refers to this custom of punishing "those who are obstinate to defend a place that by the rules of war is not tenable"[5] in time of war. Nonetheless, some writers on chivalry insisted on the prohibition of rape in all circumstances. In the terrifying catalogue of threats Shakespeare's Henry V voices at the walls of Harfleur (compare Talbot's ultimatum to Bordeaux in *1 Henry VI*, IV,ii.3–14), the word "mercy" appears four times. Eventually, going beyond the requirements the medieval law of war imposed in the event of an unconditional surrender, King Henry decided to "use mercy" (*Henry V*, III.iii.137) in his treatment of the population of Harfleur. Of course, his political motivation was not to antagonize the population of a country he claimed as his own but rather to befriend his future subjects, conveniently merging with his humanitarian behaviour.

Similarly, old Lord Clifford successfully uses the promise of mercy to entice Jack Cade's followers away from their leader, thus quelling the rebellion:

> CLIFFORD: What say ye, countrymen, will ye relent
> And yield to mercy whilst 'tis offered you,
> Or let a rebel lead you to your deaths?
> Who loves the King and will embrace his pardon,
> Fling up his cap and say 'God save his majesty'.

> (*2 Henry VI*, IV.vii.164–68)

Although rebels were not entitled to quarter, Clifford's offer advances his political goals as well as a humanitarian principle.

At the battle of Agincourt, Pistol grants quarter to a captured French nobleman in exchange for a handsome ransom. Pistol, a commoner, is a somewhat disreputable person and neither the beneficiary nor the subject of chivalric rules. Shakespeare makes it clear that his motivation to grant quarter to a nobleman lies in crude greed and not in the principles of humanity. He thus uses Pistol, a greedy and bloodthirsty antithesis of a chivalric person, to show the material underpinnings of the principle of mercy and quarter (*Henry V*, IV.iv.37, VI.iv.61).

Shakespeare occasionally presents grants of quarter untainted by extraneous, non-humanitarian considerations. Thus, Nestor the Greek describes Hector on the battlefield as a "Jupiter . . . dealing life" (*Troilus and Cressida*, IV.vii.67, 72–75). Despite this ringing endorsement of Hector's chivalry, Shakespeare still chooses not to portray an idealized knight, even for Hector, his favourite chivalric hero. Greed drives the same Hector in another situation, when he becomes a bloodthirsty hunter and killer of the Greek knight in a sumptuous armour (*Troilus and Cressida*, V.vi.27–30).

Shakespeare, ever the keen observer, shows how mercy and quarter tend to crumble under pressure in other plays as well. Chapter 9 discusses the massacre of French prisoners of war at Agincourt, which Henry attempts to justify on grounds of necessity and reprisal.[6] However one assesses Henry's order to kill the prisoners, it is impossible, either legally or morally, to excuse the threat, issued after victory had already been assured.[7] The King declares that, if the French do not depart from the battlefield but rather continue to fight, he will refuse to grant quarter to the new prisoners and will kill the prisoners already in the hands of the English:

> I was not angry since I came to France
> Until this instant. Take a trumpet, herald;

Ride thou unto the horsemen on yon hill.
If they will fight with us, bid them come down,
Or void the field: they do offend our sight.
If they'll do neither, we will come to them,
And make them skirr away as swift as stones
Enforcèd from the old Assyrian slings.
Besides, we'll cut the throats of those we have,
And not a man of them that we shall take
Shall taste our mercy. Go and tell them so.

(Henry V, IV.vii.53–63)

Henry's threat was taken seriously, thus avoiding further killing. Although Holinshed suggests that the King acted to deter a new battle, Shakespeare ascribes his order to anger over the killing of the boys at the rear camp, or even worse, the plunder of the King's possessions (Henry V, IV.vii.1–10). Under either interpretation, the threat would have violated the medieval laws of war. Modern international law, as stated in Article 23(c)–(d) of the Hague Convention (IV) with Respect to the Laws and Customs of War on Land (1907), prohibits not only killing or wounding an enemy who has surrendered, but also declaring—as Henry did—that no quarter will be given. Article 40 of Additional Protocol I to the Geneva Conventions for the Protection of Victims of War contains a similar proscription. A violation of either rule would constitute a serious war crime.

As Achilles does in the Iliad (21:99–103) (see Chapter 4), Shakespeare's Antony demonstrates the weakness and malleability of the norms pertaining to quarter and ransom, showing that they often yield to anger, vengeance or necessity (Antony and Cleopatra, III.xiii.180–84). Edward's chivalry quickly yields to Richard's insistence that vengeance for the murders of Rutland and the Duke of York, their father, prevail over the "doom of mercy" for the wounded Clifford (3 Henry VI, II.vi.46).

Shakespeare's Histories demonstrate this idea that those who deny mercy to others deserve none from their own opponents. In Henry V, the Southhampton traitors, Lord Scrope, the Earl of Cambridge and Sir Thomas Grey, advised Henry V not to show clemency to a minor offender. When his soldiers then arrest them for treason, the King rejects their pleas for mercy:

The mercy that was quick in us but late
By your own counsel is suppressed and killed.
You must not dare, for shame, to talk of mercy. . . .

(Henry V, II.ii.76–78)

This tension between vengeance and mercy continues throughout 3 Henry VI. After Clifford and Queen Margaret stab the Duke of York, Margaret orders his head to be cut off and placed, as an example, on the gates of York (3 Henry VI, I.iv.). York's severe rebuke of Margaret, before he dies, for her cruelty and unwomanly nature serves to condemn this lack of mercy (3 *Henry VI*, I.iv.114–16). Jean Howard and Phyllis Rackin note that Shakespeare goes beyond Hall's version to play up Margaret's monstrous qualities and makes her a target of invective, perhaps because she departs from a traditional female role and assumes male prerogatives. King Edward subsequently complains that York was killed "treacherously," without the opportunity to defend himself in a single combat (3 *Henry VI*, II.i.70–73). At the end of the play, King Edward, Richard of Gloucester, and George of Clarence cruelly stab and kill the captive Prince Edward, Henry VI's son, in the presence of his mother, Queen Margaret. The King himself saves Margaret's life, declaring, "Hold, Richard, hold— for we have done too much," implying that mercy has not disappeared altogether (3 *Henry VI*, V.v.42). Some writers, however, suggest that both Rutland and Prince Edward may have been killed on the battlefield, not wantonly murdered, and, being in their late teens, were "adult soldiers by medieval standards"[8] and not entitled to the protection chivalry afforded to children.

A final example of quarter yielding to revenge occurs when the Duke of Suffolk's captors at sea refuse to grant him ransom and promptly kill him. Personal revenge for the loss of an eye, along with political vengeance for Suffolk's responsibility in arranging the marriage of Margaret to Henry VI and losing Anjou and Maine to France, motivates the captain's murderous ways. However, the sailors' unchivalrous behaviour does have its limits. Absent any motive for revenge against the gentlemen accompanying Suffolk, the captors agree to ransom them in accordance with the rules of chivalry (2 *Henry VI*, IV.i). Interestingly, only one of the gentlemen is released upon the promise of ransom, while the other is held by the captors until ransom is delivered, perhaps as a reflection of the rule that a promise to pay ransom or to return to captivity was regarded as binding only between knights. As non-knights, the captors thus understood and feared that the ransom agreement might not be respected and detained one gentleman as security for payment.[9]

Protecting Women

Chivalric literature is replete with rules and anecdotes describing the respect due to women in medieval warfare. Married or not, women could not be captured or carried off as slaves.[10] As a result, when the captured Duchess of Brittany asked the Duke of Bourbon whether she was a prisoner, the Duke answered, "No, we do not war on ladies."[11] Lucrece, Cleopatra and Cressida are three of the women Shakespeare uses to portray the norms governing the treatment of women. The first is a victim of rape, the second, a captive queen, and the third, an unwilling object of an exchange for a captive Trojan warrior. Cleopatra was, of course, not only a woman and a queen but also a military leader, who would have lost her privileges and immunities under the rules of chivalry.[12]

Women are often the voice of reasonableness and the defenders of chivalry in Shakespeare. Thus, Queen Isabel adopts a peace-making role, saying, "Haply a woman's voice may do some good / when articles too nicely urged be stood on" (*Henry V*, V.ii.93–94), and offers eloquent praise of the Anglo-French peace. In *2 Henry IV*, Lady Percy pleads restraint and reasonableness to both her father and her husband, Hotspur. In *The Merchant of Venice*, Shakespeare's Portia performs brilliantly as a judge and jurist. Cassandra, although denigrated as the "mad sister" (*Troilus and Cressida*, II.ii.98), is the only honest voice predicting Troy's fall and destruction. Constance, the mother of Prince Arthur, who claimed the throne of England, challenges King John, but nevertheless insists on exhausting diplomatic remedies to avoid a bloody war:

> Stay for an answer to your embassy,
> Lest unadvised you stain your swords with blood.
> My lord Châtillon may from England bring
> That right in peace which here we urge in war,
> And then we shall repent each drop of blood
> That hot rash haste so indirectly shed.

> (*King John*, II.i.44–49)

Shakespeare shows little consideration for women in roles of military leadership, such as Margaret and Joan of Arc, the primary examples of women warriors in Shakespeare's plays. In contrast, with her military role thrust upon her, Cordelia is actually a victim. Forced to raise an army to fight for her father, she joins it on the battlefield and is captured and murdered. She is the only good and loyal daughter of King Lear. In these circumstances, Shakespeare is sympathetic to Cordelia, allowing her to retain her feminine qualities, although in terms that, today, not only feminists would decry as offensively stereotyping: "Her voice was ever soft, / Gentle, and low, an excellent thing in woman" (*King Lear*, V.iii.247–48).

Shakespeare's protagonists denigrate women as military leaders. Richard mocks Margaret, "A woman's general—what should we fear" (*3 Henry VI*, I.ii.68), and Bedford pokes fun at Joan of Arc, "A maid? And be so martial?" (*1 Henry VI*, II.i.21). Margaret and Joan are treated harshly, even with misogyny, perhaps because, in Shakespeare's view, they have abandoned traditional female roles and assumed the male roles of combatant and military leader. Although provoked by Margaret's lack of pity for others rather than the fact that she is a woman, York's condemnation of Margaret—a mother determined to protect her son's rights of succession—could not be harsher or, in modern terms, more violently misogynic:

> She-wolf of France, but worse than wolves of France,
> Whose tongue more poisons than the adder's tooth—

How ill-beseeming is it in thy sex
To triumph like an Amazonian trull
Upon their woes whom fortune captivates!
. . .
'Tis beauty that doth oft make women proud—
But, God he knows, thy share thereof is small;
'Tis virtue that doth make them most admired—
The contrary doth make thee wondered at;
'Tis government that makes them seem divine—
The want thereof makes thee abominable.
Thou art as opposite to every good
As the antipodes are unto us,
Or as the south to the septentrion.
O tiger's heart wrapped in a woman's hide!
. . .
Women are soft, mild, pitiful, and flexible—
Thou stern, obdurate, flinty, rough, remorseless.
. . .
But you are more inhuman, more inexorable,
O, ten times more than tigers of Hyrcania.

(3 *Henry VI*, I.iv.112–16, 119–38, 142–43, 155–56)

Joan of Arc also endures a litany of abuses in *1 Henry VI*. Shakespeare clearly defames Joan, making her deny her own father, admit her promiscuity,[13] and demonstrate that she lied in her claims to virginity. This latter invention is Shakespeare's own; his chroniclers did not doubt that Joan was, in fact, a virgin. This scene must have played well before an audience "as anti-Catholic as it was Francophobic."[14] Whether it was written by Shakespeare himself is unclear.[15] Early in the play, Shakespeare's portrayal of Joan is not unsympathetic. She engages the Dauphin in a single combat to try her courage (*1 Henry VI*, I.iii)—a typically chivalric practice—and fights bravely in a single combat against even the great Talbot himself (*1 Henry VI*, I.vii). In addition, the Dauphin addresses Joan in the classical language of courtly love and *Frauendienst*, typically a tribute to a noble lady ("Let me thy servant, and not sovereign be" [*1 Henry VI*, I.iii.90]). Finally, she raises the Dauphin's courage and morale, and, most importantly, persuades the Duke of Burgundy to abandon the English and return to the French (*1 Henry VI*, III.vii). Indeed, historians recognize the importance of her role in the war. Joan's rallying of the French in 1429 sparked a turning-point that eventually led to the defeat of England.

Later in the play, however, her image deteriorates and Shakespeare emphasizes her abuse of sexual attraction, her witchcraft and her claims of unnatural powers. Previous assertions of virtue are demolished, her leadership, courage and patriotism disregarded. Although Shakespeare follows Holinshed's basic tale, he embellishes it to damage Joan's reputation further. Forcing her to name one French leader after another as the man who fathered her child demonstrates both her mendacity and her promiscuity. Shakespeare's attack on Joan thus far surpasses that found in Hall, Holinshed or the Burgundian chronicler Enguerrand de Monstrelet.[16]

Shakespeare's failure to treat women warriors as favourably as men warriors reflects his chroniclers' negative view of this type of women. For example, Hall asserted that participation in wars was contrary to a woman's character.[17] Holinshed criticized Joan for shamefully rejecting her sex by dressing as a male soldier.[18] One source for this attitude was probably a letter from Henry VI to the Duke of Burgundy, which Hall included in his *Chronicles* and Shakespeare and his co-authors likely read. The letter castigates Joan for dressing in men's clothes, a thing "abhominable" to God, usurping a coat of arms, guiding men in war, committing unnatural cruelties, shedding Christian blood, stirring sedition and inducing people to rebellion, sorcery and blasphemy.[19]

At her trial[20] by a French ecclesiastical and English-dominated tribunal, Joan asked for a postponement of her execution on grounds of pregnancy:

Will nothing turn your unrelenting hearts?
Then Joan, discover thine infirmity,
That warranteth by law to be thy privilege:
I am with child, ye bloody homicides.
Murder not then the fruit within my womb,
Although ye hale me to a violent death.

(*1 Henry VI*, V.vi.59–64)

Although her claim to pregnancy was false, Shakespeare's chroniclers write that Joan's execution was in fact postponed.[21] In the play, however, Joan is promptly executed by burning (*1 Henry VI*, V.vi.86–93). Shakespeare therefore does not appear to be troubled by this difference in treatment, perhaps because his public enjoyed a xenophobic play. Although Joan was denied the protection accorded pregnant women, the prohibition on the execution of pregnant women was recognized by the common law[22] and is fully a part of modern human rights and humanitarian law.

Shakespeare's contemporary, the international jurist Alberico Gentili, showed greater fairness in his discussion of Joan. Admitting that women who perform the duties of men do not deserve special privileges from acts of war,[23] he nonetheless protested treating women with less respect than that required by the law of war merely because they dressed in man's attire.[24]

In my discussion of *Troilus and Cressida*, I noted that, in contrast to Chaucer, Shakespeare appears unaware and unconcerned by the exchange of a non-combatant Trojan woman for a Trojan warrior. This lack of interest in the protection of women from captivity also characterizes Shakespeare's treatment of Queen Margaret. Although chivalric principles prohibited taking women as prisoners, Shakespeare's protagonists do not question Suffolk's capture of Margaret. To obtain more favourable treatment, Margaret claims royal status (*1 Henry VI*, V.v.7–8), discusses the possibility of ransom (*1 Henry VI*, V.v.29–30, 36), and expresses confidence that since Suffolk is a knight, he "will not any way dishonour" her (*1 Henry VI*, V.v.58). However, she does not challenge her basic status as a prisoner of war. In contrast, Bouvet's proscription against taking women prisoner, as well as demanding ransom for their release, is clear:

> I hold firmly, according to ancient law, and according to the ancient customs of good warriors, that it is an unworthy thing to imprison either old men taking no part in the war, or women, or innocent children. Certainly it is a very bad custom to put them to ransom as it is common knowledge that they can have no part in war, for the former lack strength, the others knowledge. And in truth to capture them would show no great courage, for all gentlemen should keep them from harm, and all knights and men-at-arms are bound to do so, and whoever does the contrary deserves the name of pillager.[25]

Of course, the presumption that women did not take part in hostilities was rebuttable and, as already noted, women's participation in hostilities was not unusual.[26]

After Margaret's defeat at the end of the *Henry VI* trilogy, Shakespeare, reflecting historical fact, refers to her ransom by her father, King René. Again, the dramatist does not question whether the rules of ransom applied to women. Shakespeare's version ("Rene her father, to the King of France hath pawned the Sicils and Jerusalem, and hither have they sent it for her ransom" [*3 Henry VI*, V.vii.38–40]) draws on Hall's Chronicles, according to which René was forced to relinquish Naples, Sicily and Provence to Louis XI to obtain the enormous sum necessary to ransom Margaret.[27] In contrast to her capture by Suffolk in *1 Henry VI*, it was appropriate, at the end of the trilogy, to treat Margaret as a warrior and insist on ransom.[28]

The principal protection chivalry required for women was against rape.[29] Shakespeare, or perhaps his co-author John Fletcher, refers to the normative significance of this aspect of the laws of war when Cardinal Wolsey assures his female guests, "Nay, ladies, fear not. By all the laws of war you're privileged" (*All Is True* [*Henry VIII*], I.iv.52–53). As in modern times, rules protecting women against rape were often honoured in the breach. Franciscus de Vitoria reluctantly admitted the lawfulness of allowing soldiers to sack a city if the necessitites of war required or as a spur to the morale of the troops, even when rape would result.[30] Alberico Gentili, however, prohibited the rape of even women soldiers whom, in some circumstances, it might have been lawful to kill, and mentioned the possibility of war crimes trials for enemy leaders who allowed the rape of women.[31]

Resonating with some current discussions of rape, Christine de Pisan complained that she was "troubled and grieved when men argue that many women want to be raped and that it does not bother them at all to be raped by men even when they verbally protest."[32] Shakespeare's treatment of Lucrece demonstrates that he does not doubt that her verbal protests against rape are sincere. However, his treatment of King Henry V's threats of rape in his speech to the people of Harfleur is ambivalent:

> The gates of mercy shall be all shut up,
> And the fleshed soldier, rough and hard of heart,
> In liberty of bloody hand shall range
> With conscience wide as hell, mowing like grass
> Your fresh fair virgins and your flow'ring infants.
> What is it then to me if impious war
> Arrayed in flames like to the prince of fiends
> Do with his smirched complexion all fell feats
> Enlinked to waste and desolation?
> What is't to me, when you yourselves are cause,
> If your pure maidens fall into the hand
> Of hot and forcing violation?
> What rein can hold licentious wickedness
> When down the hill he holds his fierce career?
> We may as bootless spend our vain command
> Upon th'enragèd soldiers in their spoil
> As send precepts to the leviathan
> To come ashore. Therefore, you men of Harfleur,
> Take pity of your town and of your people
> Whiles yet my soldiers are in my command[.]
> . . .
> What say you? Will you yield, and this avoid?
> Or, guilty in defence, be thus destroyed?
>
> (Henry V, III.iii.93–112, 125–26)

Shakespeare's Henry emphasizes the sheer horror of rape, but clearly places the responsibility for the violations on Harfleur if it resists his ultimatum.

Finally, we also find in Shakespeare the traditional Roman notion that a woman cannot survive the dishonour rape brings to the victim and to her family. For this reason, Lucrece kills herself and Titus kills Lavinia (Titus Andronicus, V.iii.35–46). This sense of shame is still present in some societies in our contemporary world.

Keeping Promises: Oaths and Vows

Oaths and solemn promises were a foundation of the medieval hon-our system (Grundnorm). Some oaths involved important matters of peace and war and governance. A knight who broke an oath of loyalty to his king, his lord, his captor or others was a perjurer and a traitor. He was thus subject to the sanction of dishonour. For example, Fluellen declares that a soldier who does not keep his vow to resort to a duel is "a craven and a villain" (Henry V, IV.vii.130). Promises to pay ransom enjoyed high status and were seldom breached; violations were subject to severe punishment. A knight's oath was his word of honour, a pledge of his faith.

In the feudal system, a vassal owed allegiance to his lord, who, in turn, owed allegiance to an even higher authority, such as the king. Upon his dubbing, a newly created knight swore allegiance to his prince. A knight could also owe allegiance to an order of chivalry, similar to vows made to a religious order (some orders of chivalry—such as the Templars or the Teutonic Knights—had a strong religious character). Oaths and allegiance were at the very basis of the normative system.

Generally more individualistic than oaths, vows—to God, oneself or a lady—were equally important and binding. Indeed, there was often an overlap between the use of the two terms, "oaths" and "vows".[33] Vows often were exhibitionist and extravagant, involving feats of arms in jousting or in war, usually with religious or erotic overtones.[34] Frivolous or not, a vow required the same adherence as an oath. When Peter of Dreux, the Duke of Brittany, made an alliance with England after swearing that he would not do so, his fellow barons solemnly condemned him.[35] King John the Good of France provides a particularly important example of respect for chivalric oaths. After the French débâcle at the battle of Poitiers (1356), the captured John was released following receipt of the first installment of his ransom, but voluntarily returned to England when the French defaulted on paying the remainder, living out his days in captivity. Any other behaviour would have broken his word as a knight and a gentleman and, although an ineffective ruler, King John was a perfect knight.[36]

A knight's solemn oath was binding even in the case of rash and extravagant promises.[37] Shakespeare's plays incorporate the entire spectrum of chivalric oaths and vows. Troilus voices an example of extravagant vows made in the context of courtly love:

> Nothing but our undertakings, when we vow to weep seas, live in fire, eat rocks, tame tigers, thinking it harder for our mistress to devise imposition enough than for us to undergo any difficulty imposed.

> (Troilus and Cressida, III.ii.74–77)

The Duke of Austria vows to Prince Arthur, kissing his cheek "as seal to this indenture of my love" (King John, II.i.20), not to return to his home until Arthur has regained Angers and his other rights in France. Later, Salisbury, Pembroke and Bigot vow "never to taste the pleasures of the world" (King John, IV.iii.68) until they have revenged Arthur's death. Prince Harry vows to his father to prevail over the gallant Hotspur, the all-praised knight for whom Henry IV had a great admiration, declaring that he would "die a hundred thousand deaths ere break the smallest parcel of this vow" (*1 Henry IV*, III.ii.158–59).

Oaths of allegiance to a foreign prince might serve to complete and guarantee peace agreements, and the renunciation of such oaths would amount to *lèse majesté* and treason. The victorious Henry V requires the oaths of the Duke of Burgundy and of the French peers "for surety of our leagues" (*Henry V*, V.ii.367). Gloucester forces the Governor of Paris to swear allegiance to Henry VI:

> Now, Governor of Paris, take your oath
> That you elect no other king but him;
> Esteem none friends but such as are his friends. . . .

> (*1 Henry VI*,IV.i.3–5)

To avoid further killing, Charles the Dauphin accepts the request of Richard Duke of York that he

> swear allegiance to his majesty,
> As thou art knight, never to disobey
> Nor be rebellious to the crown of England,
> Thou nor thy nobles, to the crown of England.

> (*1 Henry VI*, V.vi.169–72)

Nonetheless, Alençon already hints at the fragility of this agreement in his whispered aside to Charles to "break [the truce] when your pleasure serves" (*1 Henry VI*, V.vi.164).

Shakespeare's treatment of oath under stress is particularly interesting. For example, in *Richard II*, York agonizes over the conflict between his oath to the King and his sense of justice, which favours Bolingbroke:

> Both are my kinsmen.
> T'one is my sovereign, whom both my oath
> And duty bids defend; t'other again
> Is my kinsman, whom the King hath wronged,
> Whom conscience and my kindred bids to right.

> (*Richard II*, II.ii.111–15)

When Cassandra and Andromache, Hector's sister and wife, try to persuade him to stop fighting and thus save his life, Hector answers that "[t]he Gods have heard me swear" (*Troilus and Cressida*, V.iii.15) to fight the Greeks. Cassandra then advances a theory of the validity of vows, suggesting that they are only binding when made for a valid purpose:

CASSANDRA: The gods are deaf to hot and peevish vows.

   . . .

ANDROMACHE: (to Hector) O, be persuaded. Do not count it holy
To hurt by being just. It is as lawful,
For we would give much, to use violent thefts,
And rob in the behalf of charity.

CASSANDRA: It is the purpose that makes strong the vow,
But vows to every purpose must not hold.
Unarm, sweet Hector.

(Troilus and Cressida, V.iii.16, 19–25)

Hector, ever chivalrous, believes that refusing to fight would be a dishonour and that honour is more important than life:

Mine honour keeps the weather of my fate. Life every man holds
dear, but the dear man holds honour far more precious-dear
than life

(Troilus and Cressida, V.iii.26–28)

The agreement in 2 Henry IV between Prince John, on behalf of Henry IV, and the Archbishop of York, leader of the rebels, raises the question of whether a promise made to rebels is binding. It can be argued that, since rebels have by definition broken their own oaths to their sovereign, the sovereign is not bound to keep a promise made to them. The question is whether a breach of promise by one side justifies a breach of promise by the other side. Having promised that the rebels' grievances will be redressed, the King's forces order the discharge of both the rebels' and the King's armies, so peace and friendship will reign again. Seemingly in direct contravention of this agreement, the King's troops then promptly arrest the Archbishop and his ally Lord Mowbray and charge them with capital treason. When Mowbray protests, "Is this proceeding just and honourable?" Westmoreland replies, "Is your assembly so?" (2 Henry IV, IV.i.335–36), denying any breach of faith, or perhaps justifying a mutual breach of faith.

Holinshed serves as Shakespeare's main source for this scene. His account confirms that the rebels were deceived, but offers nothing to support the exchange between Mowbray and Westmoreland in Shakespeare's play concerning the legality of the arrest in light of the earlier promise.[38] Having already presented a credible case for the rebels' grievances, including Worcester's claims that the King had disregarded his oath and "all faith and troth" (1 Henry IV, V.i.58, 70), Shakespeare creates the impression of unfair treatment and unjust arrest of the rebel leaders.

Failure to uphold an oath also drew scorn from one's peers and fellow combatants. Burgundy vows to continue fighting with Talbot for Rouen (1 Henry VI, III.v.44), but soon therafter yields to Joan's appeal to his

honour and patriotism to change allegiance to the French. His inability
to adhere to one vow of allegiance leads to Joan's sarcastic aside, strangely
Francophobic on her part: "Done like a Frenchman— (*aside*) turn and
turn again" (*1 Henry VI*, III.vii.85).

Henry VI's marriage to Margaret involves a breach of a promise purportedly made against state interest. In the conflict between a promise
and *Staatsraison*, the latter prevails. When Suffolk sings the praise of Margaret, Gloucester, the King's Protector, protests that the King is already
committed to marry Bona, a daughter of the Duke of Armagnac:

> You know, my lord, your highness is betrothed
> Unto another lady of esteem.
> How shall we then dispense with that contract
> And not deface your honour with reproach?

(1 Henry VI, V.vii.26–29)

He argues that agreeing to the marriage with Margaret would be "to
flatter sin" (*1 Henry VI*, V.vii.25). In contrast, Suffolk's argument justifying a breach of the earlier promise is unashamedly opportunistic, un-
chivalric and Machiavellian: promises against interest are not binding and
marriage to Margaret, the daughter of King René, would better serve the
cause of peace with France:

> SUFFOLK: As doth a ruler with unlawful oaths,
> Or one that, at a triumph having vowed
> To try his strength, forsaketh yet the lists
> By reason of his adversary's odds.
> A poor earl's daughter is unequal odds,
> And therefore may be broke without offence.

(1 Henry VI, V.vii.30–35)

Arguing that the King's will prevails over legal obligations, Suffolk
cynically adds that "marriage is a matter of more worth than to be dealt
in by attorneyship" (*1 Henry VI*, V.vii.55–56). He neglects to mention,
however, that Margaret was actually the daughter of a poor father and
was Suffolk's captive prior to the marriage agreement.

Shakespeare's story stems from Hall and Holinshed, who simply mention Gloucester's argument that it would be dishonourable for Henry to
break an earlier marriage contract and report that Suffolk prevailed.[39]
After his negative portrayal of Margaret as a queen, Shakespeare implies
that Gloucester was right and Suffolk wrong.

A more sophisticated and cynical excuse for reneging on an oath—
one akin to the more positive modern public policy justifications for in-
validating contracts and peremptory norms of international law (*jus co-
gens*) invoked as a basis for declaring treaties void—arises in Salisbury's

change of allegiance from Henry VI to the Duke of York during the War of the Roses:

> KING HENRY: Hast thou not sworn allegiance unto me?
>
> SALISBURY: I have.
>
> KING HENRY: Canst thou dispense with heaven for such an oath?
>
> SALISBURY: It is great sin to swear unto a sin,
> But greater sin to keep a sinful oath.
> Who can be bound by any solemn vow
> To do a murd'rous deed, to rob a man,
> To force a spotless virgin's chastity,
> To reave the orphan of his patrimony,
> To wring the widow from her customed right,
> And have no other reason for this wrong
> But that he was bound by a solemn oath?
>
> (2 *Henry VI*, V.i.177–88)

Queen Margaret's sarcastic retort is memorable: "A subtle traitor needs no sophister" (2 *Henry VI*, V.i.189). Shakespeare's Henry VI later agrees to change the line of succession to York—a major constitutional issue[40]—provided that York consents to Henry's reign for the rest of his life. This exchange of oaths poses the question whether Henry's oath "unnaturally . . . disinherit[ing]" his son (3 *Henry VI*, I.i.194) is valid and, because Henry was surrounded by the Yorkists at the time, whether his oath was invalid because it was made under duress and coercion. When York's sons urge him to disown the promise to let Henry rule until his death, York feels bound because he "took an oath that [Henry] should quietly reign" (3 *Henry VI*, I.ii.15). Edward replies crudely that "[b]ut for a kingdom any oath may be broken. I would break a thousand oaths to reign one year" (3 *Henry VI*, I.ii.16–17). Richard, the future Richard III, presents more formal and legal justifications based on Henry's lack of authority to receive and confirm the oath, but also alludes to the magnetism of royalty:

> RICHARD: An oath is of no moment being not took
> Before a true and lawful magistrate
> That hath authority over him that swears.
> Henry had none, but did usurp the place.
> Then, seeing 'twas he that made you to depose,
> Your oath, my lord, is vain and frivolous.
> Therefore to arms—and, father, do but think
> How sweet a thing it is to wear a crown. . . .
>
> (3 *Henry VI*, I.ii.22–29)

In his discussion of the change of succession and of Henry and York's oaths, Shakespeare drew on Holinshed and Hall's somewhat different versions, as well as on a number of literary sources.[41] Henry's encounter with the gamekeepers, more elaborate than its source in Holinshed,[42] demonstrates the centrality of a subject's oath to the sovereign. The gamekeepers are concerned about the status of their oaths of allegiance after the sovereign is deposed:

> SECOND GAMEKEEPER: You are the king King Edward hath deposed,
> And we his subjects sworn in all allegiance
> Will apprehend you as his enemy.
>
> KING HENRY: But did you never swear and break an oath?
>
> SECOND GAMEKEEPER: No—never such an oath, nor will not now.
>
> KING HENRY: Where did you dwell when I was King of England?
>
> SECOND GAMEKEEPER: Here in this country, where we now remain.
>
> KING HENRY: I was anointed king at nine months old,
> My father and my grandfather were kings,
> And you were sworn true subjects unto me—
> And tell me, then, have you not broke your oaths?
>
> FIRST GAMEKEEPER: No, for we were subjects but while you were king.
>   . . .
>
> KING HENRY: . . . But do not break your oaths, for of that sin
> My mild entreaty shall not make you guilty.
> Go where you will, the King shall be commanded;
> And be you kings, command, and I'll obey.
>
> FIRST GAMEKEEPER: We are true subjects to the King, King Edward.
>
> KING HENRY: So would you be again to Henry,
> If he were seated as King Edward is.
>
> FIRST GAMEKEEPER: We charge you, in God's name and in the King's,
> To go with us unto the officers.
>
> (3 Henry VI, III.i.69–80, 89–97)

Henry yields, allowing the gamekeepers to apprehend him, and even urges them not to break their oaths to King Edward, which would be a sin.

Keeping oaths must contend with papal pressure and the threat of excommunication in King John. King Philip of France and England's King John have just concluded a solemn pact involving the marriage of Blanche, John's niece, to Louis the Dauphin. In the treaty, the French renounced support for Prince Arthur's claim to the throne of England. Pandolph, the papal envoy, wants King Philip to abrogate the pact and resume war against John, because John objects to the Pope's appointment of Stephen Langton to the Archbishopric of Canterbury. Pandolph threatens to place a curse on Philip's head if he refuses. In response to this pressure, John appeals to nationalistic and antipapal arguments and is promptly excommunicated. Philip then invokes his obligation to honour his sacred vows underlying the pact with King John:

> Married in league, coupled and linked together
> With all religious strength of sacred vows;
> The latest breath that gave the sound of words
> Was deep-sworn faith, peace, amity, true love,
> Between our kingdoms and our royal selves;
> . . .
> I may disjoin my hand, but not my faith.
>
> (*King John*, III.i.154–58, 188)

Pandolph responds by invoking the supremacy of Philip's earlier religious vows of obedience to the Church over his later secular vows.

> So mak'st thou faith an enemy to faith,
> And like a civil war, sett'st oath to oath,
> Thy tongue against thy tongue. O, let thy vow,
> First made to heaven, first be to heaven performed;
> . . .
> It is religion that doth make vows kept;
> But thou hast sworn against religion;
> . . .
> Therefore thy later vows against thy first
> Is in thyself rebellion to thyself. . . .
>
> (*King John*, III.i.189–92, 205–06, 214–15)

Ultimately, threatened with excommunication, Philip yields and breaks his pact with King John.

All normative systems, including chivalry, have escape valves based on public policy that allow or even require the disavowal of existing obligations. Knights were excused from participating in obviously unjust wars. Similarly, they did not owe their princes the duty to engage in wars against the Church, despite vows of allegiance.[43] Sinful orders did not require compliance[44] and a person could even fight against a superior who acted unlawfully.[45] In addition, any promise obtained through threats or fraud and any oath subjecting imprisoned knights to ill treatment could be disowned.[46] For the same reasons, oaths extorted through fraud, made under misapprehension, compulsion, or in the service of injustice or tyrants did not have to be honoured.[47]

Although prisoners were bound by their chivalric oaths to obey their captors, the great English hero and paradigm of chivalry, John Talbot, disregards this obligation and rises against his captors in response to mistreatment that violated the principles of chivalry. Once he is liberated following a payment of ransom and an exchange of prisoners, he tells Salisbury that he was treated

> [w]ith scoffs and scorns and contumelious taunts.
> In open market place produced they me,
> To be a public spectacle to all.
> 'Here', said they, 'is the terror of the French,
> The scarecrow that affrights our children so.'
> Then broke I from the officers that led me
> And with my nails digged stones out of the ground
> To hurl at the beholders of my shame.
> My grisly countenance made others fly.
> None durst come near, for fear of sudden death.
>
> (*1 Henry VI*, I.vi.17–26)

Mistreatment of prisoners of war, specifically making them an object of insults and public curiosity, as often happens even in modern times, contravened the principles of chivalry, just as it violates rules of modern international law, including Article 13 of the Geneva Convention (No. III) Relative to the Treatment of Prisoners of War.

Shakespeare's treatment of oaths demonstrates a mastery of the subject and the legalisms and sophistry advanced to justify withdrawal from existing obligations. Although Shakespeare's plays abound with references to honour and dishonour, accentuating the critical importance of shame in ensuring respect for chivalry's norms, they also reveal the limitations on the effectiveness of the sanction of dishonour. The normative system could not be enforced against sovereigns and was not applicable to commoners. When it comes to high politics, kings and princes could resort to various safety valves to renege on their promises (King Harry: "O Kate, nice customs curtsy to great kings" [*Henry V*, V.ii.267]), and did so more often than ordinary knights, against whom the sanction of dishonour could more effectively be applied. As Frances Shirley observed, Shakespeare's plays demonstrate how allegiances evaporate, sometimes with legalistic justifications, sometimes with mere verbiage: "every regicide, every friend-turned rival" finds excuses for breaking oaths; men of power turn oaths to air.[48] Facing the pressure of self-interest, Shakespeare's kings show how chivalric principles often crumbled.

CRIMES AND ACCOUNTABILITY

Accountability for crimes, a theme central to Shakespeare's plays, is also extraordinarily pertinent to our times. Newspapers have reported on the care taken by the leaders of the former Yugoslavia to order atrocities against "enemy" populations only in the most indirect and euphemistic way. Even the Nazi leaders constantly resorted to euphemisms in referring to the Holocaust. No explicit written order from Hitler to carry out the final solution has ever been found. At the height of their power, the Nazis treated the data on the killing of Jews as top secret.[1] Similarly, a high-ranking member of the former security police, told the South African Truth and Reconciliation Commission that written instructions to kill anti-apartheid activists were never given; squad members who carried out the killings simply got "a nod of the head or a wink-wink kind of attitude."[2]

For a generation that grew up with the memory of the Holocaust and witnessed the genocide in Cambodia, as well as the atrocities in Kurdistan, Yugoslavia and Rwanda, no question can be more cogent than personal responsibility. Shakespeare's treatment of accountability of leaders sheds light on the antecedents of our notions of personal responsibility. Throughout recorded history, most egregious crimes, the mass atrocities, the genocides and the crimes against humanity have been ordered by leaders; it is they who must be held primarily accountable. But Shakespeare also pondered the roles of executioners and courtiers—in modern terms, aides, staffers and bureaucrats.

In this chapter, I intend to show how, in his works, Shakespeare dealt with crimes committed or ordered by leaders, as well as such related, but different, concepts as the arrogance of power, constraints on the prince's power; the leader's special responsibility; command responsibility; superior orders and the responsibility of the ruler's advisers and intermediaries; responsibility for thought alone; the observance of forms of law; capitulation to pressure to commit crimes; Richard III as a Machiavellian prince; responsibility for the massacre of French prisoners of war at Agincourt; the role of conscience; and the sins of the fathers: collective or individual responsibility.

In analyzing Shakespeare's portrayal of crimes and responsibility, I touch on the intellectual genealogy of our modern humanitarian law. Shakespeare raises critical questions, still important today, whose complexity he recognizes or prefers not to resolve. Although I relate some of his questions and answers to modern international law, I do not attempt to align them perfectly with that law. Any such attempt would be based on the false assumption that the issues—and the solutions—were the same for Shakespeare as they are for us.

Although some of the crimes I discuss were committed in international wars or their medieval or earlier counterparts, most of these offences occurred during periods of civil war, internal strife or tyrannical repression. However, "internal" crimes should bear just as much significance for international lawyers as "international" crimes, for several reasons. First, concepts of guilt and responsibility are easily carried over from one type of crime to another. Second, modern international law increasingly recognizes that crimes against humanity can be committed within a single country and without any nexus to war and that certain war crimes can be committed in civil as well international wars. Third, international human rights treaties penalize the perpetrators of egregious violations such as torture and inhuman or degrading treatment and punishment.

Arrogance, Responsibility and the Constraints on the Prince's Power

Shakespeare's tyrannical rulers demonstrate an arrogance of power by refusing to account for their acts. This arrogance of power stems both from the physical force of soldiers and from claims of legislative and judicial authority. For example, Lady Macbeth encourages her husband by reminding him that his superior forces offer ample protection. "Fie, my lord, fie, a soldier and afeard? What need we fear who knows it when none can call our power to account?" (*Macbeth*, V.i.34–36). Further, such leaders make the laws and refuse to have them interpreted and applied against themselves. Goneril makes the ultimate claim of the absolute ruler: "Say if I do, the laws are mine, not thine. Who can arraign me for't?" (*King Lear*, folio text, V.iii.149). In his famous soliloquy "To be, or not to be," Hamlet complains of "[t]he insolence of office" (*Hamlet*, III.i.75).

The plays show the resilience of the concept of accountability, which Shakespeare refers to in both secular senses (e.g., *Coriolanus*, IV,vii.18–19; *Macbeth*, V.i.34–36) and spiritual ones (e.g., *Hamlet*, I.v.79, *King John*, IV.ii.217). The tyrants' secular and political nemeses are the barons who, as in *Macbeth* and *King John*, unite against murder and tyranny and fight for the restoration of the social compact that governs relations between the sovereign and his subjects (dishonour, the most common sanction for a knight's violation of rules of chivalry, could not be enforced against mighty princes). Shakespeare understood that in the case of egregious excesses, the rudimentary system of checks and balances that existed in medieval society could direct the enforcement of these basic rules against the sovereign himself, just as in our contemporary law, violations of international humanitarian law, or war crimes, can be avenged against the rulers.

There was thus a normative system that even the mighty were bound to pay lip service to, if not to obey. On his ascension to the throne, Henry V renounces his earlier juvenile, even criminal, behaviour, and accepts the supreme authority of the law and regal obligations. The Chief Justice, concerned lest the new King make him pay for his attempts to enforce the law against Henry, when he was the Crown Prince, pleads:

> I then did use the person of your father.
> The image of his power lay then in me;
> And in th' administration of his law,
> Whiles I was busy for the commonwealth,
> Your highness pleasèd to forget my place,
> The majesty and power of law and justice,
> The image of the King whom I presented,
> And struck me in my very seat of judgement;
> Whereon, as an offender to your father,
> I gave bold way to my authority
> And did commit you.

> (*2 Henry IV*, V.ii.72–82)

And Prince Harry, now King, responds:

> You are right Justice, and you weigh this well.
> Therefore still bear the balance and the sword[.]

> (*2 Henry IV*, V.ii.101–02)

This scene was inspired by the anonymous play, *Famous Victories of Henry the Fifth*[3] and by Holinshed,[4] but Shakespeare goes further in elevating the concept of supremacy of the law over princes. Shakespeare's contemporary, the great common lawyer and Chief Justice Sir Edward

Coke, inevitably comes to mind. In his many disputes with King James I, Coke argued that the king was subject to a dual set of restraints, the orders of the Almighty and the common law. Using the thirteenth-century maxim of Henry de Bracton, Coke developed a theory of government under God and law, *non sub homine sed sub deo et lege.*[5] Although such principles were in the air, Shakespeare's play was printed in 1600, well before Coke became Chief Justice of the Court of Common Pleas in 1606.

Also in the air was the influence of the great Dutch humanist Erasmus, whose ideas, Walter Kaiser suggested, "had filtered down through the century and become a part of the ideological climate of Shakespeare's world."[6] Moreover, one of Erasmus's plays may have been amongst the inspirations for *The Taming of the Shrew*[7] and Shakespeare's Falstaff may have been influenced by Erasmus's Stultitia.[8] For me, Henry's acceptance of the supremacy of the law echoes Erasmus's *The Education of a Christian Prince,* written in 1516.[9] Although this work was first translated into English only after Shakespeare's death, Shakespeare probably knew enough Latin to read the original. According to divine law, Erasmus wrote, the prince is subject to earthly law and must obey it, even though his will has the force of law.[10] Justice "restrains bloodshed, punishes guilt, defends possessions, and keeps the people safe from oppression."[11] In contrast to Niccolò Machiavelli, whose Prince I shall discuss as a model for Richard III, Erasmus believed that "there can be no good prince who is not also a good man."[12] Our own private standards of integrity, morality and goodness should therefore govern our comportment as public officials and in the public domain generally. Machiavelli, "a hated name" in Shakespeare's England[13]—it was fashionable to highlight as cynical and amoral his espousal of the interests of the Prince—had an important impact on England of the 1590's, and, as I shall show, on Shakespeare. Invoking *The Discourses,* Gentili defended Machiavelli against calumnies triggered by *The Prince.* He described Machiavelli as a misunderstood "eulogist of democracy" and "a supreme foe of tyranny." In *The Discourses,* in contrast to *The Prince,* Machiavelli supported the democratic republic and the concept of mass consent.[14]

For his part, Erasmus argued that the prince must be religious, refrain from plunder and violence, and not let his personal ambitions override concern for the state. He should govern with "wisdom, integrity and beneficence."[15] Shakespeare's Henry V amply reflects Erasmus's ideal of a Christian prince: he is pious, worried about the right decisions and causing loss of life through war, uninterested in material pursuits, chivalrous and patriotic. Replete with warnings against tyranny, Erasmus's book expounds his justification for tyrannicide. Since tyrants void the mutual compact with the people through their oppressive behaviour, violence against them is not unlawful and can even be justified.[16]

Despite the extremely broad powers and command over law enforcement and the military apparatus of English kings, the criminalization of acts or speech against them as treason, and their claim of a divine right to govern (e.g., *Richard II*, III.ii.50–53), they did not have unlimited power. In 1215, King John was compelled by the barons to issue the Magna Carta, a foundation of English constitutional freedoms. The barons, the commons, the judges and the common law, the Church, and the need to obtain funds—all effectively limited the power of the medieval kings. The feudal system of relationships between vassals and sovereign also gave rights to the vassals.

Although Shakespeare may overstate the powers of the kings for dramatic purposes, he effectively shows that egregious violations of governing principles may have caused rebellions or strife by the barons, an important restraint on abuses by the monarch. Sometimes Shakespeare's kings thus choose to reject and disclaim illegal orders that violate the norms of chivalry and contravene the social compact between the kings and the nobility.

Shakespeare's characters advocate the right to rebel against absolutely tyrannical, evil, murderous kings in *Richard III* and *Macbeth*. However, when faced with abusive kings who do not rise to the supreme evil of his Richard III, they express qualms about rebellion, a caution that may reflect sensitivity imposed by the censorship of Elizabeth, the granddaughter of the victorious rebel Henry VII. In any event, maligning Richard III may have been the "party line" for the descendants of Henry VII.

The necessity to justify Elizabeth's and James's reigns (and the history that led up to them) required Shakespeare to do a delicate balancing act in some places. How could one justify the history of regicide and usurpation that led to the Tudor/Stuart reigns without endorsing regicide and usurpation generally, and hence destabilize those very monarchies? Although Richard III's evil tyranny served as justification for Henry of Richmond's rebellion and regicide, to sustain this justification fully required claiming that Richard was a usurper (*Richard III*, V.v.193–216).

Elsewhere in the canon, the general message is that rebellion is a serious matter; it causes great disorder and suffering, and that can be justified only in extreme circumstances. The nobles voice their complaints against Richard II's abuses: unjust taxation, the seizure of Bolingbroke's inheritance, the King's incompetence, which is central to the loss of his Crown, and the unfortunate state of the nation. Although they hold Richard responsible for these wrongs (*Richard II*, II.i), Shakespeare does not grant them a moral imprimatur for rebellion and leaves the question of the right of rebellion unanswered.

As James Boyd White argues, *Richard II* does not speak with the voice of a general theorist of constitutional law; the voices are of particular characters, addressing particular situations and positions. The play thus "works on the principle that the truth cannot be said in a single speech or language, but lies in the recognition that against one speech or claim or language is always another one."[17] White's interpretation therefore seems to be that, for Shakespeare, there cannot be a simple statement of unique truths but, rather, a continuous unresolved dialogue about fundamental questions in which it is difficult to discern a single unified position that is Shakespeare's own. My view is different. I suggest that with regard to crimes and acccountability—in contrast, perhaps, to constitutional theory—Shakespeare presents something close to his own moral voice in the language of his protagonists. Of course, Shakespeare's view is not condensed into the lines of any one character, but nevertheless it emerges by analysing the dialogue with reference to the situations of the ensemble of the characters. While one finds many emphatic statements underlying accountability, there are hardly any categorical denials of this concept. A study of the ensemble thus suggests that Shakespeare has a resolved moral view of accountability for crimes that is valid across time and in different places.

Shakespeare's Bishop of Carlisle pleads eloquently against overthrowing Richard II, God's anointed King, censures trying him *in absentia*, and warns against the social upheavals his removal would generate:

> What subject can give sentence on his king?
> And who sits here that is not Richard's subject?
> Thieves are not judged but they are by to hear,
> Although apparent guilt be seen in them;
> And shall the figure of God's majesty,
> His captain, steward, deputy elect,
> Anointed, crownèd, planted many years,
> Be judged by subject and inferior breath,
> And he himself not present? O, forfend it, God. . . .

> (*Richard II*, IV.i.112–20)

John of Gaunt also refuses to rebel against Richard II, despite the Duchess of Gloucester's entreaties that he avenge her husband and Gaunt's brother's death. He states,

> God's is the quarrel; for God's substitute,
> His deputy anointed in his sight,
> Hath caused his death; the which if wrongfully,
> Let heaven revenge, for I may never lift
> An angry arm against his minister.

> (*Richard II*, I.ii.37–41)

Pressured by Bolingbroke to join the rebels against Richard II, York, by nature a loyalist and a legalist, agonizes over his decision: "It may be I will go with you—but yet I'll pause / For I am loath to break our country's laws" (*Richard II*, II.iii.167–68).

Throughout the Histories, the protagonists engage in calculation and rationalization in deciding whether kings' wrongs justify resort to the ultimate and dangerous recourse of rebellion. In *2 Henry IV*, the Archbishop of York weighs the rights and wrongs of rebellion against an abusive monarch. York invokes the mismanagement of the kingdom, the giving away of Anjou and Maine for Margaret's hand, and the loss of France, but the principal cause of the rebellion, and the one for which Shakespeare appears to have the greatest sympathy, is York's seemingly better claim to the Crown. Henry V fears that, despite his efforts to atone, he will be held to account for his father's crime in usurping the Crown and will also bear responsibility for the death of Richard II (*Henry V*, IV.i.289–302).

Although some chivalric writers supported the right of rebellion against a prince who was acting unlawfully and outside his authority, Shakespeare made his heroes distinctly unsympathetic to rebels and rebellions, which he denigrates in particularly sharp language.[18] This approach extends beyond the Histories. Thus, in *Julius Caesar*, Shakespeare affirms stability, legitimacy and empire and voices strong reservations about the overthrow of Caesar and republicanism.

Because of the ever-present danger of an uprising by the barons, Shakespeare's kings—like other leaders throughout history—resort to euphemisms to mask their murderous orders, and disown their deeds after their execution. These practices lead to complicated issues of accountability.

The Special Responsibility of the Leader

Shakespeare concerned himself with the responsibility both of the leader, the king or prince, and of the executioner, the courtier or soldier who carries out orders that are legally or morally wrong. However, the special responsibility of the leader stood at the center of Shakespeare's interests, for it is the leader who carries the heavier obligation.

The case is most effectively made in the *Rape of Lucrece*. Attacked by Tarquinus, the tyrant of Rome, Lucrece pleads with him not to rape her, brilliantly articulating the principle of the special responsibility of leaders: their crimes cannot be covered up; they serve as a model for good or for bad.

> O be remembered, no outrageous thing
> From vassal actors can be wiped away;
> Then kings' misdeeds cannot be hid in clay.
>   . . .
> For princes are the glass, the school, the book
> Where subjects' eyes do learn, do read, do look.
> And wilt thou be the school where lust shall learn?
> Must he in thee read lectures of such shame?
> Wilt thou be glass wherein it shall discern

Authority for sin, warrant for blame,
To privilege dishonour in thy name?

(*The Rape of Lucrece*, lines 607–09, 615–21)

Arguing against the special responsibility of leaders, Cleopatra complains,

Be it known that we, the greatest, are misthought
For things that others do; and when we fall
We answer others' merits in our name,
Are therefore to be pitied.

(*Antony and Cleopatra*, V.ii.172–75)

Shakespeare's Henry V resists the attribution to the king of responsibility for the acts, and the fate, of his troops. On the eve of the battle of Agincourt, he is already exhausted and perhaps not entirely satisfied with his efforts to convince his soldiers Bates and Williams that his war is just and that he, who combines in his person kingship and mortality,[19] is therefore not responsible for soldiers' damnation in such a war. Whether evading responsibility or engaging simply in self-pity, Henry states in the famous soliloquy "Upon the King":

'Let us our lives, our souls, our debts, our care-full wives,
Our children, and our sins, lay on the King.
We must bear all. O hard condition,
Twin-born with greatness: subject to the breath
Of every fool, whose sense no more can feel
But his own wringing. What infinite heartsease
Must kings neglect that private men enjoy?
And what have kings that privates have not too,
Save ceremony, save general ceremony?

(*Henry V*, IV.i.228–36).

Henry also tries to evade responsibility in the scene before the walls of Harfleur, where he enumerates the dreadful abuses, including rape, that his troops will commit in the city if it refuses to surrender. He, their commander, will no longer be able to control them and the leaders of Harfleur will bear responsibility for the consequences:

What rein can hold licentious wickedness
When down the hill he holds his fierce career?
We may as bootless spend our vain command
Upon th' enragèd soldiers in their spoil
As send precepts to the leviathan
To come ashore. Therefore, you men of Harfleur,

Take pity of your town and of your people
Whiles yet my soldiers are in my command. . . .

(*Henry V*, III.iii.105–12)

Of course, Shakespeare emphasizes rape and its sheer horror. But in a speech which attracted feminist censure, his Henry clearly places the responsibility on Harfleur should it resist his ultimatum. Although his own ordinances prohibited rape without any qualification as to situations of siege,[20] Henry washes his hands of the results that will follow unless his terms for surrender are promptly accepted. Given the high incidence of rape in cities taken after siege, the softness of the rules prohibiting rape,[21] and the difficulty to enforce the law, there is some realism in Henry's statement. In terms of *realpolitik*, Henry tells Harfleur: "If you do not deal now with me, your one protector able only for a time to maintain discipline among this terrifying force, the force will run amok according to base human nature and I cannot be responsible for the consequences." But such arguments by their very nature are likely to incite illegal conduct by the troops, and these claims of inevitable indiscipline are thus both evasions of the moral responsibility that should continue even into battle, and affirmative encouragement to unrestrained war. Compare Henry's model statement concerning Bardolph:

> We would have all such offenders so cut off, and we here give express charge that in our marches through the country there be nothing compelled from the villages, nothing taken but paid for, none of the French upbraided or abused in disdainful language. For when lenity and cruelty play for a kingdom, the gentler gamester is the soonest winner.
>
> (*Henry V*, III.vi.108–14)

Surely a leader strong enough to insist that Bardolph be hanged for stealing a pyx from a church, so as to set an example for others and ensure humanitarian treatment of the French population under English occupation, such a leader could have threatened to punish his troops in Harfleur severely if they resorted to rape, so as to ensure the maintenance of discipline.

The ruler's responsibility for waging war is an important aspect of *Henry V*. Henry V worries about his responsibility for a war that will inevitably cause bloodshed and death. Shakespeare's discussion of Henry's accountability contains an important secular and legal element, found both in Henry's exchange with the Archbishop of Canterbury and in the "little touch of Harry in the night" scene (*Henry V*, IV.o.47) with the soldiers Bates and Williams, on the eve of Agincourt. Nonetheless, the spiritual dimension dominates, especially in Henry's conversation with Bates and Williams. The two soldiers are clearly more reflective, more doubting and more critical than the self-serving Archbishop, but do not possess the authority to give Henry approval for his recourse to war. Henry has already consulted the Archbishop, the highest spiritual authority in England, for reassurance that the war, with its awesome capacity for the shedding of innocent blood, is just. In this way, Shakespeare highlights spiritual accountability by giving the church, a spiritual authority, the role of declaring the legality and justness of the war (Henry V, I.ii.9–28). Henry then insists further, demanding, "May I with right and conscience make this claim?" (Henry V, I.ii.96). In response, Canterbury gives him what for an ecclesiastic is the strongest imaginable stamp of approval, invoking "[t]he sin upon my head, dread sovereign" (Henry V, I.ii.97–98).

As I showed in chapter 2, Shakespeare's Henry probably knows that the Church has its own interests in encouraging his involvement in foreign wars (Henry V, I.i), which diminishes the reliability of the Archbishop's assurances. As a result, doubts continue to haunt him. Bates and Williams become a mouthpiece for the common soldier, the subordinate who is ordered to fight in a war whose dynastic justifications are too complicated to understand. Worried, the two soldiers debate their spiritual end should they die fighting in Henry's war. The discussion implicates several related issues, which are not fully explored: the spiritual consequences of dying in war without last rites; the difference with regard to dying without last rites between just and unjust wars (does a soldier who dies in a just war bear spiritual responsibility for unrepented pre-war or wartime misdeeds?); the question whether and to what extent the spiritual consequences for the soldiers are assumed by the king; the relationship between the king's responsibility for spiritual welfare of the soldiers and his general responsibility for their acts; the question whether obedience to the king exonerates soldiers that participate in an unjust war.

In talking to King Henry on the eve of Agincourt, Bates suggests that obedience to the king fighting in a wrong cause "wipes the crime of it out of us" (Henry V, IV.i.131–32). Williams elaborates:

> But if the cause be not good, the King himself hath a heavy reckoning to make, when all those legs and arms and heads chopped off in a battle shall join together at the latter day, and cry all, "We died at such a place[.]" . . . I am afeard there are few die well that die in a battle, for how can they charitably dispose of anything, when blood is their argument? Now, if these men do not die well, it will be a black matter for the King that led them to it—who to disobey were against all proportion of subjection.
>
> (Henry V, IV.i.133–45)

Thus is articulated the theory of the king's absolute responsibility for all the acts of his soldiers. By obeying the king, soldiers are absolved of spiritual responsibility not only for killing enemy soldiers in an unjust war, but also for wartime felonies and prewar misdeeds. Henry's rejection of such responsibility includes both secular and spiritual aspects:

> [T]here is no king, be his cause never so spotless, if it come to the arbitrament of swords, can try it out with all unspotted soldiers. Some, peradventure, have on them the guilt of premeditated and contrived murder; some, of beguiling virgins with the broken seals of perjury; some, making the wars their bulwark, that have before gored the gentle bosom of peace with pillage and robbery. Now, if these men have defeated the law and outrun native punishment, though they can outstrip men, they have no wings to fly from God. War is his beadle. War is his vengeance. So that here men are punished for before-breach of the King's laws, in now the King's quarrel. Where they feared the death, they have borne life away; and where they would be safe, they perish. Then if they die unprovided, no more is the King guilty of their damnation than he was before guilty of those impieties for the which they are now visited. Every subject's duty is the King's, but every subject's soul is his own.
>
> (Henry V, IV.i.157–76)

Since the king, even in a truly just war, cannot solely employ only totally virtuous soldiers, he is responsible *only* for the acts of war he ordered ("Every subject's duty is the King's"), and not responsible for the soldier's pre-war or wartime sins, including pillage during the campaign ("every subject's soul is his own"). In rejecting any responsibility for the spiritual damnation of his soldiers, Henry enunciates the then prevailing legal doctrine of not holding kings to account for the wrongful private acts of their troops (*respondere non sovereign*, an exception to the general common law rule of *respondeat superior*). Nevertheless, by emphasizing the issue of Henry's accountability, Shakespeare demonstrates that perhaps leaders do have a special responsibility simply because they are in command and have the authority to declare war.

In the Henry-Bates-Williams exchange, Shakespeare raises the question of the moral responsibility of combatants involved in an unjust war.[22] Some moralists argued that a knight who feels the war is unjust need not follow his prince. Others, emphasizing the tradition of absolute obedience to the prince, believed that it was for the prince to determine whether a war was just; the subject, whose duty was to follow, would not endanger his eternal salvation.[23] As early as the fourth century, Saint Augustine argued that the duty of obedience preserved the soldier's innocence.[24] As the justness of war came to depend greatly on whether it was public, that is, declared on the authority of a prince competent to make such declarations, the dominant view held that the sin of declaring an unjust war was the prince's alone.

According to Christian doctrine, a sinner who dies without receiving communion, without confession and absolution, without a chance to repent, may be doomed to eternal damnation. When the ghost of his father, the King, reveals the circumstances of his murder by Claudius to Hamlet, the ghost expresses particular despair at not having been afforded last rites (*Hamlet*, I.v.78–80). Hamlet finds Claudius praying and is tempted to kill him, but that would be senseless. Claudius killed Hamlet's father without allowing him last rites; if Hamlet kills Claudius while Claudius is praying, Claudius might go to heaven, surely a travesty of justice. The irony is that Claudius himself recognizes the futility of his prayers: it is useless to ask God for forgiveness as long as he continues to possess the objects for which he committed the crime ("my crown, mine own ambition, and my queen" [*Hamlet*, III.iii.54–55]). His prayer is futile ("My words fly up, my thoughts remain below. / Words without thoughts never to heaven go" [*Hamlet*, III.iii.97–98]), but Hamlet, unknowingly, decides to wait for an occasion when Claudius's passage to hell will be assured (*Hamlet*, III.iii.73–95).

Command Responsibility

I turn to the overlapping issues of responsibility for acts of subordinates and for actions one had the power to prevent. This question, important to the moral and legal responsibility of everyone, not just leaders, arises in the following episode from *Antony and Cleopatra*. The triumvirs of Rome, Mark Antony, Octavius Caesar and Lepidus, are dining and drinking heavily as guests on a boat of their former adversary and competitor, Sextus Pompey. The scene presents an unparalleled opportunity for assassination, and Menas, Pompey's friend, urges him to agree to kill them:

> MENAS: Wilt thou be lord of all the world?
>
> . . .
>
> And, though thou think me poor, I am the man
> Will give thee all the world.
>
> POMPEY: Hast thou drunk well?
>
> MENAS: No, Pompey, I have kept me from the cup.
> Thou art, if thou dar'st be, the earthly Jove.
> Whate'er the ocean pales or sky inclips
> Is thine, if thou wilt ha 't.
>
> POMPEY: Show me which way!
>
> MENAS: These three world-sharers, these competitors,
> Are in thy vessel. Let me cut the cable;

And when we are put off, fall to their throats.
All there is thine.

(*Antony and Cleopatra*, II.vii.60–72)

Pompey desires nothing more than to remove the triumvirs, provided that his own chivalric honour is not soiled. He may even have considered the possibility of eliminating his competitors for power already. But once Pompey is apprised of the plot, his honour is implicated and he is forced to condemn and thus forbid the assassination:

POMPEY: Ah, this thou shouldst have done
And not have spoke on 't. In me 'tis villainy,
In thee 't had been good service. Thou must know
'Tis not my profit that does lead mine honour;
Mine honour, it. Repent that e'er thy tongue
Hath so betrayed thine act. Being done unknown,
I should have found it afterwards well done,
But must condemn it now. Desist, and drink.

(*Antony and Cleopatra*, II.vii.72–79)

Of course, Menas the pirate was not subtle in his suggestions. The very explicitness of his proposal might have made an indirect and euphemistic reaction more difficult for Pompey.

Shakespeare draws here on both the ideas and the actual language in Plutarch's *Parallel Lives*:

Now, in the midst of the feast . . . Menas the pirate came to Pompey, and whispering in his ear, said unto him: "Shall I cut the cables of the anchors, and make thee lord not only of Sicily and Sardinia, but of the whole empire of Rome besides?" Pompey, having paused a while upon it, at length answered him: "Thou shouldest have done it, and never have told it me; but now we must content us with that we have: as for myself, I was never taught to break my faith, nor to be counted a traitor."[25]

Pompey's concept of responsibility is something quite different from the concept of negative responsibility espoused by modern moral philosophy's utilitarian school.[26] At the very minimum, the Pompey episode is analogous to command responsibility, or the Yamashita principle, which I discuss further below. The special responsibility of leaders for certain crimes is recognized in modern international law. After the Second World War, only the most senior leaders of Germany and Japan were prosecuted for crimes against peace, or aggression. Responsibility for a war of aggression attached only to the acts of high-ranking officials, not to everyone who fought in such a war. Thus, soldiers fighting in wars of aggression were not prosecuted for that act alone, a policy that was both just and reasonable. In commenting in 1950 on the "Formulation of the Nuremberg Principles," the International Law Commission thus set out its interpretation of the understanding of the Nuremberg Tribunal, that the expression "waging of a war of aggression" in Article 6(a) of the Nuremberg Charter,[27] referred "only to high-ranking military personnel and high State officials."[28]

The Yamashita principle of modern international law echoes with Cleopatra's and Henry's complaints about the burdens and perils of leadership. General Tomuyuki Yamashita, the commander of the Japanese forces in the Philippines in 1944–45, was charged by the victorious American army with having failed to discharge his duty to control the operations of the persons subject to his command who had violated the laws of war by committing massacres, murder, pillage and rape against civilians and prisoners of war. Yamashita protested that he had not personally either committed or directed the commission of those atrocities. On a petition from a U.S. military commission (only government leaders were tried before the International Military Tribunal for the Far East), the Supreme Court affirmed the conviction and the capital sentence imposed on the general and held that commanders must be responsible for their subordinates.[29] Chief Justice Harlan Fiske Stone enunciated the doctrine that the law of war imposed an affirmative duty to take such measures to protect prisoners and civilians as were within the commander's power and appropriate in the circumstances.[30] The purpose of the law of war—to protect civilian populations and prisoners from brutality—would largely be defeated if the commander could get away with neglecting to take reasonable measures to that end.

In a powerful dissent, Justice Frank Murphy argued that the United States was not alleging that General Yamashita had committed or ordered the commission of atrocities, or that he had any knowledge of the commission of atrocities by members of his command. The United States had effectively destroyed Yamashita's command and communications and thus his ability to wage war. It was therefore actually charging him with the crime of inefficiency in controlling his troops, which was not recognized in international law.[31] In criticizing the decision, Michael Walzer appears to have agreed with Yamashita's defense lawyers that Chief Justice Harlan Fiske Stone established a standard of strict liability, a standard inappropriate for criminal justice.[32] However, the Chief Justice and the majority of the Court did not suggest that they were applying such a standard, believing that their standard was one of due diligence.

The exchange between Justices Stone and Murphy foreshadows that in *United States v. Park*[33] between Chief Justice Warren Burger, writing for the majority, and Justice Potter Stewart, writing for the dissenters. In *Park*, which concerned the scope of and limits on the criminal liability of senior corporate managers under the Federal Food and Drug Acts, the Justices voiced strikingly similar arguments. The Acts imposed criminal liability not only on corporate officers who themselves had committed a criminal act, but also on others who by virtue of their positions could be held responsible. The Acts did so by dispensing with the requirement of "consciousness of wrongdoing," declaring instead that failure to act was sufficient when the senior officer had the power to prevent the *unlawful conduct*.[34] The essentially utilitarian argument of Chief Justice Burger stemmed from his focus on the importance of protecting the health and well-being of the public. In contrast, Justice Stewart emphasized fairness, arguing that the jury had been instructed to find the defendant guilty merely because he had a responsible relation to the situation. Rather, the court below should have instructed the jury that the test for criminality was whether the defendant had engaged in wrongful conduct amounting at least to common-law negligence.[35]

I believe the problem was not the standard set by *Yamashita*. In his criticism of the decision, Michael Walzer recognizes that the majority Justices did not believe they were enforcing the principle of strict liability; international lawyers usually do not read *Yamashita* as introducing strict liability and interpret the standard as requiring an element of *mens rea* through either actual knowledge or the means of knowledge that the commander failed to exercise.[36] The difficulty lies in applying that standard to General Yamashita, which appeared unfair on the facts. In reality, the standard thus edged closer to strict liability. Yamashita was unable to prevent the atrocities, an inability to which U.S. actions heavily contributed. Of course, as Walzer suggests, strict liability is supported by a utilitarian argument: making senior officers automatically responsible for massive violations forces them to do everything possible to avoid such abuse. An interesting question is whether senior commanders worry about the risk of a postwar trial. However, here utilitarianism may clash with justice and fairness to the defendants.[37] Utilitarians might answer that both justice and fairness could be achieved by requiring commanders, if they are to avoid liability, to set up effective systems of control of those under their command, but this might not always be possible.

The Yamashita doctrine was not incorporated in the Geneva Conventions of 12 August 1949 and Relating to the Protection of Victims of War, but was codified as what appears to be a due diligence standard in Article 86(2) of Additional Protocol I to the Geneva Conventions ("if they did not take all feasible measures within their power to prevent or repress the breach"),[38] and, in somewhat different language, in the statutes of the international criminal tribunals for the former Yugoslavia[39] and Rwanda. The future case law of these two tribunals may further clarify the Yamashita principle and its place in customary law. I believe that Article 86(2) strikes a fair balance between the utilitarian interests of the community and the interest of justice and fairness to the defendants. A different perspective suggests that there is no conflict between community interests and the interest of justice to the defendants; the latter is also a community interest. The question is therefore one of proper balancing of several community interests.

The Yamashita principle was the first authoritative articulation of the modern rule of command responsibility: if a superior did not take all feasible measures to prevent or repress a breach, acts of subordinates would implicate his responsibility if he knew, or had information that should have enabled him to conclude, that the subordinates were about to commit, or had committed, a breach. Under that principle, the commander must enforce the law and make persons subject to his command accountable for compliance with the norms.

If Shakespeare is viewed in this light, we note that the triumvirs are guests on Pompey's boat, and that Menas is his friend. Pompey is both the host and the commander of his troops and the pirates on board. The fact that he is also the host makes his responsibility even more compelling. Since Menas informs Pompey of his criminal intent and in fact asks for Pompey's consent, consent or even acquiescence would make Pompey an accessory to the crime or a party to the conspiracy to commit a crime.

Under the Yamashita principle, Pompey's obligations as a commander-host might nevertheless have been violated even if Menas had murdered the triumvirs without Pompey's advance knowledge. However, if they had been murdered elsewhere, by someone else, and without Pompey's involvement in any way as host or commander, the attribution of accountability would be different. In that case, Pompey would regard the murder as his good fortune and not an act triggering his responsibility. Alternatively, he might not hold himself responsible even if he had learned of such a plot in advance and simply failed to warn the triumvirs. On the assumption that a warning was feasible and that he could therefore have saved them, Pompey would still bear only negative and not positive responsibility for the deaths. As a result, those who do not regard negative responsibility as morally significant, would consider him blameless.

Pompey is of course a leader. Most of us believe that, generally speaking, standards of private morality are applicable to public life and public personalities. Public morality thus includes individual private morality. Thomas Nagel posits, however, that public officials could be held to different standards, so that in some respects these standards might be more demanding than those applicable to ordinary people, but in other respects they might allow acts that would be impermissible if measured by the standard of individual morality.[40] To say that standards of private morality are applicable to public personalities does not rule out the possibility that further moral requirements apply to public officials by virtue of their official responsibilities, which derive not from private morality alone but from additional principles of political theory. Yet, even if the public function may modify the moral standards applicable to the leader, as Thomas Nagel suggests, when the limits, perhaps the outer limits, of public morality are transgressed, as in the case of murder, the leader must refuse to cross the line.[41] Thus, political killing can never be justified. By preventing Menas from murdering the triumvirs, Pompey meets these standards of morality. In another respect, however, Pompey appears morally wrong.

His express willingness to applaud Menas's crime so long as he, Pompey, has not heard about it beforehand is morally objectionable. If Pompey is obligated to prevent the murder, then surely he should be obligated to deplore the crime after the fact.

Superior Orders: The Ruler's Advisers and Intermediaries

Pompey's obligation in *Antony and Cleopatra* contrasts with that of Sir Robert Brackenbury in *Richard III*. Brackenbury, the Lieutenant of the Tower of London, is given a written order to hand over the imprisoned Duke of Clarence to the hired thugs of Richard, Duke of Gloucester. The two intruders have just entered and accosted Brackenbury:

(*Enter two Murderers*)

FIRST MURDERER: Ho, who's here?

BRACKENBURY: What wouldst thou, fellow? And how cam'st thou
    hither?

SECOND MURDERER: I would speak with Clarence, and I came hither
    on my legs.

BRACKENBURY: What, so brief?

FIRST MURDERER: 'Tis better, sir, than to be tedious. (*To Second
    Murderer*) Let him see our commission, and talk no more.
    (*Brackenbury reads*)

BRACKENBURY: I am in this commanded to deliver
    The noble Duke of Clarence to your hands.
    I will not reason what is meant hereby,
    Because I will be guiltless of the meaning.
    There lies the Duke asleep, and there the keys.
    (*He throws down the keys*)
    I'll to the King and signify to him
    That thus I have resigned to you my charge.

FIRST MURDERER: You may, sir; 'tis a point of wisdom.
(*Exit Brackenbury*)

(*Richard III*, I.iv.80–95)

Brackenbury represents the submissive collaborator who knows, or at least suspects, the murderous, unarticulated goal of the warrant. He prefers not to think, not to question, even in the privacy of his mind. He collaborates with evil while trying not to sully his hands, or his conscience, by considering what is really involved. Can Brackenbury be compared to the French policeman who follows written orders to round up Jews and deliver them for deportation to the Vel d'Hiv (the round-ups in Paris on July

16–17, 1942 pursuant to written directives to the French police from the German High Command)?[42] He does not ask where, why, for what purpose—resettlement, forced labour, or worse? Rather the approach is—do not ask, "be guiltless of the meaning."

The failure of Brackenbury to question the purpose of the order appears morally reprehensible as deliberate self-deception, different from ignorance or lack of awareness.[43] Brackenbury's ignorance, if any, results from his refusal to ask questions because he expects the answer to be unpalatable. I recognize that for some commentators it might not be morally culpable to fail to ask a question when there is nothing the person can do about the answer. In my view, even if there is nothing that Brackenbury could do to save Clarence, he may be guilty of moral negligence by not questioning the morality of what he does.[44]

Legally, both the French policeman and Brackenbury may have a good defence. The order to deliver Jews, in one case, and Clarence, in the other, may not have been manifestly illegal and the agents may not have been sufficiently aware of any illegality. Morally, however, their situation is quite different. The French policeman had far greater latitude to evade the order. He could have sought out the Jews less diligently, or otherwise sabotaged the order. In contrast, Brackenbury's options were quite limited. He could either obey or refuse, and in the latter case, his own fate would be death.

The penal codes of civil law systems, with some exceptions, recognize duress as a complete defence for all crimes. In common law countries, however, duress is not a complete defense for murder. Common law cases typically concerned situations where an accused had a choice between his own life and the life of another, as distinct from cases where the choice was either the death of another or the death of both, as in Erdemović's case, which I discuss below. Duress, involving lack of moral choice and the risk of death, may provide a moral justification. In modern humanitarian law, such duress provides, at the very least, powerful mitigation and, according to some cases (the case law on the subject is not uniform) complete exoneration. Although the appeals chamber of the International Criminal Tribunal for the former Yugoslavia recently ruled that duress does not provide a complete defense to a soldier charged with a crime against humanity and/or a war crime involving the killing of innocent human beings, the narrowness of the majority (three to two) and the cogency of Antonio Cassese's dissent may suggest that the jury is still out on this question.[45]

The jurisprudence of the Nuremberg Tribunals under Control Council Law No. 10 on the responsibility of senior staff officers of the German army (Wehrmacht) who transferred illegal orders from senior commanders to field units or who delivered Soviet war prisoners to Nazi authorities such as the Sicherheitsdienst (SD), is not quite clear. Senior commanders who gave clearly illegal orders and the subordinates who carried them out were found responsible. In the *High Command Case*, the Tribunal found that execution of orders to the Wehrmacht to turn over prisoners of war to the Nazi SD, an organization in which all accountability for them would have evaporated, when it was suspected or known that their ultimate fate was extermination, was criminal. On the other hand, tribunals found that, absent command responsibility, staff officers were not responsible for either criminal acts in the command in which they performed staff duties or the mere transfer of commands to the field. But they were responsible if they put the basic idea, which was criminal, into the form of a military order, or took personal action to see that the order was properly distributed. As regards field commanders, the tribunals held that to hold such a commander criminally responsible for the transmittal of an order down the chain of command, the order had to be criminal on its face, or one that the commander knew was criminal.[46]

Of course, there are important differences between medieval and modern channels for the communication of commands. Medieval kings often gave orders directly to the executioners. Instructions were frequently delivered in person and usually not by written message. However, in Shakespeare's plays written warrants were frequently invoked. In the German security and extermination apparatus, one could trace at least four stages: from Hitler to Himmler to Heydrich to the camp commanders and finally to the block wardens. Criminal orders such as the Kommandobefehl went through many more command levels in the Wehrmacht, greatly complicating questions of knowledge and responsibility. That order, issued by Hitler on October 18, 1942, provided that enemy troops on commando missions, whether in uniform or not, whether armed or not, and whether in battle or in flight, were to be slaughtered to the last man.[47]

The Wehrmacht officers' latitude for evasion of orders probably exceeded Brackenbury's. By agonizing over his "guiltlessness," Brackenbury reveals that he is aware of the moral dilemma, which the strength of his legal defence cannot resolve. Imagine, however, that Brackenbury definitely knows that Clarence will be murdered. If he delivers Clarence, will Brackenbury become an accessory to the murder, at least on the moral plane? Under the absolutist prong of modern moral philosophy, certain egregious acts such as murder and torture are never allowed, regardless of the benefit they may generate. The prohibition of murder should thus prevail over any other consideration, including a utilitarian conception of consequences. But perhaps the distinction between actual participation in the murder and mere obedience to the order to deliver Clarence to the murderers is significant, especially given the implicit coercion and the absence of any options for evasion. As Thomas Nagel suggested, absolutism forbids doing certain things to people, rather than bringing about certain results through one's own actions.

Whatever his situation under the absolutist theory may be, under a utilitarian view of moral responsibility Brackenbury may be justified in handing over the keys. If he refuses, Clarence will be killed anyway and he will die as well. In a utilitarian-consequentialist sense he is not responsible for Clarence's death, since he cannot do anything to prevent it. Therefore, he should act in such a way that the result will be one death instead of two. The absolutist-utilitarian controversy was brilliantly illuminated in the appeals chamber of the International Criminal Tribunal for former Yugoslavia in a recent exchange between President Antonio Cassese and Judges Gabrielle Kirk McDonald and Lal Chand Vohrah (the Erdemović case) pertaining to a soldier who was allegedly coerced by threats of immediate execution into participating as a member of a firing squad in the massacre of a large number of innocent civilians. The utilitarian argument voiced by Cassese was that, because the massacre would have proceeded in any event, Dražen Erdemović's refusal to participate in the killings, which would have led to the sacrifice of his life, would have benefited no one and would have simply added one more victim. The law, Cassese argued, could not require Erdemović to forfeit his life, which, apart from setting a heroic example, would be of no avail. The absolutist argument echoed by McDonald and Vohrah rejected any balancing of harms and rested on the categorical prohibition of killing innocent people even under duress. In addition, however, to the absolutist prohibition of killing innocent people even when the killing results from duress, McDonald and Vohrah invoked the policy consideration of deterring future offenders, thus themselves drawing on a utilitarian argument. Nevertheless, if Cassese's focus was on the facts of the Erdemović case, their's was on the broader impact of the sentence.[48] Under the McDonald-Vohrah view, Jews in Nazi concentration camps compelled to assist in operating the crematoria would have been denied the defense of duress. Would this be just?

I would like to mention another aspect. There can be cases where a person's refusal to participate in a collective massacre may inspire others to resist orders to kill. When this happens, commanders might find it difficult to carry the massacres out and the absolutist argument could merge with the utilitarian. In the case of Erdemović, prospects of this happening may have been utopian; in the case of Brackenbury's encounter with the two hired murderers it would have been impossible.

However, Shakespeare provides no evidence that Brackenbury is willing to justify his conduct to himself in a utilitarian way. Presumably, this means that if he were ordered to kill Clarence himself, he would feel some reluctance, even if he could not save the Duke by refusing to carry out the orders. Were Brackenbury thinking only of choosing the lesser evil, he would not have had to elude full awareness of his role as an active agent in the murder.

In some ways, Shakespeare is quite kind in his treatment of Brackenbury's failure to prevent Clarence's delivery to his murderers. Perhaps he sympathizes with Brackenbury's predicament and realizes that there is a limit to a person's ability to challenge the apparatus of the state in an environment of terror. Or perhaps the dramatist shows leniency because he learned from the chroniclers that Brackenbury had resisted an earlier attempt to kill the two Princes (discussed below).

In *Richard II*, Shakespeare introduces further questions of responsibility. Richard banishes Henry Bolingbroke, the Duke of Hereford and eldest son of John of Gaunt, the Duke of Lancaster and fourth son of Edward III. After John's death, Richard decides to confiscate his entire property, allegedly to finance his Irish campaign, and does so in total disregard of Bolingbroke's inheritance rights. Richard's uncle, the Duke of York, warns the King that this lawless confiscation will expose him to tremendous risks. Richard's rights to the Crown depend on lawful succession; his encroachment on the legitimate succession rights of the nobility will inevitably endanger his own rights as well. Thus argues York:

> Take Hereford's rights away, and take from Time
> His charters and his customary rights:
> Let not tomorrow then ensue today;
> Be not thyself, for how art thou a king
> But by fair sequence and succession?
> Now afore God—God forbid I say true!—
> If you do wrongfully seize Hereford's rights,
> Call in the letters patents that he hath
> By his attorneys general to sue
> His livery, and deny his offered homage,
> You pluck a thousand dangers on your head,
> You lose a thousand well-disposèd hearts. . . .

(Richard II, II.i.196–207)

Despite this warning that violation of the law by the King will destroy the legal foundation on which the King himself rests, the arrogance of power proves blinding yet again: Richard replies, "Think what you will, we seize into our hands / His plate, his goods, his money, and his lands" (*Richard II*, II.i.210–11).

As York has warned in vain, the confiscation of Bolingbroke's property arouses the barons' fear that they will suffer a similar fate. They thus decide to support Bolingbroke against the King.

> ROSS: The commons hath he pilled with grievous taxes,
>   And quite lost their hearts. The nobles hath he fined
>   For ancient quarrels, and quite lost their hearts.
>
> WILLOUGHBY: And daily new exactions are devised,
>   As blanks, benevolences, and I wot not what.

(Richard II, II.i.247–51)

Clearly, Bolingbroke is not the only victim of the King's excesses; in fact, the whole population is already suffering from Richard's actions.

Richard's growing unpopularity and prolonged absence while campaigning in Ireland help shift the balance of power to Bolingbroke. The latter quickly expands his goals so that he not only claims his rightful inheritance, but also seeks the Crown itself. Richard, though ultimately forced to abdicate in Henry's favour and imprisoned in Pomfret, is still regarded as a danger. A deposed monarch, as long as he breathes, and—as in *Richard III*—his children are a threat to those who deposed and displaced them, because of the overriding legality of their entitlement to the Crown. In the end, Richard II is assassinated by Exton, one of Henry's courtiers.

The order to kill Richard is never explicitly stated but is implied by the courtiers, who transform what they understand as Henry's desire into an operational order. Sir Piers of Exton interprets the King's words with chilling clarity. Shakespeare makes Henry's words resemble the statement attributed by oral tradition to Henry II in 1170 before the murder of Thomas à Becket in the Canterbury Cathedral: "Will no one rid me from this turbulent priest?"

> (*Enter Sir Piers Exton, and his Men*)
>
> EXTON: Didst thou not mark the King, what words he spake?
>   "Have I no friend will rid me of this living fear?"
>   Was it not so?
>
> [FIRST] MAN: Those were his very words.
>
> EXTON: "Have I no friend?" quoth he. He spake it twice,
>   And urged it twice together, did he not?
>
> [SECOND] MAN: He did.
>
> EXTON: And speaking it, he wishtly looked on me,
>   As who should say "I would thou wert the man
>   That would divorce this terror from my heart",
>   Meaning the King at Pomfret. Come, let's go.
>   I am the King's friend, and will rid his foe.
>   (*Exeunt*)
>
> (*Richard II*, V.iv.1–11)

Exton and his men proceed to Pomfret and assassinate Richard. Typically of most of Shakespeare's executioners, remorse comes quickly and the spiritual aspect dominates. Immediately after striking the deadly blow, Exton exclaims,

> O, would the deed were good!
> For now the devil that told me I did well
> Says that this deed is chronicled in hell.
>
> (*Richard II*, V.v.114–16)

The most intriguing aspect of this episode is King Henry's reaction when Exton and his men arrive with Richard's body and Exton claims credit for his deed ("within this coffin I present / Thy buried fear" [*Richard II*, V.vi.30–31]). Henry disowns the act and punishes the courtier with exile, despite Exton's attempt to exonerate himself by invoking the defence of superior orders.

> KING HENRY: Exton, I thank thee not, for thou hast wrought
> A deed of slander with thy fatal hand
> Upon my head and all this famous land.
>
> EXTON: From your own mouth, my lord, did I this deed.
>
> KING HENRY: They love not poison that do poison need;
> Nor do I thee. Though I did wish him dead,
> I hate the murderer, love him murderèd.
> The guilt of conscience take thou for thy labour,
> But neither my good word nor princely favour.
> With Cain go wander through the shades of night,
> And never show thy head by day nor light.
> (*Exeunt Exton and his men*)
>
> (*Richard II*, V.vi.34–44)

Exton's fate is reminiscent of the complaint voiced by the Second Knight, one of the murderers of Archbishop Thomas à Becket in T.S. Eliot's *Murder in the Cathedral*: "King Henry—God bless him—will have to say, for reasons of state, that he never meant this to happen; and there is going to be an awful row; and at the best we shall have to spend the rest of our lives abroad."[49]

Having banished Exton, Henry remains with his lords and for the first time admits responsibility for Richard's death, offering repentance by making a voyage to the Holy Land.

> Lords, I protest my soul is full of woe
> That blood should sprinkle me to make me grow.
> Come mourn with me for what I do lament,
>
> . . .
>
> I'll make a voyage to the Holy Land
> To wash this blood off from my guilty hand.
> March sadly after.
>
> (*Richard II*, V.vi.45–51)

In recounting Henry's wish to have Richard killed and his subsequent murder by Exton, Shakespeare followed Holinshed closely.[50] He also drew on various additional sources.[51] However, the above exchange between Exton and the King, which highlights issues of accountability, is not based on historical sources. This scene, focusing as it does on a ruler's denial of responsibility for an order he did not explicitly issue, may thus have special significance as a reflection of Shakespeare's own attitudes. Obviously, Shakespeare regards Henry as responsible.

Exton's punishment has both a spiritual and a physical component (the "guilt of conscience," and banishment[52]), again highlighting Shakespeare's focus on spiritual accountability as a viable complement of accountability (*Richard II*, V.vi.41–42).

King John reintroduces the issue of distributing accountability between a leader and his subordinate. In contrast to Richard II, King John takes a more direct and explicit role in ordering a crime. King John is at war with Philip of France, who asserts the claims to the English throne of Prince Arthur, the son of the deceased Geoffrey, John's older brother. During a battle, Arthur is taken prisoner. John entrusts custody of Arthur to Hubert, a courtier, hinting that as long as Arthur is alive, John's entitlement to the Crown of England will not be secure. The obvious conclusion is that Arthur must be killed. Pandolph, the papal envoy, cynically predicts the inevitability of the murder in his conversation with the French King's son, Louis the Dauphin. In his statement (*King John*, III.iv.118, 123–34, 138–67), a marvel of Machiavellian *realpolitik*, Pandolph also highlights the French gains that will result from the crime. The murder will not only strengthen the Dauphin's claim to England through his wife, Blanche, but also will incite the barons to rebel against John.

By this time, John has enlisted Hubert as Arthur's executioner.

KING JOHN: Yet I love thee well,
    And by my troth, I think thou lov'st me well.

HUBERT: So well that what you bid me undertake,
    Though that my death were adjunct to my act,
    By heaven, I would do it.

KING JOHN: Do not I know thou wouldst?
    Good Hubert, Hubert, Hubert, throw thine eye
    On yon young boy. I'll tell thee what, my friend,
    He is a very serpent in my way,
    And wheresoe'er this foot of mine doth tread,
    He lies before me. Dost thou understand me?
    Thou art his keeper.

HUBERT: And I'll keep him so
    That he shall not offend your majesty.

KING JOHN: Death.

HUBERT: My lord.

KING JOHN: A grave.

HUBERT: He shall not live.

KING JOHN: Enough.
I could be merry now. Hubert, I love thee.
Well, I'll not say what I intend for thee.
Remember.

(*King John*, III.iii.54–69)

Despite this atmosphere of terror, legal formalities are not forgotten in *King John*. King John gives Hubert a warrant and the executioner Hubert finds to carry out the deed insists on seeing it. He says, demonstrating the continued reliance on legal niceties, "I hope your warrant will bear out the deed" (*King John*, IV.i.6). Hubert also shows the warrant to Arthur as a way to justify his bloody mission, asking, "Is it not fair writ?" To which Arthur replies, "Too fairly, Hubert, for so foul effect" (*King John*, IV.i.37–38).

Ultimately, when King John disowns the order, Hubert will produce the warrant as formal legal protection from the King's wrath, saying "Here is your hand and seal for what I did" (*King John*, IV.ii.216). Although the warrant provides authority and disobedience will be dangerous, Hubert yields to Arthur's pleas for mercy (*King John*, IV.i.126–33).

The executioner is actually pleased with Hubert's decision to spare Arthur. Revealing his distaste for the King's demand and perhaps his sense of morality, he says, "I am best pleased to be from such a deed" (*King John*, IV.i.85). Nonetheless, Hubert returns to King John and reports that he has complied with the order, because anything different would entail too much danger. King John's reaction to the report that Arthur was killed, which he believes to be true, shows the ambivalence between his desire simply to deny responsibility and thus appease the nobles and his twinges of conscience and fear of damnation. King John places the responsibility for the crime on Hubert, bemoaning courtiers who, anxious to please, anticipate their masters' orders and do not hesitate to murder to humour them and win their gratitude. They, like Hubert, certainly do not try to dissuade the leaders from their evil designs, even though they might be able to do so.

Throughout history, the courts of princes and the chanceries of world leaders have been staffed with opportunistic aides and sycophants. How many advisers actually resign to protest egregiously immoral or illegal orders? How many are prepared to tell the leaders that their designs are unethical or illegal? Some have surely resigned, or been demoted or worse, rather than cravenly follow the improprieties of their rulers. Although King John is both self-serving and hypocritical in this exchange with Hubert, his comments about advisers and courtiers still ring true, for many cases. Had Hubert expressed some doubts, or even restated the King's orders in different terms, perhaps John would have rescinded the order.

In her early fifteenth-century *Book of Fayttes of Armes and of Chyvalrye*, translated into English in 1489 by William Caxton, Christine de Pisan urged that a prince consult impartial advisers before deciding whether the war under consideration was just.[53] Humanists, especially More, bared open the adviser's dilemma. The temptation to enter a prince's service was great especially since the humanists aspired to reform the political system through educating the rulers and thus could justify their action by what they perceived to be an obligation of service. In More's *Utopia*, in the conversation with More and Giles, the imaginary Raphael Hythlodaeus warns that in the prince's court, the independent expert is bound to lose his independence; that the status- and advancement-oriented councillor is bound to tell the prince what he wants to hear; that he is likely to sink in sycophancy, and that tampering with truth "is the very condition of service in the councils of the mighty."[54]

Although advising on war and warning against crime present different issues, both turn on the integrity of the adviser. As *King John* demonstrates, finding such honest advisers must have been a difficult task.

KING JOHN: Why seek'st thou to possess me with these fears?
  Why urgest thou so oft young Arthur's death?
  Thy hand hath murdered him. I had a mighty cause
  To wish him dead, but thou hadst none to kill him.

HUBERT: No had, my lord? Why, did you not provoke me?

KING JOHN: It is the curse of kings to be attended
  By slaves that take their humours for a warrant
  To break within the bloody house of life,
  And on the winking of authority
  To understand a law, to know the meaning
  Of dangerous majesty, when perchance it frowns
  More upon humour than advised respect.

HUBERT: Here is your hand and seal for what I did.

(*King John*, IV.ii.204–16)

Hubert then reminds the King that he had given him the warrant, showing him a piece of paper. John, fearing his damnation for having issued the order, attempts to shift the blame to the opportunistic courtier, all too willing to commit evil to ingratiate himself with his lord. The King continues:

Hadst thou but shook thy head or made a pause
When I spake darkly what I purposèd,
Or turned an eye of doubt upon my face,
As bid me tell my tale in express words,
Deep shame had struck me dumb, made me break off,
And those thy fears might have wrought fears in me.
But thou didst understand me by my signs,
And didst in signs again parley with sin;
  . . .

Out of my sight, and never see me more!
My nobles leave me, and my state is braved,
Even at my gates, with ranks of foreign powers;
Nay, in the body of this fleshly land,
This kingdom, this confine of blood and breath,
Hostility and civil tumult reigns
Between my conscience and my cousin's death.

(*King John*, IV.ii.232–49)

Hubert bears a heavy moral responsibility for having failed even to attempt to discourage the King.[55] Furthermore, he cannot benefit from a defence of superior orders. Even if the order to kill or blind Arthur was not illegal on its face—to use a modern law-of-war term—because it emanated from an absolute monarch, Shakespeare suggests that John had not coerced Hubert into accepting the order.[56] Rather, Hubert's motivation came from his desire to endear himself to the King and to reap the unspecified advantages the King had promised him.

Shakespeare's kings usually do not order murders but, rather, buy promises to kill. In *Richard III*, Buckingham's initial hesitation to become the instrument for killing King Edward's children leads to Richard's anger, creating an immediate threat to Buckingham's survival in the royal court. By this time, his hands are already dirty. But it is Buckingham's decision to join a rebellion that leads, after his defeat and capture, to his execution, not the initial hesitation. As a result, we cannot know if, for Shakespeare, Buckingham's execution has resulted from Richard's desire to get rid of a courtier who can no longer be trusted and knows too much, or if it is merely a punishment for treason. Perhaps Buckingham could have declined to cooperate earlier on, before his complacent immersion in the evil doings of the tyrannical regime made him too dangerous to be ignored. However, for Richard, though perhaps not for John or other leaders, any refusal may not have been tolerable.

The rest of the episode from *King John* demonstrates the complexities of these issues of responsibility. Although they attribute Arthur's possibly accidental death to John, the barons understand that John is not made of Richard III's wholly immoral fabric. Salisbury, one of the nobles, recognizes that the King is troubled by his desire to kill Arthur: "The colour of the King doth come and go / Between his purpose and his conscience" (*King John*, IV.ii.76–77). A modern commentator observed that "Shakespeare's monster [King John] is a terribly human one. . . . He is plagued with all-too-recognizable uncertainties and guilts."[57] He struggles to pit his private conscience against his political ambition.

Nonetheless, it is too late for John to escape responsibility. As in *Richard III*, the barons provide the counterbalance to lawless tyranny. They swear to break their obedience to the King and resort to vengeance (*King John*, IV.iii.60–73). Yet, in the end, despite their vows, the barons do not depose John; rather, he dies poisoned by a monk.

Although the rebellious barons do not succeed in their revolt, their fate merits additional comment. Count Melun warns them that, should the French win, they will be delivered to King John to face a traitor's punishment (*King John*, V.iv.10–20). Consequently, they agree to return and seek John's mercy. Shakespeare's Melun implies that there was a deal between John and the French, saying, "Fly, nobel English, you are bought and sold" (*King John*, V.iv.10). But Shakespeare's source, Holinshed, suggests another explanation for this treatment of the seemingly honourable nobles. The French would act on their own in enforcing, even against interest, the international rules of chivalry that condemned as treason and rebellion a knight's disavowal of an oath of allegiance to his sovereign.[58] These chivalric rules certainly did not make rebellion any easier. The party line against rebellions is harshly voiced by the Bastard, who, addressing the English lords, calls them "degenerate," "ingrate revolts," "bloody Neros," "ripping up the womb [o]f your dear mother England" (*King John*, V.ii.151–53).

However, perhaps because the nobles rebelled only in reaction to the violation of chivalric rules by the King, Shakespeare attributes their plight to an unsavoury deal between John and the French rather than to the normative rules of chivalry. Shakespeare thus refrains from undermining the barons' noble motivation. Significantly, his Melun calls them "noble English."

The historical basis of the story of Arthur is still shrouded in some mystery.[59] Shakespeare's version of Arthur's disappearance generally incorporates both Holinshed's story and *The Troublesome Raigne of King John*. The moral-ethical discussion of responsibility in Shakespeare, however, tracks the story in *The Troublesome Raigne of King John*, where Hubert initially shows little hesitancy to carry out his warrant and in fact reads it loud to Arthur. Eventually, he allows his conscience to triumph by accepting Arthur's entreaties, which bear an important resemblance to Arthur's pleas for pity in Shakespeare's *King John*. In fact, the sophisticated discussion of the tension between the moral duty of the individual and the legal obligation of an official in *The Troublesome Raigne of King John* appears to have influenced Shakespeare's treatment of conscience.

At the very beginning of scene xii, Hubert and the three executioners are morally troubled by their assigned task. Hubert shows them the warrant, as he does in *King John*, and explains that the king "threatneth torture for the default."[60] Throughout the scene, Hubert declares his intention to obey his King's command because it is an order, so that "I must not reason why he is your foe, / But doo his charge since he commaunds it so."[61] Echoing Shakespeare's Brackenbury, Hubert thus invokes the need to comply with orders and laws, which is rooted in good order, stability and obedience, saying, "Why then no execution can be lawfull, / If Judges doomes must be reputed doubtfull."[62] Therefore, a subject must comply with superior orders, because "a subject dwelling in the land / is tyed to execute the kings commaund."[63]

Arthur argues, however, that illegal orders to commit murder cannot be obeyed and that orders of execution are valid only when in compliance with the substance and form of law. He states,

[N]o commaund should stand in force to murther.
. . . [W]here in forme of Lawe in place and time,
The offender is convicted of the crime.[64]

In the end, Hubert tells Arthur that his "conscience bids desist"[65] and he will, therefore, save Arthur. The distinction in *The Troublesome Raigne of King John* between the secular effect of the warrant and its inability to protect the executioner from divine law is echoed by the murderers of Clarence in *Richard III*, I.iv. Hubert says, "My King commaunds, that warrant sets me free: / But God forbids, and he commaundeth Kings."[66] Again, the role of conscience and divine accountability comes to the fore.

The questions raised in *King John* and its sources remain central to modern international law. The Nuremberg Charter provides that the defence of superior orders shall not free a defendant from responsibility, although it may be considered in mitigation of punishment if the Tribunal determines that justice so requires.[67] However, Nuremberg jurisprudence subsequently tempered the severity of this provision.[68] The Nuremberg Charter's approach was followed by the Statutes of the International Criminal Tribunals for the former Yugoslavia and Rwanda.

In addressing the criminal liability of East German officials for killing those who tried to escape to the West over the Berlin Wall, German courts have dealt much more harshly with members of the National Defence Council who issued or transmitted orders to shoot pursuant to the laws in force, than with border guards who carried out those orders.[69] Guards who initially did not agree to shoot were assigned to inferior maintenance work and reproached for being uncomradely, but they were not threatened with physical risk to themselves or their families.[70] Thus, the defence of duress was not available to the guards.[71] In another case, which involved high officials, the Federal Supreme Court (Bundesgerichtshof) ruled that any justification arising from the statute had to be disregarded by the courts when it implied a patent violation of overriding fundamental principles of justice and humanity. The Court held that the accused officials who drafted, adopted, and saw to the implementation of the orders to eliminate persons attempting to flee from the German Democratic Republic, which permitted the intentional killing of fugitives to prevent them from escaping, had no justification in view of the obvious, intolerable violations of the elemental demands of justice and human rights protected by international law.[72]

Shakespeare's Hubert felt that the King's warrant provided him with a legal justification, but not a moral one. That warrant, however, was only an authorization; given the consensual circumstances in which it was isued, it was not an order. Had Hubert believed that his moral objections tainted the legality of the warrant, he might have invoked the defence of duress, recognizing that disobeying the King's warrant would expose him to danger. In modern international law, however, he would fail. International tribunals do not accept pleas of duress lightly.

The International Criminal Tribunal for the former Yugoslavia recently considered the related questions of superior orders and duress in the sentencing judgement of Dražen Erdemović, a Croat member of the Bosnian Serbian forces. As noted above, Erdemović pleaded guilty to crimes against humanity for having participated in a firing squad, during the infamous Srebrenica massacre of July 11, 1995.[73] The defendant argued that, although he had initially refused to carry out the order, he was threatened with instant death and was sure that if he had not obeyed, he would have been killed or his wife and child directly threatened.[74] The trial chamber's review of the Nuremberg jurisprudence suggested that the Nuremberg Tribunals had accepted the defence of superior orders as grounds for mitigating responsibility, showed greater leniency when the accused held a low rank in the military or civilian hierarchy, and recognized the defence of duress as a mitigating circumstance entailing a more lenient sentence.[75] The Tribunals' test for the defence of superior orders was "whether moral choice was in fact possible."[76] However, in the absence of evidence supporting the plea of extreme necessity, the chamber did not accept Erdemović's claim.[77] Sentencing him to a prison term of ten years, subsequently reduced to five years, the chamber balanced the gravity of the offence against the mitigating circumstances of his youth, low rank and cooperation with the prosecutor's office.[78] Thus, neither the defence of superior orders nor that of duress was ultimately considered in the sentencing calculus. The appeals chamber, as already noted, altogether rejected duress as a defence for crimes against humanity and war crimes involving the killing of innocent persons. The case illustrates the reluctance of international tribunals to accept a plea of duress.

Responsibility for Thought Alone

Responsibility for thought alone, or imagining evil deeds is one of the interesting issues to which 2 *Henry VI* gives rise. Henry VI exemplifies the good, meek, even saintly, but totally ineffectual leader,[79] not able or willing to assert his authority to stop the impending crime, the murder of Humphrey, the Duke of Gloucester, and the King's Protector. Although the facts surrounding the death of Humphrey, remain to be uncovered by historians, and the conflicts and power struggle between him and his opponents at the court are quite complex, Shakespeare presents a clear and simplified version of the episode. For him, the murder of Gloucester is fact and the responsible principal obvious. By portraying Suffolk, whom Shakespeare describes as the Queen's lover, as the main culprit and moving spirit of a plot by Queen Margaret and some of her courtiers, including the Duke of York and Cardinal Beaufort, Shakespeare creates the necessary elements for the unfolding drama.

Margaret, York and Beaufort are determined to eliminate an honest man, who, as the young King's Protector and guardian, is close to the King, by falsely accusing him of treason. Henry protests, but all too gently, hardly acting like a sovereign:

> KING HENRY: ... shall I speak my conscience?
> Our kinsman Gloucester is as innocent
> From meaning treason to our royal person
> As is the sucking lamb or harmless dove.
> The Duke is virtuous, mild, and too well given
> To dream on evil or to work my downfall.
>
> (2 Henry VI, III.i.68–73)

In denying the trumped-up charges against him, Gloucester alludes to the chivalric virtue of mercy: "Pity was all the fault that was in me" (2 Henry VI, III.i.125). As prisoner, Gloucester is entrusted to the Cardinal's custody and the King capitulates, effectively renouncing his authority: "My lords, what to your wisdoms seemeth best / Do or undo, as if ourself were here" (2 Henry VI, III.i.195–96).

Henry does not eliminate his moral responsibility by reiterating his confidence in Gloucester's innocence, which may be an attempt to assuage his own conscience. Indeed, his awareness of the certitude of the impending crime makes his passivity still more reprehensible:

> Ah, uncle Humphrey, in thy face I see
> The map of honour, truth, and loyalty;
> And yet, good Humphrey, is the hour to come
> That e'er I proved thee false, or feared thy faith.
> What louring star now envies thy estate,
> That these great lords and Margaret our Queen
> Do seek subversion of thy harmless life?
> Thou never didst them wrong, nor no man wrong.
> And as the butcher takes away the calf,
> And binds the wretch, and beats it when it strains,
> Bearing it to the bloody slaughterhouse,
> Even so remorseless have they borne him hence[.]
>
> (2 Henry VI, III.i.202–213)

Despite the King's timidity, the anti-Gloucester faction is not confident that his attitude will endure. Outside Henry's presence, Margaret insists that because of the danger that Gloucester represents—"the fear we have of him" (2 Henry VI, III.i.234)—he must be eliminated quickly. The Cardinal agrees to this "policy" of eliminating Gloucester. Characteristic of Shakespeare's protagonists who insist on adhering to the forms of the law, the Cardinal argues that "yet we want a colour for his death. / 'Tis meet he be condemned by course of law" (2 Henry VI, III.i.236–37). Suffolk, however, is concerned that the King will "labour" (2 Henry VI, III.i.239), and perhaps even the commons will rise, to save Gloucester. He recognizes that Gloucester is innocent, because there is neither evidence nor crime. Although Gloucester may have intended to commit a crime, he has not acted on that intention. Nonetheless, they decide to deprive Gloucester of the presumption of innocence and treat him as guilty, perhaps because they fear that a fair trial will reveal his innocence.[80]

Without a legal case, the results of a trial are uncertain, but the plotters decide Gloucester's fate quickly, anyway. Thus, although Gloucester's "purpose is not executed," he must die because "he is a fox," who "[b]y nature proved an enemy to the flock" (2 Henry VI, III.i.256–58). Gloucester is therefore punished for, at most, his intents or thoughts. Even though the plot to kill him is both legally and morally wrong, it is, ironically, the clergyman, the Cardinal, who agrees to provide the executioner.

Shakespeare demonstrates his opposition to criminalizing thought in other plays. When, for example, in Richard III, King Edward learns from Richard of Gloucester that Clarence is dead, having been killed in pursuance of Edward's first order, the King complains:

Have I a tongue to doom my brother's death,
And shall that tongue give pardon to a slave?
My brother slew no man; his fault was thought;
And yet his punishment was bitter death.

(Richard III, II.i.103–106)

As Herbert Morris argued, the maxim that law is concerned with external conduct while morality is concerned with internal conduct is misleading because states of mind such as criminal intent and mens rea are relevant to law as an element of various crimes, and conduct is relevant to morality.[81] However, Shakespeare's distaste for guilt based on intent alone is not hard to justify. Even if we assume that Gloucester did intend to assassinate English public officials, a thought or intent not accompanied by attempts or any other substantial steps cannot—from our contemporary legal perspective—rise to a legal offence. If intent to assassinate public officials, without more, were criminalized through legislation, prosecution would fail for lack of evidence, since only God can know what is in the hearts of men. Morris believed that the eighteenth-century legal commentator William Blackstone would not have been troubled by laws making certain mental states criminal and accepting confessions as reliable evidence—note that, although the right not to be penalized for our thoughts alone is now taken for granted, this was not the case in the Middle Ages, especially in prosecutions for heresy. Modern readers may need to be reminded that under the English Treason Act of 1352 imagining and compassing the King's death was treason, as John Bellamy pointed out.[82] Nevertheless, it seems reasonable to believe that, even if Shakespeare's Gloucester confessed his intent to kill public officials, most lawyers would be uncomfortable with a conviction based only on this admission of thought. Despite Shakespeare's apparent antipathy to criminalization of thought, I do not suggest that he had a clear conception of a right to privacy, or that the issues for him and for us are the same. After all, he wrote in an era of developing conceptions of freedom of conscience, which really took form only in the eighteenth century.

Morris correctly argues that laws criminalizing thought alone would certainly trouble the moral philosopher.[83] A person who only intends to commit a crime does not interfere with the liberty of others. No less important, his own liberty to think freely should be protected by law, not prohibited. Our mental processes should enjoy absolute immunity from criminal prosecution even if some future technology (e.g., the "thought police" of George Orwell's *Nineteen Eighty-Four*) could reliably bare our thoughts and thus dismantle the evidentiary obstacles. Our inner thoughts must remain at the core of our privacy rights, rights whose protection from the state and others is absolute. This protection is enshrined in modern human rights law, especially in Articles 18 and 19 of the Universal Declaration of Human Rights and Articles 18 and 19 of the International Covenant on Civil and Political Rights, as well as in modern constitutions, and must be supported on the moral plane as well.

Shakespeare's King Henry actually does hold a trial. At the trial, he tries to save Gloucester or perhaps establish a favourable historical record. He urges the full application of due process of law:

> Proceed no straiter 'gainst our uncle Gloucester
> Than from true evidence, of good esteem,
> He be approved in practice culpable.

> (*2 Henry VI*, III.ii.20–22)

Margaret hypocritically supports Henry, saying,

> God forbid any malice should prevail
> That faultless may condemn a noble man!
> Pray God he may acquit him of suspicion!

> (*2 Henry VI*, III.ii.23–25)

At this, Henry himself joins in the farce: "I thank thee, Meg. These words content me much" (*2 Henry VI*, III.ii.26).

Suffolk then enters the trial chamber to report that Gloucester has been found dead in his bed. Although the play depicts Suffolk as responsible for ordering the Duke of Gloucester's murder, the chroniclers are less categorical. They emphasize that "hatred and mistrust of [Suffolk] were widely spread."[84] Both Hall and Holinshed describe Gloucester's death as a murder, but do not name the perpetrator. Despite this lack of clear proof, Shakespeare's authority for attributing the responsibility to Suffolk may have been Hall's statement that among the various accusations against Suffolk voiced in the commons was that he was "the chief procurer of the death of the good duke of Gloucester."[85]

Forms of Law

I have already mentioned the role of a warrant in *King John*. Even in an environment of terror like Richard III's England as depicted by Shakespeare, forms of law are not totally ignored. Frequently it is the executioners, or leaders, but sometimes even the victims, that invoke them. Richard, Duke of Gloucester, tries to persuade the Mayor of London that the summary execution of Hastings "against the form of law" was compelled by supreme necessity ("the extreme peril of the case, / The peace of England, and our person's safety / Enforced us to this execution" [*Richard III*, III.v.40–44]). The Mayor obligingly promised to "acquaint our duteous citizens / With all your just proceedings in this cause" (*Richard III*, III.v.63–64).

In an earlier scene, the two murderers hired to kill the Duke of Clarence, who is already incarcerated in the Tower on the orders of King Edward, come to Richard, Duke of Gloucester, for instructions.

RICHARD GLOUCESTER: But soft, here come my executioners.—
How now, my hardy, stout, resolvèd mates!
Are you now going to dispatch this thing?

A MURDERER: We are, my lord, and come to have the warrrant,
That we may be admitted where he is.

RICHARD GLOUCESTER: Well thought upon; I have it here about
me.
(*He gives them the warrant*)

(*Richard III*, I.iii.337–42)

Despite the warrant, Richard is concerned that the murderers might have second thoughts. He instructs them to hurry and to refrain from any discussion with Clarence (dehumanizing the victim completely, he calls him a "thing"), as the Duke might effectively plead for mercy. Richard is promptly reassured by one of the murderers:

Tut, tut, my lord, we will not stand to prate.
Talkers are no good doers. Be assured,
We go to use our hands, and not our tongues.

(*Richard III*, I.iii.348–50)

The murderers produce the warrant ("commission") to persuade the Lieutenant of the Tower, Sir Robert Brackenbury, to give them custody of Clarence. Brackenbury, as already mentioned, prefers to hide behind the language of the commission and not raise questions about its true purpose, so that he can be "guiltless of the meaning" (*Richard III*, I.iv.91).

Nevertheless, the warrant does not remedy the problems of account-ability. It may satisfy the demands of human law, but not those of either divine law or conscience. The existence of a warrant also fails to allocate accountability. The Second Murderer hesitates, recognizing the warrant's insufficiency as a means to absolve him of responsibility. His conscience is an obstacle to his bloody designs. The First Murderer urges him on:

FIRST MURDERER: What, art thou afraid?

SECOND MURDERER: Not to kill him, having a warrant, but to be damned for killing him, from the which no warrant can defend me.

(*Richard III*, I.iv.106–109)

At this point, the origin of the warrant is ambiguous. But the play explains soon thereafter that King Edward had issued it. He thus shares responsi-bility with Richard for the killing.

FIRST MURDERER: My voice is now the King's; my looks, mine own.

   . . .

What we will do, we do upon command.

SECOND MURDERER: And he that hath commanded is our king.

(*Richard III*, I.iv.165,188–89)

In a legal sense, the murderers thus enunciate a defence that, in modern terminology, is the justification of superior orders, relying on the King's orders.

Although Richard and Edward both incur some blame for the murder, the responsibility is not equally divided. Following Holinshed, Shake-speare recognizes that they share responsibility: On the one hand, the murderers discuss reporting back to Richard and being paid by him (*Rich-ard III*, I.iv.112–13,125,269–78). On the other hand, they tell Clarence that King Edward ordered the murder (*Richard III*, I.iv.188–89). But Shakespeare then parts company with Holinshed and more modern his-torians, portraying Richard as the principal culprit. Shakespeare's Edward reverses the order (*Richard III*, II.i.87), and Richard arranges through his manipulations that "by [the King's] first order [Clarence] died" (*Richard III*, II.i.87–88). Modern historians usually attribute the entire responsibility for Clarence's death to King Edward. The chroniclers suggest only complicity.[86]

In presenting Clarence's complaint that he has been deprived of due process of law, since both evidence and conviction are absent, Shakespeare also departs from his sources. According to the chroniclers and historians, Clarence was charged with treason, attainted by Parliament, convicted, and sentenced to death.[87] He was executed a month later on February 18, 1478.[88] The process therefore followed at least some forms of law. Shakespeare's decision to disregard the chroniclers concerning both the measure of Edward's blame and those forms of law that were in fact followed was deliberate. He must have sensed that the more depraved and evil Richard appeared, the greater the dramatic scope to demonize him in a superb morality tale, and, as already noted, to serve the legitimating purposes of the Tudor court. It was primarily Sir Thomas More's image of the evil Richard, followed by the major chroniclers, that inspired the almost caricatured and ahistorical Richard III of Shakespeare's play.[89] In reality, forms of law were as well observed in Richard III's reign, as in Edward IV's or Henry VII's.

Even in the terrifying murder scene, Shakespeare's Clarence invokes due process of law. He thus challenges his assassins:

> Are you drawn forth among a world of men
> To slay the innocent? What is my offence?
> Where is the evidence that doth accuse me?
> What lawful quest have given their verdict up
> Unto the frowning judge, or who pronounced
> The bitter sentence of poor Clarence' death?
> Before I be convict by course of law
> To threaten me with death is most unlawful.

> (*Richard III*, I.iv.176–83)

Once this invocation of secular law proves unable to deter the assassins, Clarence resorts to religious law, which is equally ineffective:

> Erroneous vassals, the great King of Kings
> Hath in the table of his law commanded
> That thou shalt do no murder. Will you then
> Spurn at his edict, and fulfil a man's?
> Take heed, for he holds vengeance in his hand
> To hurl upon their heads that break his law.

> (*Richard III*, I.iv.190–95)

The Second Murderer's earlier comment that he is afraid of damnation, from which "no warrant can defend me" (*Richard III*, I.iv.107–109), addresses this notion of spiritual accountability as separate from legal accountability. Thus, although an order by the King can provide a legal defence, for spiritual responsibility, the King's order would not constitute a justification.

Shakespeare found some authority for his approach in the chronicles and literary sources and additional authority in the legend of Richard's unlimited evil.[90] When Richard III hires Tyrrell, a "discontented gentleman" whom "corrupting gold / Will tempt unto a close exploit of death" (*Richard III*, IV.ii.35–37), the King tells him that the "bastards in the Tower" are his "sweet sleep disturbers" (*Richard III*, IV.ii.74–76)—even in the Tower they are a threat to his aspirations—Tyrrell readily agrees to rid Richard "from the fear of them" (*Richard III*, IV.ii.78). Interestingly, like Clarence's assassin, Tyrrell also wants some form of authorization, stating, "Let me have open means to come to them" (*Richard III*, IV.ii.77). Richard then gives him a sign of authority, saying, "Go, by this token" (*Richard III*, IV.ii.80). Nevertheless, apparently no written document implicates Richard in the murder of the Princes, a crime lacking any colour of legality, in contrast to the murder of Clarence, for which the first warrant was issued by King Edward.

Holinshed served as the primary historical source for the murder of the Princes and for Shakespeare's Richard III. In writing this part of his chronicle, Holinshed drew extensively on Thomas More and Hall, More being the key source for the chroniclers' treatment of Richard.[91] According to the chroniclers, Richard made two attempts to kill the Princes. Holinshed, following More, provides a useful description of the first attempt: because the people would not recognize his right to the throne as long as his nephews were alive, Richard sent one John Greene to the Tower's constable, Sir Robert Brackenbury, ordering him to put the Princes to death.[92] The most interesting and surprising part of More's story, as reported by Holinshed, is that Brackenbury refused to cooperate with Greene, in contrast to his behaviour in Shakespeare's treatment of the murder of Clarence. More explained, "he [Brackenbury] would neuer put them to death."[93] However, this episode is not reflected in Shakespeare's drama. Hall's account of the second attempt, based on More, is different from Shakespeare's. Here Richard gives Tyrrell not only a token, but a letter to Brackenbury; a letter with which Brackenbury complied,[94] much as he did in the murder of Clarence. In Shakespeare's *Richard III*, there is no mention of Brackenbury in the context of the Princes' murder, a murder of which we learn through Tyrell's report to Richard (*Richard III*, IV.iii). Shakespeare departs from his sources, perhaps to exonerate Brackenbury from responsibility.

The Cardinal and the Sanctuary: Yielding to Pressure

Shakespeare is at pains to show in his plays how good men yield to pressure. The episode of the sanctuary, which occurs just before the murder of the Princes, closely reflects the chronicles that Shakespeare read, providing an interesting example. Queen Elizabeth, afraid that Richard will murder her children, has taken the young Duke of York to a sanctuary under the Lord Cardinal's promise of protection and care (*Richard III*, II.iv.65–72). On his return to London, Prince Edward, the heir to the throne, is informed by Hastings that his brother York is in a sanctuary and therefore cannot welcome him. Edward does not appear to suspect that anything is amiss and wants his brother to come to him.

Buckingham, still Richard's willing accomplice, demands that the Cardinal persuade the Queen to leave the sanctuary and send the Duke of York to his brother. Should persuasion fail, he declares, he will resort to the alternative of brute force: Shakespeare's Hastings would "from her jealous arms pluck him perforce" (*Richard III*, III.i.36). Hall reports that in the council, Richard demanded that the Prince be forcibly removed if the Queen refused to surrender him.[95] In both the chronicles and Shakespeare, the Cardinal demurs. He is prepared to try persuasion, but would not dare to violate the holy sanctuary:

> My lord of Buckingham, if my weak oratory
> Can from his mother win the Duke of York,
> Anon expect him. But if she be obdurate
> To mild entreaties, God in heaven forbid
> We should infringe the sacred privilege
> Of blessèd sanctuary. Not for all this land
> Would I be guilty of so deep a sin.
>
> (*Richard III*, III.i.37–43)

Insisting on the privileges of sanctuary in a place of religious worship, Shakespeare's Cardinal thus reflects not only ancient ecclesiastical practice but also the customs of chivalry and the common law. Shakespeare's sources, such as Hall,[96] emphasized these normative rules, declaring that both the secular and the ecclesiastical authorities were obligated to respect the privileges of sanctuary.

Not satisfied with the Cardinal's response, Buckingham resorts to a menacing tone. In both Shakespeare and the chronicles, he plays the lead role in pressuring the Cardinal and invokes legal arguments to support his claim that York does not qualify for sanctuary. By arguing for the inapplicability of the rules protecting sanctuaries in this case, Buckingham is effectively preparing a justification for a forcible removal of York. He says to the Cardinal:

> You are too senseless-obstinate, my lord,
> Too ceremonious and traditional.
> Weigh it not with the grossness of this age.
> You break not sanctuary in seizing him.
> The benefit thereof is always granted

To those whose dealings have deserved the place,
And those who have the wit to claim the place.
This prince hath neither claimed it nor deserved it,
And therefore, in my mind, he cannot have it.
Then taking him from thence that 'longs not there,
You break thereby no privilege nor charter.
Oft have I heard of "sanctuary men",
But "sanctuary children" ne'er till now.

(*Richard III*, III.i.44–56)

Again, the chronicles provided a ready source for Shakespeare's treatment of this episode. Buckingham's "legal" arguments, which may have a strong basis in the common law, closely reflect Holinshed's rendition:

Against unlawful harms, never pope nor king intended to privilege any one place, for that privilege hath every place. . . . But where a man is by lawful means in peril, there needs he the tuition of some special privilege, which is the only ground and cause of all sanctuaries. From which necessity, this noble prince is far, whose love to his king, nature and kindred proveth; whose innocency to all the world, his tender youth proves; and so sanctuary, as for him, neither none he needs, nor also none can have. . . . He must ask it himself that must have it, and reason: since no man has cause to have it but whose conscience of his own fault makes him fain need to require it.

And if no body may be taken out of sanctuary, that says he will bide there. . . . And verily, I have often heard of sanctuary men, but I never heard erst of sanctuary children. . . .

But he can be no sanctuary man that neither has the wisdom to desire it nor malice to deserve it; whose life or liberty can by no lawful process stand in jeopardy. And he that takes one out of sanctuary to do him good, I say plainly, that he breaks no sanctuary.[97]

The speed with which Shakespeare's Cardinal, the supreme spiritual authority of England, yields to pressure is shocking. After Buckingham's intimidation, behaviour that was a flagrant sin a moment earlier becomes religiously neutral. Shakespeare may have intended here to cast doubts on the moral probity of Catholic clergy or perhaps simply to demonstrate that heroes are hard to find in an atmosphere of total terror. Even more important, he may have wanted to show how principles crumble under pressure. Thus, the Cardinal immediately responds to Buckingham's "legal" arguments: "My lord, you shall o'errule my mind for once. / Come on, Lord Hastings, will you go with me?" And Hastings obediently replies "I come, my lord" (*Richard III*, III.i.57–59).

In Hall, the Cardinal's surrender is more subtle.[98] However, as he does throughout his plays, Shakespeare exaggerates his character's actions and behaviour to dramatize his goal more effectively.

Shakespeare deliberately does not tell us anything about the pressure the Cardinal exerts on the Queen. He leaves the scene in the sanctuary to our imagination. Nonetheless, Hastings's presence is a clear hint of the alternative means, that is, brute force, that would be introduced if the Queen were to demur. There is no doubt that the Queen was forced to consent to York's release, so that he would join his older brother and ultimately be murdered in the Tower.[99]

Richard III as Machiavelli's Prince

The landscape of Shakespeare's plays is not filled only with strong and determined villains like Richard III. There are also wanton kings, such as Richard II and Henry IV, kings who are evil but incompetent, inconsistent and essentially humane, such as King John; and good but weak kings, such as Henry VI.[100] Some kings represent a composite of these characteristics. Michael Manheim argued that in Shakespeare's time, under the Tudors, the medieval image of the Christian knightly king was abandoned in favour of the Machiavellian model of a ruthless, calculating, successful king, bent on creating a positive, even if deceptive, image that would appeal to the people. Despite his many virtues, Henry V is almost Machiavellian in effectively manipulating public opinion.[101] But the master of image-making is Shakespeare's arch-Machiavellian, Richard III. Consider the scene with the two Bishops, staged to persuade the citizens of London of Richard's Christian virtues (Buckingham: "Two props of virtue for a Christian prince / To stay him from the fall of vanity" *Richard III*, III.vii.96–97).

Among the players are also well-meaning but weak princes and, as always, opportunistic courtiers. Each is conscious of what is happening, understands the trend of the events and foresees the inevitable crime, but lacks either the will or the courage to stand up and resist. Finally, there are the executioners, some only too willing to carry out their orders and others resisting orders, even at risk to their lives.

In the first section of this Chapter, I touched on the role of Niccolò Machiavelli's *Prince* in inspiring Shakespeare's *Richard III*. The early sixteenth-century *Prince* and *The Discourses* (1513) were translated into English only in 1640 and 1636 respectively, but Shakespeare most likely had a working knowledge of Italian and may have read these works in the original, or at least may have read about them in secondary sources circulating in England in his time. In any event, as Max Lerner points out, Elizabethan authors made frequent references to Machiavelli.[102]

In contrast to Erasmus's Christian Prince, Machiavelli's Prince is not bound to have, or always to observe, the virtues that are esteemed good in people's private lives. To serve his interests however, he should seem to be endowed with these qualities and thus appear to be merciful, faithful, humane, sincere and religious. Nevertheless, to maintain the state, a prince is often obliged to act against faith, charity, humanity and religion.[103] A prudent ruler should not keep faith when doing so would be against his interest.[104] Interestingly, as noted in Chapter 8, some of Shakespeare's figures voice similar sentiments in the discussion of oaths that can be breached for *Staatsraison*. A ruler can always find a colourable excuse for the non-fulfilment of a promise.[105] For example, a prince cannot live securely in a state as long as those whom he has deposed survive. It is therefore dangerous to deprive a ruler of his kingdom and yet leave him his life, requiring the new leader to resort to violence. New benefits can never cancel old injuries, even less so when the benefits are small in comparison to the injuries inflicted.[106]

Shakespeare's Richard III and the Prince are thus a perfect fit. Richard despises the virtues respected in private life but works hard at appearing to have them. His ascent to the throne and reign are ruthless and devoid of ethical standards, his power, survival and security the only goals. Anyone who is, or could be, a threat must be eliminated. Moreeover, references to Machiavelli actually appear several times in Shakespeare's plays. In discussing his plans to obtain the throne of England through killing and scheming, Richard of Gloucester mentions Machiavelli as someone to whom he, Richard, could teach a lesson:

> Torment myself to catch the English crown.
> And from that torment I will free myself,
> Or hew my way out with a bloody axe.
> Why, I can smile, and murder whiles I smile,
> And cry "Content!" to that which grieves my heart,
> And wet my cheeks with artificial tears,
> And frame my face to all occasions.
> I'll drown more sailors than the mermaid shall;
> I'll slay more gazers than the basilisk;
> I'll play the orator as well as Nestor,
> Deceive more slyly than Ulysses could,
> And, like a Sinon, take another Troy.
> I can add colours to the chameleon,
> Change shapes with Proteus for advantages,
> And set the murderous Machiavel to school.
> Can I do this, and cannot get a crown?

> (3 *Henry VI*, III.ii.179–94)

Richard III's defeat at the hands of Henry of Richmond, soon to become Henry VII, is inevitable in Shakespeare's paradigm of the barons rising against bloody tyrants in a just, and therefore winning, cause. Richmond's moving oration to his soldiers before the battle addresses several aspects of Richard's accountability.

> Yet remember this:
> God and our good cause fight upon our side.

The prayers of holy saints and wrongèd souls,
Like high-reared bulwarks, stand before our forces.
Richard except, those whom we fight against
Had rather have us win than him they follow.
For what is he they follow? Truly, friends,
A bloody tyrant and a homicide;
One raised in blood, and one in blood established;
One that made means to come by what he hath,
    . . .
Then if you fight against God's enemy,
God will, in justice, ward you as his soldiers.
If you do sweat to put a tyrant down,
You sleep in peace, the tyrant being slain.
If you do fight against your country's foes,
Your country's foison pays your pains the hire.
If you do fight in safeguard of your wives,
Your wives shall welcome home the conquerors.
If you do free your children from the sword,
Your children's children quites it in your age.

(*Richard III*, V.v.193–216)

In effect, Richmond presents a strong justification for the right of revolt against a tyrant, especially one that usurped the Crown and is thus an illegitimate monarch. By comparing Richard III to Machiavelli, the counselor of evil, Shakespeare emphasizes that in Elizabethan times, Richard was an approved target and a ruler against whom rebellion was, exceptionally, justified.

Accountability for the Agincourt Massacre: Henry V

Accountability is also an important aspect of *Henry V*. In two scenes, discussed above, the King consults the Archbishop of Canterbury about the justness of the war (*Henry V*, I.ii.9–32), and tries to persuade the sceptical soldiers Bates and Williams, and perhaps reassure himself as well, that the war is just (*Henry V*, IV.i).

Henry V is about war with an external enemy, in which, on the whole, the rules applied to the French were rules of chivalry and the international law of arms, rather than the law of England governing treason. As a result, there is less room for tyrannical abuse. Shakespeare's treatment of the laws of war here shows that he was well aware of the difference between internal strife and international wars.[107] Accordingly, the Southampton plot is described as "dangerous treason" and "high treason" by men who "[j]oined with an enemy proclaimed and fixed" (*Henry V*, II.ii.145, 164, 183). In contrast, Shakespeare refers to the conflict with the French as "a fair and lucky war" (*Henry V*, II.ii.181). Similarly, *Richard*

III unambiguously demonstrates Shakespeare's understanding of the difference between domestic and international wars, when King Richard urges,

> March on, march on, since we are up in arms,
> If not to fight with foreign enemies,
> Yet to beat down these rebels here at home.

> (*Richard III*, IV.iv.459–61)

The scene at the battle of Agincourt presents a penetrating view of Henry's accountability for the effects of the war. Henry's order to kill the French prisoners involves no euphemisms or code words, perhaps because it is arguably justified as made in reprisal for the killing of the boys guarding the rear encampment, and as impelled by the necessity of war—Henry's fear that the French are regrouping for another attack and that the multitude of prisoners will rise against their captors in aid of the attackers. These justifications clearly distinguish the killing of the prisoners at Agincourt from the obvious crimes of kings discussed above. However, the plea of necessity for the killing of French cavalry is weakened when Pistol, who is not a knight, calls it throat-cutting:

> KING HARRY: (*Alarum*)
> But hark, what new alarum is this same?
> The French have reinforced their scattered men.
> Then every soldier kill his prisoners.
> (*The soldiers kill their prisoners*)
> Give the word through.

> [PISTOL]: *Coup' la gorge.*

> (*Henry V*, IV.vi.35–39)

Gower's scathing sarcasm further highlights Shakespeare's substantial doubts about the legality of the order. Gower thus undermines the justification and raises questions of credibility:

> FLUELLEN: Kill the poys and the luggage! 'Tis expressly against the law of arms. 'Tis as arrant a piece of knavery, mark you now, as can be offert. In your conscience now, is it not?

> GOWER: 'Tis certain there's not a boy left alive. And the cowardly rascals that ran from the battle ha' done this slaughter. Besides, they have burned and carried away all that was in the King's tent; wherefore the King most worthily hath caused every soldier to cut his prisoner's throat. O 'tis a gallant king.

> (*Henry V*, IV.vii.1–10)

I argued elsewhere that the English rear camp constituted a lawful object of attack and that the French raid was unlikely to have violated any laws of war.[108] Without a manifest breach of law by the French, Henry could not claim the defence of reprisal, which was then generally permissible. However, because Henry believed that the battle had not been won and danger persisted, and that the captured French prisoners posed a threat to his forces, his order to kill the prisoners probably did not violate medieval legal standards. Nevertheless, it clashed with the views of some of the writers disposed to take a more humanitarian view of the law, including Gentili,[109] an Italian Protestant who took refuge in England and in 1587 became the Regius Professor of Civil Law at Oxford, and, later, an adviser to the Crown. In modern humanitarian law, reprisals against prisoners of war are absolutely prohibited.[110]

Those of us who consider Henry's order to be barbaric may need to revisit the law in force during the American Civil War. The well-known Lieber's Code, the military law promulgated by President Lincoln and proposed by Francis Lieber of Columbia College Law School, which was generally admired for its humanitarian and enlightened nature, allowed the denial of quarter on grounds of necessity to enemy, that is, Confederate, prisoners: "a commander is permitted to direct his troops to give no quarter, in great straits, when his own salvation makes it impossible to cumber himself with prisoners."[111] This rule, which was law for the United States Army in the mid-nineteenth century, appears almost designed to legitimate the massacre Henry V ordered at Agincourt. Article 62 of the Lieber Code even authorized a savage form of reciprocity, declaring that troops that gave no quarter, would receive none in return. Article 66 extended reciprocity and retribution to the period after the battle, when there could no longer be any semblance of necessity. It allowed killing of enemy prisoners if within three days after the battle it was discovered that they belonged to a corps that gave no quarter.[112]

The tolerance of the Lieber Code for denial of quarter did not long survive in the evolution of modern international humanitarian law. Article 23(d) of the Hague Regulations emphasizes that declaring that no quarter will be granted is particularly forbidden.[113] Today, the denial of quarter and killing of captured prisoners of war constitutes one of the most obvious and absolute war crimes.

Shakespeare's Henry V does not try subsequently to disclaim the order, leaving us uncertain about his own feelings as regards the massacre. No less, a look at the sources offers little enlightenment. The real Henry's chronicler, an anonymous chaplain attached to his court who left posterity the only eye-witness account of Agincourt, the wonderful *Gesta Henrici Quinti* (1416–17), does not even mention the order to kill the prisoners. He describes the killing as almost an act of nature.[114] This may mean that the King was not proud of the order and did not want it to be highlighted. Shakespeare himself probably did not read the *Gesta*, which remained in manuscript form in the sixteenth century.

Conscience: The Unwanted Intruder

The dominant theme in Shakespeare's treatment of accountability is a moral-psychological one. It concerns the mysteries and power of conscience, not an exclusive preserve of noble courtiers, but one that belongs to hired guns as well. It shows conscience as an important instrument for ensuring accountability.

Let us turn once more to *Richard III*, the scene in the Tower of London, and to the two murderers who came to kill George, the Duke of Clarence. The Second Murderer understands the limitations of the written warrant and the criminal order. It can protect him from human justice, but not from his fear of damnation or his pangs of conscience. An additional worry for a modern executioner might be that the warrant would not protect him from international justice or prosecution by foreign states. The First Murderer reminds his colleague of the promised reward:

FIRST MURDERER: Where's thy conscience now?

SECOND MURDERER: O, in the Duke of Gloucester's purse.

FIRST MURDERER: When he opens his purse to give us our reward, thy conscience flies out.

SECOND MURDERER: 'Tis no matter. Let it go. There's few or none will entertain it.

FIRST MURDERER: What if it come to thee again?

SECOND MURDERER: I'll not meddle with it. It makes a man a coward. A man cannot steal but it accuseth him. A man cannot swear but it checks him. A man cannot lie with his neighbour's wife but it detects him. 'Tis a blushing, shamefaced spirit, that mutinies in a man's bosom. It fills a man full of obstacles. It made me once restore a purse of gold that by chance I found. It beggars any man that keeps it. It is turned out of towns and cities for a dangerous thing, and every man that means to live well endeavours to trust to himself and live without it.

(*Richard III*, I.iv.124–41)

The Second Murderer's morality appears to yield to his partner's cynical rationality. But Clarence does not only plead for mercy, invoking both secular and religious law. He somberly and realistically warns the murderers not to expect gratitude from Richard: "O sirs, consider: they that set you on / To do this deed will hate you for the deed" (*Richard III*, I.iv.249–50). The reader is reminded here of Henry IV's treatment of Exton, disowning and banishing him rather than rewarding him.

The First Murderer symbolizes the wholly cynical murderer for whom relenting would be "cowardly and womanish" (*Richard III*, I.iv.252). In contrast, the Second Murderer has a conscience that he tries to stifle without success. He ultimately refuses to carry out the criminal order and even tries to save Clarence, but his effort is too late and too little to prevent the murder. Nevertheless, he issues a challenge to Richard, refusing the payment and wanting Richard to know that he did not participate in the murder, although he understands the dangers inherent in his calling:

> SECOND MURDERER: I would he knew that I had saved his brother.
> Take thou the fee, and tell him what I say, For I repent me that
> the Duke is slain.
> (Exit)
>
> (Richard III, I.iv.271–73)

He thus proves morally superior to the courtier Hubert in King John, who hides his mercy and reveals it opportunistically only later, when it appears that it would serve John's interests if Arthur were still alive. The dialogue between the two murderers concludes with the First Murderer's surprising recognition that after he has been paid, he too will have to disappear (Richard III, I.iv.277–78).

The power of conscience is demonstrated again after the murder of the Princes. The thugs Tyrrell hires to kill the Princes suddenly feel such remorse for their crime that they cannot even discuss it, as Tyrrell describes in his soliloquy while awaiting Richard (Richard III, IV.iii.1–22). Even when he is in the presence of the King, Tyrrell remains ambivalent and reserved about the murder, showing the effect of his conscience as well.

> KING RICHARD: Kind Tyrrell, am I happy in thy news?
>
> TYRRELL: If to have done the thing you gave in charge
> Beget your happiness, be happy then,
> For it is done.
>
> (Richard III, IV.iii.24–27)

The significance of conscience as an instrument of accountabiity is perhaps best seen in Richard himself, who does not fear any retribution, whether human or divine. His only fear is his own conscience, represented by the ghosts of his victims, who appear to him on the night before the battle with Richmond, in which he dies.

> Have mercy, Jesu!—Soft, I did but dream.
> O coward conscience, how dost thou afflict me?
> . . .
> My conscience hath a thousand several tongues,
> And every tongue brings in a several tale,
> And every tale condemns me for a villain.
> Perjury, perjury, in the high'st degree!

Murder, stern murder, in the dir'st degree!
All several sins, all used in each degree,
Throng to the bar, crying all, "Guilty, guilty!"

(*Richard III*, V.v.132–33,147–53)

Despite this fear and despair, on the day of the battle, Richard, in an act of bravery and defiance, decides not to yield to conscience—which would be cowardice—and rather to be faithful to himself to the very end:

Go, gentlemen, each man unto his charge.
Let not our babbling dreams affright our souls.
Conscience is but a word that cowards use,
Devised at first to keep the strong in awe.
Our strong arms be our conscience; swords, our law.
March on, join bravely! Let us to 't, pell mell—
If not to heaven, then hand in hand to hell.

(*Richard III*, V.vi.37–43)

This is reminiscent of the penultimate scene of Da Ponte's libretto of Mozart's Opera *Don Giovanni*, when Don Giovanni refuses to repent in his fatal encounter with the Commendatore, because to do so would be cowardice. When Shakespeare's Richard III rejects conscience and refuses repentance, any possibility of reconciliation disappears and the only avenue for the satisfaction of the victims' grievances is the justice, retribution and force that the rising barons dispense.[115]

The Macbeths' power proves inadequate to defeat the barons, who fight the murderous and tyrannical couple. Conscience is the dominant element in *Macbeth*: it can send the ghosts of one's victims to haunt one's dreams, and deprive one of that essential element of survival and sanity, sleep. Even before Macbeth's defeat on the battlefield, he and his wife are destroyed by their consciences. The ghosts of their victims take over the night, suggesting that Macbeth has murdered sleep: "Macbeth shall sleep no more" (*Macbeth*, II.ii.34–41). The ambitious and steely Lady Macbeth surprisingly succumbs to a mental illness. Her constant washing of her hands cannot "clea[r] [her] of this deed" (*Macbeth*, I.ii.65), nor can the physician help her overcome her problems.

MACBETH: (*to the doctor*)
Canst thou not minister to a mind diseased,
Pluck from the memory a rooted sorrow,
Raze out the written troubles of the brain,
And with some sweet oblivious antidote
Cleanse the fraught bosom of that perilous stuff
Which weighs upon the heart?

DOCTOR: Therein the patient
   Must minister to himself.

MACBETH: Throw physic to the dogs; I'll none of it.

(Macbeth, V.iii.42–49)

Lady Macbeth's conscience eventually kills her by forcing her to suffer her own tormented memories and ghosts. Again, Shakespeare emphasizes the role of conscience, rather than secular law, as an arbiter of accountability.

Sins of the Fathers: Collective or Individual Responsibility?

If Shakespeare believes in the principle of individual responsibility and acccountability, as shown above, references in his plays to a different and conflicting principle, that the sins of the fathers are visited on the sons, are difficult to explain. Does Shakespeare believe in the personal responsibility of the responsible leader and the executioner or in the collective responsibility of the family, group or nation? In the Middle Ages, the period on which Shakespeare focuses in his Histories, the latter concept could be expressed in the Old Testament's warning in *Deuteronomy* 5:9, *Numbers* 14:18 and *Exodus* 20:5, 43:7, that God is "visiting the iniquity of the fathers upon the children unto the third and fourth generation."[116] An evil or criminal ancestor could thus escape a punishment that would instead afflict an innocent descendant. This is a counter-individualistic approach to accountability, wholly in conflict with our modern notions of justice.

As Phillis Rackin points out, in the second half of the sixteenth century, historiography was changing and history was gradually being separated from theology. Although God's will was still regarded as the first cause, human actions and their consequences were increasingly considered as another, sometimes dominant cause. Renaissance historians explained events in light of both providential and rational causes. Hall, who may have influenced Shakespeare's providentialism, regarded Henry VI's misfortunes as punishment for the usurpation of the Crown by his grandfather, Henry IV, even though others attributed the misfortune to his own personal failings.[117]

The Old Testament prophet Jeremiah challenges the idea of the sins of the fathers frontally and rejects it fully: "[I]n those days they shall say no more, the fathers have eaten a sour grape, and the children's teeth are set on edge. But every one shall die for his own iniquity: every man that eateth the sour grape, his teeth shall be set on edge" (*Jeremiah* 31:29–30). Another Old Testament prophet, Ezekiel, takes the same position, declaring that "the person who sins, only he shall die. . . . A child shall not share the burden of a parent's guilt, nor shall a parent share the burden of a child's guilt; the righteousness of the righteous shall be accounted to him alone, and the wickedness of the wicked shall be accounted to him alone" (Ezekiel 18:1–4, 20).

Although rooted in the Old Testament, this concept of the sins of the fathers is not part of the Jewish tradition, which is one of individual responsibility. The rabbis of the Talmud (Berakhot 7a) and medieval Jewish commentators such as Rashi and Seforno interpreted the sins of the fathers concept as attaching responsibility to the succeeding generations only if they continued to sin. This interpretation drastically transformed the concept from one of collective responsibility to one of individual responsibility. Furthermore, although Exodus and Deuteronomy cite the sins of the fathers concept in the august Ten Commandments, rabbis nevertheless dropped it from the liturgy.[118]

In any event, the concept of the sins of the fathers addresses only divine accountability. For the administration of justice, individual responsibility is the only valid principle, as recognized in Deuteronomy 24: 16: "Fathers shall not be put to death for children; neither shall children be put to death for fathers. Every man shall be put to death for his own sin."

Separate from the issue of original sin, the Catholic tradition is rather similar. Saint Thomas Aquinas teaches that a son is not punishable for his father's sin and "a person is punished only for his own sin, because sinning is a personal act."[119] Much like the Jewish commentators, Saint Thomas interprets the sins of the fathers concept in Exodus as applying only in those cases in which the sons also sin.[120] Therefore, no one can contract a sin "by way of origin from any ancestor."[121] Only if the son shares in the fault of the father will he be punished for his father's sins.[122] Finally, parents do not transmit their merits to the children, much less their sins.[123] Modern Catholic commentators agree that the sins of the fathers are not visited on children "who are in no sense partakers of their parents's sins."[124]

In contrast to our perspective, people in the Middle Ages may have believed in the reality of the sins of the fathers. Given the widespread illiteracy, lack of information, superstitions and strong, often fanatical religious beliefs, it is not surprising that people would interpret the bad fortune that befalls some people or families as unexplainable except as a just punishment for the sins of earlier generations, or as a result of potent curses on future generations.[125]

The sins of the fathers principle is, of course, the very opposite of modern principles of individual responsibility. Throughout history, it has been invoked as a justification for glaring injustices, such as the persecution of countless generations of Jews allegedly responsible for the death of Jesus Christ. A Bosnian-Serb lawyer at the International Criminal Tribunal for the former Yugoslavia at The Hague answered accusations that his client, Duško Tadić, committed atrocities against Bosnian Muslims with claims that Muslims in Bosnia have been committing crimes against Christians for centuries. The lawyer was not concerned with the religious or spiritual effects of the sins of the fathers concept. He advocated, in effect, vengeance for acts of former generations, supporting a similar principle of collective responsibility in the secular domain.

Shakespeare's plays include several episodes that speak about the sins of the fathers being visited on subsequent generations. Henry V fears that despite his efforts to atone, he will be held to account for his father's crime in usurping the Crown and will bear responsibility for the death of Richard II.

> Not today, O Lord,
> O not today, think not upon the fault
> My father made in compassing the crown.
> I Richard's body have interrèd new,
> And on it have bestowed more contrite tears
> Than from it issued forcèd drops of blood.
> Five hundred poor have I in yearly pay
> Who twice a day their withered hands hold up
> Toward heaven to pardon blood. And I have built
> Two chantries, where the sad and solemn priests
> Sing still for Richard's soul. More will I do,
> Though all that I can do is nothing worth,
> Since that my penitence comes after ill,
> Imploring pardon.
>
> (*Henry V*, IV.i.289–302)

Neither Holinshed's nor Hall's accounts contain anything about the sins of the fathers relevant to this soliloquy. Shakespeare may have found the concept itself in Robert Fabyan's *New Chronicles of England and France*, which were compiled in 1495 and printed in 1516 and 1559. Fabyan reports that Henry arranged that a weekly mass and a yearly requiem be held, and three houses of religion established, on Richard's behalf.[126] A modern commentator speaks of the "end of the curse of [Bolingbroke's] usurpation" that came only with the victory of Henry VII over Richard III.[127]

In *King John*, in a heated argument with Queen Eleanor, King John's mother, Constance complains that Eleanor's sins are visited on the tragic hero of the play, Constance's son, Prince Arthur. This argument serves to castigate Eleanor for taking a position in favour of her son King John and against the dynastic claims of her grandson Arthur:

> Thy sins are visited in this poor child;
> The canon of the law is laid on him,
> Being but the second generation
> Removèd from thy sin-conceiving womb.
>
> (*King John*, II.i.179–82)

The third example of Shakespeare's use of the sins of the fathers idea appears in *1 Henry VI*, when Somerset tries to triumph over against Rich-

ard Plantagenet. Here, as in the previous episode, the objective in introducing the sins of the fathers is to curse or reprove one's adversaries.

> SOMERSET: Was not thy father, Richard Earl of Cambridge,
> For treason executed in our late king's days?
> And by his treason stand'st not thou attainted,
> Corrupted, and exempt from ancient gentry?
> His trespass yet lives guilty in thy blood,
> And till thou be restored thou art a yeoman.
>
> (*1 Henry VI*, II.iv.90–95)

Thus, in both *King John* and *1 Henry VI*, the notion of sins of the fathers
is used as an offensive argument in quarrels with adversaries and can be
seen as a means of damaging the son's reputation or status in society.
Nevertheless, following Somerset's tirade above, Henry VI decides to "res-
tor[e] Richard to his blood . . . [s]o shall his father's wrongs be recom-
pensed" (*1 Henry VI*, III.i.164–65) and create him the Duke of York.
However, Richard actually did suffer from a punishment imposed on his
father by not inheriting the title, which had no relation to the sins of
the fathers concept.[128]

The fourth example is Richard II threatening Bolingbroke's ally
Northumberland that God will strike his "children yet unborn and un-
begot" (*Richard II*, III.iii.87). Shakespeare's actual commitment to the
belief that the sins of the fathers are visited on their sons might not be
serious, as this exchange between Lancelot the clown and Jessica in *The
Merchant of Venice* shows:

> LANCELOT: Yes, truly; for look you, the sins of the father are to be
> laid upon the children, therefore I promise you I fear you. I was
> always plain with you, and so now I speak my agitation of the
> matter, therefore be o' good cheer, for truly I think you are
> damned. There is but one hope in it that can do you any good,
> and that is but a kind of bastard hope, neither.
>
> JESSICA: And what hope is that, I pray thee?
>
> LANCELOT: Marry, you may partly hope that your father got you not,
> that you are not the Jew's daughter.
>
> JESSICA: That were a kind of bastard hope indeed.
> So the sins of my mother should be visited upon me.
>
> LANCELOT: Truly then, I fear you are damned both by father and
> mother. Thus, when I shun Scylla your father, I fall into Cha-
> rybdis your mother. Well, you are gone both ways.
>
> (*The Merchant of Venice*, III.v.1–16)

The exchange preceding Clifford's killing of Rutland in *3 Henry VI*
is not an example of the sins of the fathers principle, but rather a ven-

detta. Rutland, still a child, is accompanied by his tutor, a chaplain, who appeals to Clifford to "murder not this innocent child / Lest thou be hated both of God and man" (3 *Henry VI*, I.iii.8–9). Clifford spares the tutor's life because of his priesthood, but rejects his and Rutland's cries for mercy. He must kill Rutland because Rutland's father, Richard Duke of York, killed Clifford's father.

RUTLAND: I never did thee harm—why wilt thou slay me?

CLIFFORD: Thy father hath.

RUTLAND: But 'twas ere I was born.
    . . .

CLIFFORD: No cause? Thy father slew my father, therefore die.
    (*He stabs him*)

RUTLAND: *Dii faciant laudis summa sit ista tuae.*
    (*He dies*)

(3 Henry VI, I.iii.39–40, 47–48)

While Rutland exemplifies individual innocence, Clifford invokes a claim to intergenerational revenge. The dialogue between Clifford and Rutland does not leave any doubt as to where Shakespeare's sympathy lies with regard to vendettas. Shakespeare shows how the cycle of violence spreads: Clifford kills Rutland in revenge for his father's death at the hands of York, Rutland's father. Although King Edward had just enunciated the chivalric principle of mercy towards the vanquished (3 *Henry VI*, II.vi.44–45), Richard and Warwick are then allowed to kill Clifford in revenge for his murder of York and Rutland. As Warwick claims, "measure for measure must be answered" (3 *Henry VI*, II.vi.55).[129]

Romeo and Juliet is another example of a vendetta. It emphasizes the suffering of the young lovers, culminating in their death, as a result of the ancient grudge between the Capulets and the Montagues (*Romeo and Juliet*, Chorus, Prologue 1–11). In the play's final lines, the Prince further highlights the futility of wars purportedly to revenge the crimes of the former generations and the price one pays for vengeance:

Where be these enemies? Capulet, Montague,
See what a scourge is laid upon your hate,
That heaven finds means to kill your joys with love.
And I, for winking at your discords, too
Have lost a brace of kinsmen. All are punishèd.

(Romeo and Juliet, V.iii.290–94)

Ultimately, Shakespeare's philosophy is to emphasize individual merit and one's own achievements rather than one's inheritance, and to favour nobility of merit over nobility of birth. This individualistic approach, discussed in chapter 7, is wholly inconsistent with any notion of collective responsibility.

Concluding Observations

Written during the period of Elizabethan absolutism, Shakespeare's plays, despite their complexity and often ironic structure, appear to advocate a society in which the law should be respected and leaders held to high standards of civilized behaviour. In the constant tension between the interests of power and ethical responsibilities, Shakespeare appears to support the latter, even if with occasional equivocation. Condemnation of crimes and euphemisms for crimes is strong. The canon emphasizes moral duties and the role of conscience as a guide to civilized behaviour by the leader and citizen. Furthermore, suggesting that crimes do not, or at least should not, go unpunished, the dramatist creates a potent image of accountability. However, he also shows how both the principle and the ideal occasionally give way in the face of stress and pressure.

Shakespeare's discussion of accountability sparks questions of both legal and moral responsibility. There are several levels of discussion, including the political-secular, the religious-spiritual, and the moral-psychological, each of which reflects the others. Leaders, even kings, who order the killing of innocent victims cannot escape responsibility for their acts. Emphasizing the religious-spiritual dimension, Shakespeare uses conscience as a particularly powerful weapon for ensuring compliance with norms.

EPILOGUE

Returning to Professor Roberts's questions, I agree that the Hague, Geneva and other Conventions have brought uniformity and clarity to the rules. No less, they have obtained the formal assent of virtually all states. In the process, however, the modern conventions have created a complicated and technical system of humanitarian law that only experts can master. A normative system, like chivalry, based largely on custom and a few rules of relative generality, would not suffice in the face of the frequent disintegration of states, the multiplicity of powerful actors on the domestic and international scene, and the modern weapons and technology of today's world. Nonetheless, due to the very fact of codification encompassing a myriad detailed provisions, we may have assigned greater legitimacy to treaties and conventions over uncodified norms. In any event, as Roberts writes, "we have also lost something: the sense that rules arise naturally out of societies, their armed forces, and their rulers on the basis of experience; the flexibility that came from their essentially customary character; and the value attached to honor, chivalry and mercy."[1]

In Algeria and other conflicts around the world, combatants kill women and children and, even worse, are proud of such killings. To combat this unlawful and dishonourable behaviour, we must revive our ability to feel shame and guilt. Technical rules have greatly replaced a culture of individual responsibility; restoring such a culture is one of the challenges we face. Shakespeare's poetic texts can help us to meet this challenge. Without neglecting our existing system of international humanitarian law, we need to refocus on broad, simple and comprehensible principles of humanity. Broad principles and norms can sometimes be more effective than technical rules in ostracizing and shaming violators and, therefore, in influencing bahaviour. While a utopian attempt to revive chivalry would have little effect, I believe we need to reinvigorate chivalry's concept and culture of values, especially the notion of individual honour and dishonour as motivating factors for the conduct of both warriors and citizens.[2]

NOTES

INTRODUCTION

1. 89 Am. J. Int'l Law 224, 226–27 (1995).

2. All references to the canon will be to William Shakespeare, The Complete Works (Stanley Wells & Gary Taylor eds., Clarendon 1988).

3. Theodor Meron, Henry's Wars and Shakespeare's Laws 7–16, 75–120, 142–71 (1993).

4. Charles Lethbridge Kingsford, English Historical Literature in the Fifteenth Century (1913).

5. Eric S. Mallin, *Emulous Factions and the Collapse of Chivalry: Troilus and Cressida*, 29 Representations 145, 154–55 (Winter 1990).

6. William Henry Schofield, Chivalry in English Literature 183–266 (1912 repr. 1964).

7. Philippe Contamine, War in the Middle Ages 257 (1984).

8. G.I.A.D. Draper, *The Interaction of Christianity and Chivalry in the Historical Development of the Law of War*, 46 International Review of the Red Cross 3, 11, 13 (No. 46, Jan. 1965).

9. Contamine, *supra* note 7, at 256.

10. Meron, *supra* note 3, at 203–204.

11. Alberico Gentili, De Jure Belli Libri Tres 212 (Carnegie ed., John C. Rolfe trans., 1933). Alberico Gentili, an Italian Protestant, took refuge in England and in 1587 became the Regius Professor of Civil Law at Oxford.

12. *See generally* Howard Mancing, The Chivalric World of Don Quixote (1982).

13. On New Historicism, see, for example, Hunter Cadzow, in The Johns

Hopkins Guide to Literary Theory and Criticism 539 (1994); Gary Taylor, Reinventing Shakespeare 346–55 (1991) (discussing the work of Stephen Greenblatt); Annabel Patterson, Shakespeare and the Popular Voice (1989); The Norton Shakespeare (Stephen Greenblatt gen. ed., Walter Cohen, Jean E. Howard & Katharine Eisaman Maus, eds., 1997); Mallin, *supra* note 5.

14. Katharine Eisaman Maus, *Henry V*, in Norton Shakespeare, *supra* note 13, at 1445.

15. See Curtis Brown Watson, Shakespeare and the Renaissance Concept of Honor 168–73 (1560).

CHAPTER ONE

1. Philippe Contamine, War in the Middle Ages 250–59, 289–90 (1984); Malcom Vale, War and Chivalry 1 (1981).

2. Vale, *supra* note 1.

3. Maurice Keen, Chivalry 249 (1984).

4. *Id.* at 240. 417 U.S. 733, 752–59 (1974).

5. Diane Bornstein, Mirrors of Courtesy 9 (1975).

6. Edgar Prestage, Chivalry 2 (1928).

7. Léon Gautier, Chivalry 5 (D.C. Dunning trans., 1959).

8. Prestage, *supra* note 6, at 26.

9. Pierre-Clement Timbal, La Guerre de cent ans vue à travers les registres du Parlement (1337–69) 269 (1961).

10. Theodor Meron, Henry's Wars and Shakespeare's Laws 142–53 (1993).

11. Marjorie Reeves & Stephen Medcalf, *The Ideal, the Real and the Quest for Perfection*, in The Later Middle Ages 56, 87 (Stephen Medcalf ed., 1981).

12. G.I.A.D. Draper, *The Interaction of Christianity and Chivalry in the Historical Development of the Law of War*, in 5 Int'l Rev. Red Cross 3 (No. 46, Jan. 1965).

13. Abraham Lincoln, Selected Speeches and Writings 389, 391 (Library of America Paperback 1992).

14. Art. 4, Issued as General Orders No. 100, *reprinted in* Dietrich Schindler & Jiří Toman, The Laws of Armed Conflicts 3 (1988); Theodor Meron, *Francis Lieber's Code and Principles of Humanity*, in Politics, Values and Functions: International Law in the 21st Century, Essays in Honour of Professor Louis Henkin 249, 252–53 (Jonathan I. Charney, Donald K. Anton, & Mary Ellen O'Connell eds., 1997), and in 36 Colum. J. Transnat'l L. 269, 273 (1997).

15. Lieber Code, *supra* note 14, at Art. 11.

16. *Id.* at Art. 15.

17. *Id.* at Art. 16.

18. *Id.* at Art. 22.

19. *Id.* at Art. 44.

20. *Id.* at Art. 60.

21. Art. 23. *Reprinted in* Schindler & Toman, *supra* note 14, at 69; 36 Stat. 2277; TS 539; 1 Bevans 631. For the principal provisions on the obligation to grant quarter, see Hague Convention (No. IV) Respecting the Laws and Customs of War on Land, with Annex of Regulations, Art. 23, Oct. 18, 1907, 36 Stat. 2277; TS 539; 1 Bevans 631; Convention Relative to the Treatment of Prisoners of War (Geneva Convention No. III), Aug. 12, 1949, Arts. 3, 4, 13, 14, 6 UST 3316, TIAS No. 3364, 75 UNTS 135; Protocol Additional to the Geneva Conventions of 1 August 1949, and Relating to the Protection of Victims of Inter-

national Armed Conflicts (Protocol I), Art. 40, opened for signature 12 Dec. 1977, 1125 UNTS 3; Protocol Additional to the Geneva Conventions of 12 August 1949, and Relating to the Protection of Victims of Non-International Armed Conflicts, Art. 4, opened for signature 12 Dec. 1977, 1125 UNTS 609.

22. *Id.* at Preamble.

23. Theodor Meron, *supra* note 10, at 152–53.

24. Department of the Army, The Law of Land Warfare, Field Manual No. 27-10, 3 (1956).

25. Department of the Air Force, International Law—The Conduct of Armed Conflicts and Air Operations, AF Pamphlet 110-31, at 1-6 para. 3 (1976).

26. Canada's Army CFP 300 at 2.07 (Version 6.1: 1 October 1997).

27. George S. Prugh, Law at War: Vietnam 1964–1973, at 74–76 and Annex H (1975).

28. International Committee of the Red Cross, Rules for Combatants.

CHAPTER TWO

1. Saint Augustine, City of God XXX(7), XIX(12) (first published 1467, Henry Bettenson trans., 1972).

2. Philippe Contamine, War in the Midde Ages 263 (1984).

3. *Id.* at 264–65.

4. Maurice Keen, Chivalry 44–50 (1984).

5. Malcolm Vale, War and Chivalry 8–9 (1981), citing Johan Huizinga, *Homo Ludens.*

6. Contamine, *supra* note 2, at 265–66.

7. M.H. Keen, "Chivalry, Nobility and the Man-at-Arms," *in* War, Literature and Politics in the Late Middle Ages 40–44 (C.T. Allmand ed., 1976).

8. Johan Huizinga, The Autumn of the Middle Ages 81 (Rodney J. Payton & Ulrich Mammitzsch trans., 1996) (emphasis added).

9. Giovanni da Legnano, Tractatus de bello, de represaliis et de duello (James Brierly trans., Thomas Erskine Holland ed., 1917). Giovanni da Legnano completed his work in 1360, but it was published in 1477 and in the better-known editions of 1487 and 1584.

10. *Id.* at 224.

11. *Id.*

12. *Id.* at 224–31.

13. Arthur B. Ferguson, The Indian Summer of English Chivalry 175 (1960).

14. Honoré Bouvet (Bonet), The Tree of Battles 192 (G.W. Coopland ed., 1949). This is a translation of the Ernest Nys edition of 1883.

15. *Id.* at 125.

16. *Id.*

17. *Id.*

18. *Id.*

19. Christine de Pisan, The Book of Fayttes of Armes and of Chyvalrye 10 (William Caxton trans., 1489, A.T.P. Byles ed., 1932).

20. Maurice H. Keen, The Laws of War in the Late Middle Ages 9 (1965).

21. Saint Thomas Aquinas, Summa Theologiae, Question 40 on War 83 (Blackfriars ed. 1972).

22. Robert P. Adams, The Better Part of Valor: More, Erasmus, Colet, and Vives, on Humanism, War, and Peace 1496–1535, at 100–17 (1962).

23. Franciscus de Vitoria, De Indis et de iure belli relectiones 174 (John Pawley Bate trans., Ernest Nys ed., 1917). These lectures were first published posthumously in 1557.

24. Id. at 173.

25. Contamine, *supra* note 2, at 285. Regarding Charles V's consultations with the estates and jurists to ensure that he had just cause to resume the war, see Christine de Pisan, *supra* note 19, at 17.

26. Contamine, *supra* note 2, at 284.

27. Theodor Meron, Henry's Wars and Shakespeare's Laws 21 (1993).

28. Christine de Pisan, *supra* note 19, at 13.

29. Vitoria, *supra* note 23, at 173–74.

30. J.H. Hexter, The Vision of Politics on the Eve of the Reformation 82–93 (1973)

31. For a further discussion of the role of courtiers in Shakespeare, see Chapter 9.

32. Christine de Pisan, *supra* note 19, at 13.

33. Michael Powicke, Military Obligation in Medieval England 232, 242–43, 250 (1962).

34. Paul C. Jorgensen, Shakespeare's Military World 180 (1956).

35. On the medieval requirement of declaring war, see Keen, *supra* note 20, at 70, 72; Bouvet, *supra* note 14, at 128–29; Christine de Pisan, *supra* note 19, at 13, Giovanni da Legnano, *supra* note 9, at 232–34, chs. 13–16. See also George Keeton, Shakespeare's Legal and Political Background 89 (1967); George Keeton, Shakespeare and His Legal Problems 72–73 (1930).

36. Christine de Pisan, *supra* note 19, at 13.

37. Francisco Suárez, Selections from Three Works 816 (Gwladys L. Williams, Ammi Brown & John Waldron eds. & trans., Carnegie ed. 1944). De legibus, ac deo legislatore, a treatise on Law and God the Legislator, was published in 1612; Defensio Fidei Catholicae ed Apostolicae Adversus Anglicanai Sectae Errores was published in 1613; and De Triplici virtute theologica, fide, spe, et charitate, The Three Theological Virtues, Faith, Hope, and Charity, which focused on the law of war, was published posthumously in 1621.

38. Id.

39. In *Henry V*, the French herald Montjoy defies Henry on behalf of Charles VI: "To this add defiance, and tell him for conclusion he hath betrayed his followers, whose condemnation is pronounced" (*Henry V*, III.vi.132–35).

40. Edward Hall, Hall's Chronicle: Containing the History of England, during the Reign of Henry the Fourth, and the Succeeding Monarchs, to the End of the Reign of Henry the Eighth 57 (1809, repr. 1965.) This edition collates the editions of 1548 and 1550. Original title: The Union of Two Noble and Illustre Famelies of Lancastre and Yorke (1548).

41. Vitoria, *supra* note 23, at 171.

42. Id. at 173.

43. Katharine Eisaman Maus, *Henry V*, in the Norton Shakespeare 1445 (Stephen Greenblatt gen. ed., Walter Cohen, Jean E. Howard & Katharine Eisaman Maus eds., 1997).

44. Other examples include the following: in *1 Henry IV*, Hotspur both assures his followers and reassures himself, saying, "Now for our consciences: the arms are fair / when the intent of bearing them is just" (*1 Henry IV*, V.ii.87–88). Henry VI declares:

What stronger breastplate than a heart untainted?
Thrice is he armed that hath his quarrel just;
And he but naked, though locked up in steel,
Whose conscience with injustice is corrupted.

(2 *Henry VI*, III.ii.232–35).

Similarly, Queen Margaret urges her troops on against Edward's army, saying, "you fight in justice; then in God's name, lords, be valiant, and give signal to the fight" (3 *Henry VI*, V.iv.81–82). Pompey also relies on divine assistance, remarking that "if the great gods be just, they shall assist the deeds of justest men" (*Antony and Cleopatra*, II.i.1–2).

45. Contamine, *supra* note 2, at 266.

46. Bouvet, *supra* note 14, at 156–57. *See also* Saint Augustine, *supra* note 1, at V(21)–(22).

47. Balthazar Ayala, De jure et officiis bellicis et disciplina militari libri III 23 (John Pawley Bate trans., John Westlake ed., 1912).

48. Keen, *supra* note 20, at 71.

49. Meron, *supra* note 27, at 39, n.88, citing William Safire, Freedom 787 (1987) (emphasis in the original).

50. Alberico Gentili, De iure belli libri tres 32 (John C. Rolfe ed. and trans., 1933).

51. *Id.*

52. *Id.*, at 485. These developments, while tending towards a broader legalization of the recourse to war, *jus ad bellum*, also had the positive effect of enlarging the list of those entitled to combatants' privileges under the law of nations, thus paving the way for modern humanitarian law's important principle of extending its protective umbrella to all those involved in war, *jus in bello*, regardless of its justness. *See also* Meron, *supra* note 27, at 10.

53. *Id.* at 192–93.

54. Gentili, *supra* note 50. Note, however, that Alberico Gentili advocates a broader concept of self-defence, not limited by necessity or proportionality. *Id.* at 58–59.

55. Hugo Grotius, De jure belli ac pacis libri tres 575–76 (Francis Kelsey trans., Carnegie ed. 1925). This edition is a translation of the 1646 edition rather than the first edition of 1625.

56. Suárez, *supra* note 37, at 816.

57. Vitoria, *supra* note 23, at 171.

58. Oscar Schachter, *United Nations Law in the Gulf Conflict*, 85 Am. J. Int'l L. 452, 460 (1991).

59. Charles T. Wood, The Age of Chivalry 55 (1970).

60. Theodor Meron, *The Authority to Make Treaties in the Late Middle Ages*, 89 Am. J. Int'l L. 1, 17 (1995).

61. Gentili, *supra* note 50, at 299.

62. *Id.* at 298–302.

63. *Id.* at 353.

64. W.G. Boswell-Stone, Shakespeare's Holinshed: The Chronicle and the Plays Compared 240 (1968).

65. *Id.* at 200–201.

66. Meron, *supra* note 27, at 182–84.

67. Gentili, *supra* note 50, at 356.

68. *Supra* note 34 at 197.

69. Steven Marx, *Shakespeare's Pacifism*, 65 Renaissance Quarterly 49 (No. 1, Spring 1992).

70. *Id.* at 65.

71. *Id.* at 59, 61

72. See generally, Dominic Baker-Smith, Moore's Utopia 59, 106 (1991).

73. Marx, *supra* note 69, at 70–71.

CHAPTER THREE

1. The Song of Roland 30, lines 24–25 (Glyn Burgess trans., 1990).

2. Johan Huizinga, The Autumn of the Middle Ages 75 (Rodney J. Payton & Ulrich Mammitzsch trans., 1996).

3. Arthur B. Ferguson, The Indian Summer of English Chivalry 87 (1960).

4. Maurice Keen, Chivalry 102–24 (1984).

5. Charles Martindale & Michelle Martindale, Shakespeare and the Uses of Antiquity 144–53(1990).

6. 6 Plutarch's Lives of the Noble Grecians and Romans 189 (Sir Thomas North trans., 1579, repr. 1896, George Wyndham ed.).

7. *Id.* at 192.

8. Derek Traversi, Shakespeare: The Roman Plays 9 (1963).

9. Martindale & Martindale, *supra* note 5, at 47.

10. William Shakespeare, The Complete Works 909 (Stanley Wells and Gary Taylor eds., 1988). Such sources included Holinshed, and a number of contemporary plays and poems. *See also* William Shakespeare, The Complete Works of William Shakespeare 1167 (David Bevington ed., 1992) (hereinafter Bevington).

11. Richard S. Ide, Possessed with Greatness (1980).

12. J.L. Simmons, Shakespeare's Pagan World 7–8 (1973).

13. *Id.* at 8.

14. Makers of Rome: Nine Lives of Plutarch 41 (Ian Scott-Kilvert trans., 1965).

15. Bevington, *supra* note 10, at 941.

16. Michael Walzer, Just and Unjust Wars 5–6 (1977).

17. 2 Coleman Phillipson, The International Law and Custom of Ancient Greece and Rome 179–82 (1911). However, Roman doctrine did actually concede that wars of aggression could in principle be just. Jonathan Barnes, "Ciceron et la guerre juste," *in* 80 Bull. Soc. Française de Philosophie 4, 38–39 (Jan. 25, 1986).

18. Phillipson, *supra* note 17, at 195. On Greek law practices, see *id.* at 207–22; Pierre Ducrey, Le Traitement des prisonniers de guerre dans la Grèce antique (1968); Pierre Ducrey, Guerre et guerriers dans la Grèce antique (1985).

19. Walzer, *supra* note 16, at 3.

20. Shakespeare's Plutarch, Vol. II: Containing the Main Sources of *Antony and Cleopatra* and of *Coriolanus* 199 (C.F. Tucker Brooke ed., 1909).

21. Regarding medieval practices of distribution of spoils of war, see Theodor Meron, Henry's Wars and Shakespeare's Laws 121, 162 (1993).

22. Shakespeare's Plutarch, *supra* note 20, at 153.

23. *Compare* Derek Traversi, *supra* note 8, at 226.

24. Bevington, *supra* note 10, at 938.

25. *Id.* at A-41.

26. *Id.*

27. Marion Wynne-Davies, *'The Swallowing Womb': Consumed and Consuming Women in Titus Andronicus,* 27 Shakespearean Criticism Yearbook 263, 274 (1995).

28. The History of Titus Andronicus, *in* 6 Narrative and Dramatic Sources of Shakespeare 40–41 (Geoffrey Bullough ed., 1966).

29. Bevington, *supra* note 10, at 939.

30. On the *problematique* of the innocence of pages, see Meron, *supra* note 21, at 159, 164–65.

31. Meron, *supra* note 21, at 162–63.

32. Hugo Grotius, De jure belli ac pacis libri tres, Bk. III, Ch. IV, Pt. XII (Francis W. Kelsey trans., Carnegie ed. 1925) (1646 edition).

33. Meron, *supra* note 21, at 68–74.

34. Plutarch's Lives, *supra* note 6, at 233.

35. *Id.* This episode provides a clear source for Shakespeare's version of Lucillus' capture in *Julius Caesar,* V.iv.

36. Meron, *supra* note 21, at 95–96.

37. See Phillipson, *supra* note 17, at 182, 187–89.

38. Meron, *supra* note 21, at 172–80, Keen, *supra* note 4, at 134.

39. *The Song of Roland, supra* note 1, at 35, line 213.

40. Plutarch's Lives, *supra* note 6, at 76.

41. Martindale & Martindale, *supra* note 5, at 151–52.

42. Makers of Rome, *supra* note 14, at 38; Shakespeare's Plutarch, *supra* note 20, at 181.

CHAPTER FOUR

1. *See generally,* the Introduction by Richard Lattimore to The Iliad of Homer, 11–54 (Richard Lattimore trans. and ed., 1951). There is a rich literature on chivalry. I have benefited, particularly, from Maurice H. Keen, The Laws of Chivalry in the Late Middle Ages (1965) and Chivalry (1984); Malcolm Vale, War and Chivalry (1981); Johan Huizinga, The Autumn of the Middle Ages (Rodney J. Payton & Ulrich Mammitzsch trans., 1996); War, Literature and Politics in the Late Middle Ages (C.T. Allmand ed., 1976); Honoré Bonet (otherwise known as Bouvet), The Tree of Battles (G.W. Coopland ed., 1949), composed ca. 1387, a translation of the Ernest Nys edition of 1883; Giovanni da Legnano, Tractatus de bello, de represaliis et de duello (Thomas Erskine Holland ed., 1917), completed in 1360, but published in 1477, with better known editions in 1487 and 1584; Balthazar Ayala, Three Books on the Law of War and on the Duties Connected with War and on Military Discipline (1582) (John Pawley Bate trans., Vol. II, Carnegie ed. 1912); Christine de Pisan, The Book of Fayttes of Armes and of Chyvalrye (1408–09) (William Caxton trans., 1489, A.T.P. Byles ed., 1932).

2. Shakespeare's principal source was probably the 1596 revised edition of Raoul le Fèvre's rendition of Guido de Colonne, Le Recueil des Histoires de Troie, translated and printed by William Caxton, ca. 1475. A New Variorum Edition of Shakespeare: Troilus and Cressida 424 (Harold N. Hillebrand ed., 1953) (hereinafter referred to as Variorum). For an edition of Caxton's translation, see Raoul le Fèvre, The Recuyell of the Historyes of Troye, Vol. I (William Caxton trans., H. Oskar Sommer ed., 1894) (hereinafter referred to as Caxton). In addition,

Shakespeare also drew on Lydgate's Hvstorye Sege and Destruccyon of Troye, written between 1412 and 1420. Variorum, at 424. For a modern edition of Lydgate, see Lydgate's Troy Book, Parts I–IV (Henry Bergen ed., 1935), published for the Early English Text Society and based on manuscript sources (hereinafter referred to as Lydgate); Shakespeare probably used the edition published by Pynson in 1513 and Marshe in 1555 under the title The Auncient Historie and onely trewe and syncere Cronicle of the Warres. Introduction by Sommer, in Caxton, at xlii. Shakespeare certainly read Chaucer's Troilus and Criseyde. Variorum, at 419. See Geoffrey Chaucer, Troilus and Criseyde (George Philip Knapp trans., 1932) (hereinafter referred to as Chaucer). For a further discussion of Shakespeare's sources and the Trojan wars, see also The Works of William Shakespeare 1–38 (Kenneth Palmer ed., Arden ed. 1982); the Introduction by Bernard Knox to Homer, The Iliad 3–64 (Robert Fagles trans., 1990); the Introduction to The Iliad of Homer, supra note 1, at 11–54; the Introduction to Troilus and Cressida (K. Muir ed., 1994); and Charles Martindale & Michele Martindale, Shakespeare and the Uses of Antiquity 91–120 (1990). Cites to Shakespeare in the text will always refer to William Shakespeare: The Complete Works (Stanley Wells & Gary Taylor eds., 1988) and cites to the Iliad in the text will always refer to the Lattimore edition, supra note 1.

3. Theodor Meron, Henry's Wars and Shakespeare's Laws 203–04 (1993).

4. Eric S. Mallin, Emulous Factions and the Collapse of Chivalry: Troilus and Cressida, 29 Representations 145, 146 (Winter 1990).

5. Id. at 152, 154.

6. 2 Coleman Phillipson, The International Law and Custom of Ancient Greece and Rome 179 (1911). On Greek law practices, see id. 207–22; Pierre Ducrey, Le Traitement des prisonniers de guerre dans la Grèce antique (1968); Pierre Ducrey, Guerre et guerriers dans la Grèce antique (1985).

7. Meron, supra note 3, at 17–46.

8. Christopher Marlowe, Dr. Faustus: the A-Text 143 (David Ormerold & Christopher Wortham eds., 1985).

9. For a discussion of this episode, see Meron, supra note 3, at 27–32.

10. Franciscus de Vitoria, De Indis et de jure belli relectiones 171–72 (1557) (John Pawley Bate trans., Ernest Nys ed., Carnegie ed. 1917); Francisco Suárez, Selection from Three Works 820 (1612, 1613, 1621) (Gwladys L. Williams, Ammi Brown & John Waldron trans., Carnegie ed. 1944).

11. Variorum, supra note 2, at 442.

12. James O'Rourke, "Rule in Unity" and Otherwise: Love and Sex in Troilus and Cressida, 22 Shakespearean Criticism Yearbook [1992] 58, 59.

13. Meron, supra note 3, at 37–40.

14. Variorum, supra note 2, at 426–28. In William Caxton, the discussions in the court of Troy end with a decision to send a naval expedition led by Paris to Greece, a mission during which Paris will eventually abduct Helen and trigger the war. First, Priam presented the issue, arguing that no peaceful means could be found to bring about his sister's restitution. Therefore, he was contemplating sending the navy to revenge the injury and shame caused by his father's murder and his sister's servitude. As his eldest son, Hector was asked to state his opinion first and he urged caution, stressing that although the Trojan cause merited vengeance, the war may have an "evil end." Id. at 426. He was moved not by cowardice, but by the need to have wise counsel. Greece was extremely powerful and the war might lead to the destruction of Troy.

Paris disagreed. The Trojans could cause damages to Greece, take prisoners, and bring back a noble Greek lady who could be exchanged for Exione. For his part, Helenus warned that a Trojan war of revenge would lead to the destruction of Troy and Priam's family. In support of the war, Troilus invoked courage and the strength of Trojan chivalry and denigrated Helenus as a coward, saying that priests belong in a temple, not in war councils.

The following day, Priam started the preparations for war. Although his decision appears to have been made, he convened the citizens of Troy, explained his intentions and asked for their advice. Only one person spoke against the war, warning that Troy would be destroyed. But the citizens were against him, and Priam, with the approval of both the council and the people, directed Paris to proceed with the expedition to Greece.

15. M. J. Finley, The World of Odysseus 113–17 (2nd rev. ed. 1978).

16. *Compare* Thomas Mowbray in *Richard II*, I.i.166–69, 175–85.

17. Martindale & Martindale, *supra* note 2, at 102–03.

18. Richard S. Ide, Possessed with Greatness: The Heroic Tragedies of Chapman and Shakespeare 34–35 (1980). See also Curtis Brown Watson, Shakespeare and the Renaissance Concept of Homer (1960).

19. *See generally*, Bernard Williams, Shame and Necessity (1993). *See also* Finley, *supra* note 15, at 113–18.

20. Arthur W. H. Adkins, Merit and Responsibility 30–60 (1960).

21. David Sylvan, *A World without Security and Foreign Policy: Thinking about the Future by Reflecting on Ancient Greece*, 6 J. Global Studies 92, 107–09 (No. 2, Spring 1995).

22. Keen, Chivalry, *supra* note 1, at 59–63.

23. Meron, *supra* note 3, at 101–04.

24. On the treatment of women in the Middle Ages, see *id.* at 111–13.

25. *Compare* Military and Paramilitary Activities in and against Nicaragua (Nicar. v. U.S.) Merits, 1986 ICJ Rep. 14, 98 (Judgement of 27 June).

26. O'Rourke, *supra* note 12, at 59.

27. *Id.* at 64.

28. Philip Brockbank, *Troilus and Cressida: Character and Value 1200 B.C. to A.D. 1985*, 13 Shakespearean Criticism Yearbook [1989] 59.

29. Stephen Wall, *Bridging the Homeric Gap*, Times Literary Supplement, July 12, 1985, p. 775.

30. Mallin, *supra* note 4, at 161.

31. Variorum, *supra* note 2, at 438; Caxton *in* Lydgate, *supra* note 2, at 604.

32. Chaucer, *supra* note 2, at 185. The traditional version appears in Geoffrey Chaucer, The Book of Troilus and Criseyde 241 (Robert Kilburn Root ed., 1926):

Ector, which that wel the Grekis herde,
For Antenor how they wolde han Criseyde,
Gan it withstonde, and sobrely answerde:
"Sires, she nys no prisoner," he seyde;
I not on yow who that this charge leyde,
But, on my part, ye may eftsone hem telle,
We usen here no wommen for to selle."

33. Eric S. Mallin, in Emulous Factions and the Collapse of Chivalry: Troilus and Cressida, 29 Representations 145, 162 (Winter, 1590)

34. *See*, for example, Convention for the Amelioration of the Condition of the Wounded and Sick in Armed Forces in the Field (Geneva Convention No. I), Art. 15, Aug. 12, 1949, 6 UST 3114, TIAS No. 3362, 75 UNTS 31; Protocol Additional to the Geneva Conventions of 1 August 1949, and Relating to the Protection of Victims of International Armed Conflicts (Protocol I), opened for signature 12 Dec. 1977, Arts. 33–34, 1125 UNTS 3, 16 ILM 1391 (1977); Protocol Additional to the Geneva Conventions of 12 August 1949, and Relating to the Protection of Victims of Non-International Armed Conflicts, opened for signature 12 Dec. 1977, Art. 8, 1125 UNTS 609, 16 ILM 1442 (1977).

35. 6 Plutarch's Lives of the Noble Grecians and Romans 21 (Sir Thomas North trans., 1579, reprint 1896).

36. 2 Alberico Gentili, De jure belli libri tres 278 (John C. Rolfe trans., Carnegie ed. 1933).

37. John Campbell, *The Greek Hero*, in Honor and Grace in Anthropology 129, 131–32 (J. G. Peristiani & Julian Pitt-Rivers eds. 1992).

38. *Cf.* Homer, The Iliad, (Robert Fagles trans.), *supra* note 2, at 22: 308–14.

39. Regarding the granting of quarter under rules of chivalry, see Meron, *supra* note 3, at 108–11. For a legal discussion of the killing of the French prisoners of war at Agincourt, see *id*. at 154–71.

40. Variorum, *supra* note 2, at 440; *see also* Caxton, *supra* note 2, at 613–14.

41. Variorum, *supra* note 2, at 441, n. *.

42. *Id.*; Lydgate, *supra* note 2, at 550.

43. Lydgate, *supra* note 2, at 551.

44. Variorum, *supra* note 2, at 308, n.12; Lydgate, *supra* note 2, at 641–46.

45. Lydgate, *supra* note 2, at 472.

46. *Id.* at 642.

47. *Id.*

48. *Id.* at 645–47.

49. *Id.* at 549.

50. *Id.* at 550.

51. Variorum, *supra* note 2, at 425.

52. Sir Thomas Malory, Le Morte d'Arthur, lines 1511–12, 1603–06 in Le Morte d'Arthur: The Seventh and Eighth Tales 161 (P.S.C. Field ed., 1977).

53. *The Works of William Shakespeare, supra* note 2, at 283, nn. 37–38. In *Natural History*, Pliny wrote that the lion is gentle to those that humble themselves before him. Variorum, *supra* note 2, at 289, nn. 43–44.

54. Variorum, *supra* note 2, at 434.

55. *Id.* at 434. *See also* the note citing Lydgate's comments to the same effect, *id.*

56. *Id.* at 432.

57. Herodotus: The History 513 (David Grene trans., 1987).

58. *Id.*

59. Spies are also harshly treated under modern humanitarian law, but are entitled to a trial nonetheless. Hague Convention (No. IV), Respecting the Laws and Customs of War on Land, with Annex of Regulations, Arts. 29–30, signed Oct. 18, 1907, 36 Stat. 2277; TS 539; 1 Bevans 631; Geneva Protocol I, *supra* note 34, at Arts. 45–46.

60. *See*, for example, Books 7 and 24.

61. Huizinga, *supra* note 1, at 107.

62. *Gesta Henrici Quinti* 57–59 (Frank Taylor & John S. Roskell eds., 1975).

63. Meron, *supra* note 3, at 132–34.

64. *Id.* at 131–41.

65. Plutarch, "Parallel Lives," *in* Joseph Satin, Shakespeare and His Sources 603 (1966); Shakespeare's Plutarch, Vol. II: Containing the Main Sources of *Antony and Cleopatra* and of *Coriolanus* 118–19 (C. F. Tucker Brooke ed., 1909).

66. For a detailed discussion of various types of duels in Shakespeare and in the chivalric tradition, see Meron, *supra* note 3, at 131–41.

67. Phillipson, *supra* note 6, at 209–10.

68. Shakespeare's Nestor makes the same point:

Who may you else oppose,
That can from Hector bring his honour off,
If not Achilles? Though't be a sportful combat,
Yet in this trial much opinion dwells,
For here the Trojans taste our dear'st repute
With their fin'st palate.
                                        (*Troilus and Cressida*, I.iii.327–32)

69. Shakespeare's satirical approach to vain and frivolous chivalry is further exemplified in the episode in which Diomedes captures Troilus' horse and claims that now he can pretend to Cressida that he prevailed over Troilus and is thus a proven knight:

DIOMEDES: Go, go, my servant, take thou Troilus' horse.
Present the fair steed to my Lady Cressid.
Fellow, commend my service to her beauty.
Tell her I have chastised the amorous Trojan,
And am her knight by proof.
                                        (*Troilus and Cressida*, V.v.1–5)

70. This scene is reminiscent of Edgar's challenge to Edmond in *King Lear*, when Edgar refuses to answer the herald's question about his "name" and "quality" (*King Lear*, V.iii.111).

EDMOND: In wisdom I should ask thy name,
But since thy outside looks so fair and warlike,
And that thy tongue some say of breeding breathes,
What safe and nicely I might well demand
By rule of knighthood I disdain and spurn.
. . .

GONERIL: This is practice, Gloucester.
By th' law of arms thou wast not bound to answer
An unknown opposite.
                                        (*King Lear*, V.iii.132–44)

71. Seamus Heaney, The Cure at Troy: a Version of Sophocles' *Philoctetes* 24–25 (1991).

72. *The Song of Roland* 144, lines 3615–17 (Glyn Burgess trans. and ed., 1990).

73. For a discussion of the theme of revenge in Shakespeare, see Richard A. Posner, Law and Literature 40–70 (1988).

74. Lydgate, *supra* note 2, at 420, 449, 550.

75. Huizinga, *supra* note 1, at 76.

CHAPTER FIVE

1. Regarding Shakespeare's sources, *see* William Henry Schofield, Chivalry in English Literature: Chaucer, Malory, Spenser and Shakespeare (1912 repr. 1964); 3 & 4 Narrative and Dramatic Sources of Shakespeare (Geoffrey Bullough ed., 1966); John Satin, Shakespeare and His Sources (1966); W.G. Boswell-Stone, Shakespeare's Holinshed: The Chronicle and the Plays Compared (1968) (hereafter Boswell-Stone).

2. Schofield, *supra* note 1, at 190.

3. *See* Meron, Henry's Wars and Shakespeare's Laws 155 (1993). The exchange is also reported in an eyewitness account of a priest accompanying Henry in Agincourt, Gesta Henrici Quinti 79 (Frank Taylor & John S. Roskell eds., 1975).

4. Shakespeare's Holinshed 199 (Richard Hosley ed., 1968) (hereafter Shakespeare's Holinshed).

5. Maurice Keen, Chivalry 51 (1984).

6. Shakespeare's Holinshed, *supra* note 4, at 165.

7. Keen, *supra* note 5, at 105.

8. *Id.* at 33.

9. The Song of Roland 9 (Glyn Burgess trans., 1990). Hereafter all the references to the poem will appear in the text in parentheses.

10. *See generally* Hugh Talbot, The English Achilles (1981); A. J. Pollard, John Talbot and the War in France 1427–1453, 35 Royal Historical Society Studies in History (1983).

11. Shakespeare's Holinshed, *supra* note 4, at 168.

12. Hall's Chronicle 229 (1548 and 1550) (1809 ed., repr. 1965)

13. Phyllis Rackin, Anti-Historians: Women's Roles in Shakespeare's. Histories, 37 Theatre Journal 329, 330, 334 (No. 3, Oct. 1985).

14. *Id.* at 335.

15. Keen, *supra* note 5, at 104 (1984).

16. E.F. Jacob, The Fifteenth Century: 1399–1485 at 506 (1961). *See also* Pollard, *supra* note 10; Talbot, *supra* note 10 (1982).

17. Honoré Bouvet [Bonet], The Tree of Battles 122 (G.W. Coopland ed., 1949), based on an 1883 translation by Ernest Nys. The book was composed ca. 1387.

18. *Id.*

19. *Id.*

20. Giovanni da Legnano, Tractatus de bello, de represaliis et de duello, ch. XXVIII, 251–52 (Thomas Erskine Holland ed., 1917, Bologna manuscript ca. 1390). Giovanni da Legnano completed his work in 1360, but it was published in 1477 and in better-known editions of 1487 and 1584.

21. Chivalric myth abounded with vows, even more artificial and esoteric than Charles's, often associated with tourneying. For example, a Polish knight swore that he would not sit to eat until he had fought an infidel, and two English gentlemen each covered one eye until he could achieve a feat of arms in France. Keen, *supra* note 5, at 213.

22. Bouvet, *supra* note 17, at 132.

23. Christine de Pisan, The Book of Fayttes of Armes and of Chyvalrye 18–19 (William Caxton trans., 1489, A.T.P. Byles ed., 1932) (composed 1408–09).

24. Bouvet, *supra* note 17, at 184.

25. Meron, *supra* note 3, at 141.

26. Johan Huizinga, The Autumn of the Middle Ages 111 (Rodney J. Payton & Ulrich Mammitzsch trans., 1996).

27. *Id.*

28. Meron, *supra* note 3, at 7.

29. Keen, *supra* note 5, at 175.

30. 3 Narrative and Dramatic Sources of Shakespeare, *supra* note 1, at 59–60.

CHAPTER SIX

1. Malcolm Vale, War and Chivalry 1 (1981).

2. This summary of Ramon Lull's chivalric virtues draws on Maurice Keen, Chivalry 9–10 (1984).

3. *Id.* at 11.

4. Theodor Meron, Henry's Wars and Shakespeare's Laws 141 (1993).

5. Sidney Painter, French Chivalry 30 (1940).

6. Arthur B. Ferguson, The Chivalric Tradition in Renaissance England 17 (1986).

7. *Id.* at 57.

8. *Id.* at 47.

9. Arthur B. Ferguson, The Indian Summer of English Chivalry 142 (1960).

10. Ferguson, Chivalric Tradition, *supra* note 6, at 46–47.

11. Ferguson, Indian Summer, *supra* note 9, at 39.

12. Meron, *supra* note 4, at 17–46.

13. *Id.* at 23, 154–55.

14. Steven Gunn, *Chivalry and the Politics of the Early Tudor Court, in* Chivalry in the Renaissance 107, 108 (Sydney Anglo ed., 1990).

15. Vale, *supra* note 1, at 167–69. See also Frank Chapman Sharp, Shakespeare's Portrayal of the Moral Life, 41–42 (1971).

16. Ferguson, Chivalric Tradition, *supra* note 6, at 98–99.

17. William Henry Schofield, Chivalry in English Literature 260 (1912, repr. 1964).

18. Joan Simon, Education and Society in Tudor England 64 (1966).

19. Annabel Patterson, Shakespeare and the Popular Voice 1 (1989).

20. M.H. Keen, *Chivalry, Nobility and the Man-at-Arms, in* War, Literature and Politics in the Middle Ages 44 (Christopher T. Allmand ed., 1976). *See also id.* at 39–45.

21. Ferguson, Chivalric Tradition, *supra* note 6, at 97.

22. Vale, *supra* note 1, at 27.

23. Richard Barber, The Knight and Chivalry 124 (1974).

24. Protocol Additional to the Geneva Conventions of 12 Aug. 1949, and Relating to the Protection of Victims of International Armed Conflicts (Protocol I), Arts. 32–34, 1125 UNTS 3; Protocol Additional to the Geneva Conventions of 12 Aug. 1949, and Relating to the Protection of Victims of Non-International Armed Conflicts (Protocol II), Art. 8, 1125 UNTS 609.

25. Alexander Leggatt, Shakespeare's Political Drama 83 (1988).

26. Johan Huizinga, The Autumn of the Middle Ages 120 (Rodney J. Payton & Ulrich Mammitzsch trans., 1996).

27. Id. at 103–04.

28. Keen, supra note 20, at 32, 40.

29. Id. at 44.

CHAPTER SEVEN

1. Johan Huizinga, The Autumn of the Middle Ages 103–04 (Rodney J. Payton & Ulrich Mammitzsch trans., 1996).

2. Philippe Contamine, War in the Middle Ages 256–57 (1984).

3. Theodor Meron, Henry's Wars and Shakespeare's Laws 162–63 (1993).

4. W.G. Boswell-Stone, Shakespeare's Holinshed: The Chronicle and the Plays Compared 218 (1968).

5. 3 Narrative and Dramatic Sources of Shakespeare 27 (Geoffrey Bullough ed., 1966).

6. Phyllis Rackin, Anti-Historians: Women's Roles in Shakespeare's Histories, 37 Theatre Journal 329, 332 (No. 3, Oct. 1985).

7. Huizinga, supra note 1, at 107–11.

8. Sidney Painter, French Chivalry 57 (1940).

9. Arthur B. Ferguson, The Chivalric Tradition in Renaissance England 74 (1986); H. R. Fox Bourne, Sir Philip Sidney: Type of English Chivalry in the Elizabethan Age 341 (1891).

10. Boswell-Stone, supra note 4, at 233.

11. Richard F. Hardin, Chronicles and Mythmaking in Shakespeare's Joan of Arc, 42 Shakespeare Survey 25, 31 (1990).

12. Maurice Keen, Chivalry 200–18 (1984).

13. Painter, supra note 8, at 142 (1940).

14. Ferguson, supra note 9, at 74.

15. Id. at 73.

16. Id.

17. The Portable Cervantes 85 (Samuel Putnam ed. and trans., 1976).

18. Id. at 86.

19. Ferguson, supra note 9, at 124.

20. E.R. Rauchut, Hotspur's Prisoners and the Laws of War in 1 Henry IV, 45 Shakespeare Quarterly 96 (1994).

21. William Henry Schofield, Chivalry in English Literature 209–10 (1912, repr. 1964).

22. Michel Eyquem de Montaigne, The Essays, at xiv (Charles Cotton trans., W. Carew Hazlitt ed., 1952; first ed. 1580). I am grateful to Justice Stephen Breyer for drawing my attention to this source.

23. Victor Skretkowicz, Chivalry in Sydney's Arcadia, in Chivalry in the Renaissance 161, 164 (Sidney Anglo ed., 1990).

24. Robert P. Adams, The Better Part of Valor: More, Erasmus, Colet, and Vives on Humanism, War and Peace 1496–1535, at 77, 277 (1962).

25. Huizinga, supra note 1, at 111–13.

26. Cervantes, supra note 17, at 136, 83, 84–85, 179, 249. See also Howard Mancing, The Chivalric World of Don Quijote 13 (1982).

27. Cervantes, supra note 17, at 392.

28. *Id.* at 28–29.

29. *Id.* at 140.

CHAPTER EIGHT

1. Theodor Meron, Henry's Wars and Shakespeare's Laws 90, 108–11, 166–67 (1993).

2. Saint Thomas Aquinas, 35 Summa Theologiae, Questions 40 and 44 (Thomas R. Heath trans., Blackfriars ed. 1972).

3. Saint Thomas Aquinas, De regimene principum, ch. 12, in Aquinas, Selected Political Writings 67 (A.P. D'Antrèves ed., J.G. Dawson trans., (Blackwell ed. Oxford, 1965); 5 Summa Theologiae, Question 21; 37 *id.*, Question 58; 34 *id.*, Questions 25, 27, 30. See also 2 Philippe de Meziere, Le Songe du Viel Pelerin 158 (bk. 3) (G. W. Coopland ed., 1969); Myra Stokes, Justice and Mercy in Piers Plowman 1–2, 154 (Croom Helm ed. 1984); Anna P. Baldwin, the Theme of Government in Piers Plowman 15–16 (D. S. Brewer ed., 1981); Gerald R. Harriss, *Introduction: The Examplar of Kingship in* Henry V: The Practice of Kingship 11–13 (Gerald L. Harriss ed., 1985).

4. Maurice Keen, The Laws of War in the Late Middle Ages 119–22 (1965).

5. Michel Eyquem de Maintaigne, The Essays 22, Essay XIV (Charles Cotton trans., W. Carew Hazlitt ed., 1952; 1st ed. 1580). I am grateful to Justice Stephen Breyer for drawing my attention to this source.

6. For a detailed discussion, see Meron, *supra* note 1, at ch. 9.

7. Holinshed's Chronicles 39 (R. S. Wallace & Alma Hansen eds., 1923, repr. 1978); Raphael Holinshed, Chronicles of England, Scotland, and Ireland, Vol. III, at 82 (1587 ed., repr. 1808) (hereinafter Holinshed).

8. Peter Saccio, Shakespeare's English Kings 153 (1977).

9. The circumstances of the capture at sea are still shrouded in mystery. While Shakespeare describes the captors as pirates, this is far from clear.

10. Philippe Contamine, War in the Middle Ages 289 (1984).

11. Sidney Painter, French Chivalry 145 (1940).

12. For a discussion of chivalric rules concerning the protection of women and the loss of privileges by women combatants, see Meron, *supra* note 1, at 91–96.

13. *See generally* Phyllis Rackin, *Foreign Country: The Place of Women and Sexuality in Shakespeare's Historical World, in* Enclosure Acts 68, 71 (Richard Burt and John Michael Archer eds., 1994); Phyllis Rackin, *Anti-Historians: Women's Roles in Shakespeare's Histories,* 37 Theatre Journal 329 (1985).

14. Richard F. Hardin, *Chronicles and Mythmaking in Shakespeare's Joan of Arc,* 42 Shakespeare Survey 25, 31 (1990).

15. *See* Introduction by Gary Taylor to *1 Henry VI, in* William Shakespeare: The Complete Works 153 (Stanley Wells & Gary Taylor eds., 1988) (who believes that this scene was not written by Shakespeare) and The Complete Works of Shakespeare 497–98 (David Bevington ed., updated 4th ed. 1997) (David Bevington supports the theory of Shakespeare's authorship of the whole play). Bevington observes that in the play, Joan embodies a domineering Amazonian woman with demonic sexuality. *Id.* at 499.

16. 3 Narrative and Dramatic Sources of Shakespeare 31, 41 (Geoffrey Bullough ed., 1966); W. G. Boswell-Stone, Shakespeare's Holinshed 238–39 (1968).

17. *See,* for example, Edward Hall, Hall's Chronicle 249–50 (1809).

18. Holinshed, *supra* note 7, at 171.

19. Hall, *supra* note 17, at 157–59.

20. Hardin, *supra* note 14, at 25; W. T. Waugh, *Joan of Arc in English Sources of the Fifteenth Century, in* Historical Essays in Honour of James Tait 387 (J. G. Edwards, V. H. Galbraith & E. F. Jacob eds., 1933); Régine Pernoud, The Retrial of Joan of Arc (J. M. Cohen trans., 1955).

21. Boswell-Stone, *supra* note 16, at 238–39.

22. James C. Oldham, *On Pleading the Belly: A History of the Jury of Matrons,* 6 Criminal Justice History 1 (1985).

23. 2 Alberico Gentili, De jure belli libri tres 252–53, 259 (Carnegie ed., John C. Rolfe trans., 1933).

24. *Id.* at 253.

25. Honoré Bouvet (Bonet), The Tree of Battles 185 (ch. XCIV) (composed ca. 1387).

26. Since many feudal customs gave women the right to succession, the participation of noble armed ladies in hostilities was not unusual. Contamine, *supra* note 10, at 241.

27. Bullough, *supra* note 16, at 167, 206; Boswell-Stone, *supra* note 16, at 341–42.

28. Sidney Painter suggests that in the fifteenth century, nobles began to hold gentlewomen for ransom, a thing practically unheard of in the fourteenth century. Painter, *supra* note 11, at 61.

29. For a discussion of the principal rules, see Meron, *supra* note 1, at 111–13.

30. Franciscus de Vitoria, De Indis et de jure belli relectiones 184–85 (para. 52) (John Pawley Bate trans., Ernest Nys ed., Carnegie ed. 1917). Franciscus de Vitoria's lectures were published posthumously in 1557.

31. Gentili, *supra* note 23, at 257–59.

32. Christine de Pisan, The Book of the City of Ladies 160–61 (E.J. Richards trans., 1982).

33. *See*, for example, *King John*, III.i.191–215.

34. Maurice Keen, Chivalry 212–16 (1984).

35. Sidney Painter, *supra* note 11, at 40–41.

36. Charles T. Wood, The Age of Chivalry 149 (1970)

37. Richard Barber, The Knight and Chivalry 44, 110 (1974).

38. Boswell-Stone, *supra* note 16, at 151–55; Joseph Satin, Shakespeare and His Sources 171–73 (1966); 4 Bullough, *supra* note 16, at 272–74 (1966).

39. Boswell-Stone, *supra* note 16, at 241; Bullough, *supra* note 16, at 71–72.

40. There appears to have been no contemporary comment on the constitutional theory underlying the arrangement of 1460. The principal source is the account in *Rot. Parl.* v. 375–79 (reprinted in S. B. Chrimes & A. L. Brown, Select Documents 313–18 [1961]. When the Duke of York made his claim of right by descent, the judges and sergeants declined to comment, saying it was "above the law and past their learning"; it is hardly surprising that no one ventured a legal comment at the time. Older writers expressed the view that Edward IV did not assert any new theory of kingship in taking the Crown but merely a better title than Henry VI. More recently, scholars have suggested that the 1460 arrangement indicates the establishment of parliamentary sovereignty, since the arrangement was made in Parliament and approved by it. W. H. Dunham & C. T. Wood, *The Right to Rule in England: Depositions and the Kingdom's Authority, 1327–1485*, 81 Am. Hist. Rev. 738, 748–52 (1976). Stanley Chrimes, however, viewed this ep-

isode essentially as an inheritance dispute, based on the absence of any embodiment of the accord in an Act of Parliament. S.B. Chrimes, English Constitutional Ideas in the Fifteenth Century 23, 26–31 (1966). John McKenna has also argued against William Dunham and Wood in J.W. McKenna, *The Myth of Parliamentary Sovereignty in Late-Medieval England*, 94 Eng. Hist. Rev. 481, 494–96 (No. 372, July 1979). In a more recent comment, Ralph Griffith suggested that the 1460 accord was unique, and not supported by the precedents of Edward II or Richard II. R. A. Griffith, The Reign of King Henry VI, at 868–69 (1981).

In 1470 Edward IV left England and Henry VI resumed the throne by a process which contemporaries called readeption (*readeptio*). The plea rolls of the central courts refer to Edward IV's accession as a violent usurpation of royal power and a forcible expulsion of Henry VI. 47 Selden Soc. xiv: Year Books of Edward IV (N. Neilson ed.) The record likely would not include such a comment without judicial approval. Of course, this does not reflect directly on the 1460 arrangement, since it was not necessary to state whether Henry VI was claiming "in fee" or merely resuming his life estate, since the agreement provided for forfeiture if he did not comply with all the terms.

I am grateful to Professor John Baker for his help in preparing the material for this note.

41. Bullough, *supra* note 16, at 158–59, 172–77 (for literary sources, see *id.* 211–17); Boswell-Stone, *supra* note 16, at 289–95; Hall, *supra* note 17, at 245–49. *See also* E.F. Jacob, The Fifteenth Century, 1399–1485, at 520–22 (1961).

42. Boswell-Stone, *supra* note 16, at 308–09.

43. Giovanni da Legnano, Tractatus de bello, de represaliis et de duello, 234, ch. xv (Thomas Erskine Holland trans., Carnegie ed. 1917)

44. Bouvet, *supra* note 25, at 169, ch.LXXII.

45. *Id.* at 289 (ch. LXXXIX).

46. Meron, *supra* note 1, at 14–15.

47. Gentili, *supra* note 23, at 152–53 (Bk. II., Ch.V). Gentili argued that kings were not allowed to alienate their subjects. *Id.* at 373. *See also* Meron, *supra* note 1, at 15–16, 189.

48. Frances A. Shirley, Swearing and Perjury in Shakespeare's Plays 80–81 (1979).

CHAPTER NINE

1. Philippe Burrin, Hitler et les Juifs 142, 148, 163, 166–67, 172 (1989).

2. N.Y. Times, Nov. 6, 1996, at A5.

3. 4 Narrative and Dramatic Sources of Shakespeare 260, 324–25 (Geoffrey Bullough ed., 1966).

4. W.G. Boswell-Stone, Shakespeare's Holinshed: The Chronicle and the Plays Compared 161–63 (1968).

5. Theodore F. T. Plucknett, A Concise History of the Common Law 49 (5th ed. 1956). The issues pertaining to the authority of the king, judges and Parliament were clearly joined in 1607, when the King argued that Sir Edward Coke's views on the supremacy of the common law and the judges' authority to be the uncontrolled interpreters of the law meant that "I shall be under the law, which it is treason to affirm; to which, says Coke, I replied that Bracton saith, *quod Rex non debet esse sub homine, sed sub Deo et lege.*" 5 W.S. Holdworth, A History of English Law 430 & nn. 2–3 (4th rev. ed. 1927). Although this is not

the place to discuss the dynamics of executive acceptance of decisions of the judiciary, one might consider President Harry Truman's acceptance of the decision of the U.S. Supreme Court in Youngstown Sheet & Tube Co. v. Sawyer, 343 U.S. 579 (1952), that the confiscated steel mills should be returned to the owners; and President Richard Nixon's eventual surrender of the tapes in response to the Court's ruling in United States v. Nixon, 418 U.S. 683 (1974). See Stanley I. Kutler, The Wars of Watergate 409, 513–16 (1990). On "culture of compliance," see Louis Henkin, International Law: Politics, Values and Functions (General Course on Public International Law) 216 Collected Courses 71 (1989–IV).

6. Walter Kaiser, Praisers of Folly: Erasmus, Rabelais, Shakespeare 210 (1963).

7. David Bevington, The Complete Works of Shakespeare A-25 (1997).

8. Kaiser, supra note 6, at 209–10.

9. Desiderius Erasmus, The Education of a Christian Prince (Lester K. Born, trans., 1936) (1540).

10. Id. at 113.

11. Id. at 122–23.

12. Id. at 189.

13. Bevington, supra note 7, at xxiv.

14. Alberico Gentili, De legationibus libri tres 156 (Gordon J. Laing trans., Carnegie ed. 1924). Max Lerner, Introduction to Niccolò Machiavelli, The Prince and the Discourses xxxvi–xxxvii (Max Lerner ed., 1950).

15. Erasmus, supra note 9, at 163.

16. Id. at 113, 117.

17. James Boyd White, Acts of Hope 50 (1994). Shakespeare's Richard II's views on absolute kingship can be regarded as an anachronism, Robin Headlam Wells, Shakespeare, Politics and the State 45 (1986).

18. Theodor Meron, Henry's Wars and Shakespeare's Laws 199–202 (1993). See also Jack Benoit Gohn, Richard II: Shakespeare's Legal Brief on the Royal Prerogative and the Succession to the Throne, 70 Geo. L.J. 943 (1982).

19. See Ernst H. Kantorowicz, The King's Two Bodies: A Study in Medieval Political Theology (1957).

20. Meron, supra note 18, at ch. 8. For a discussion of modern humanitarian law, see Theodor Meron, Rape as a Crime under International Humanitarian Law, 87 Am. J. Int'l. L. 424 (1993). For a feminist view, see Jean E. Howard & Phyllis Rackin, Engendering a Nation 5–8 (1997).

21. While urging generals to prohibit and prevent rape during the sacking of a city, Franciscus de Vitoria reluctantly admitted the lawfulness of allowing soldiers to sack a city if "the necessities of war" required it, or "as a spur to the courage of the troops," even when rape would result. Franciscus de Vitoria, De Indis et de jure belli Relectiones 184–85 (52) (John Pawley Bate trans., Ernest Nys ed., Carnegie ed. 1917) 1557, posthumous. Alberico Gentili categorically rejected the permissibility of rape. 2 Alberico Gentili, De jure belli libri tres 257 (John C. Rolfe trans., Carnegie ed.). This is the 1931 translation of the 1612 edition. The first part of the book was first published in 1588, the second and third parts in 1589. See also Theodor Meron, Common Rights of Mankind in Gentili, Grotius and Suárez, 85 Am. J. Int'l L. 110, 115–16 (1991).

22. Philippe Contamine wrote that this question was discussed only infrequently in medieval sources. Philippe Contamine, War in the Middle Ages 287 (1984). It was, however, a significant topic in the Catholic just war tradition.

23. *Id.* at 288.

24. *Id.* at 264, 267. Saint Augustine, The City of God I(21), I(26) (Henry Bettenson trans., Pelican Books 1972) (1467).

25. Plutarch, Parallel Lives (Thomas North trans., 1579), *in* Joseph Satin, Shakespeare and His Sources 582 (1966).

26. Thomas Nagel, *War and Massacre, in* War and Moral Responsibility 3, 5 (Marshall Cohen, Thomas Nagel & Thomas Scanlon eds., 1974); Bernard Williams, A *Critique of Utilitarianism*, in Utilitarianism: For and Against 77, 94–95 (J.J.C. Smart & Bernard Williams eds., 1963).

Because utilitarianism-consequentialism attaches value to states of affairs, a person is as responsible for things that he/she allows or fails to prevent (negative responsibility) as for things that he/she causes (positive responsibility). However, critics of utilitarianism and supporters of the deontological theory of ethics, who stress individual rights and responsibilities in contrast to utilitarianism's emphasis on consequences, accord negative responsibility much weaker significance than positive responsibility. Most non-utilitarians think it would be wrong to fail to throw a life preserver to someone drowning, if this involved little cost. But if the cost of preventing the death of another is substantial, the requirement disappears, unlike the prohibition against killing.

27. The Nuremberg Charter was adopted by the Agreement for the Prosecution and Punishment of the Major War Criminals of the European Axis, Aug. 8, 1945, 59 Stat. 1544, 82 UNTS 279.

28. [1950] 2 Y. B. Int'l L. Comm'n 376, UN Doc. A/CN.4/SER.A/1950/Add.1 (1957).

29. *In re* Yamashita, 327 U.S. 1 (1945).

30. *Id.* at 16.

31. *Id.* at 34–35 (Murphy, J., dissenting).

32. Michael Walzer, Just and Unjust Wars 320 (1977).

33. 421 U.S. 658 (1974).

34. *Id.* at 671.

35. *Id.* at 683 (Stewart, J., dissenting).

36. See, e.g., William H. Parks, *Command Responsibility for War Crimes,* 62 Mil. L. Rev. 1, 37, 40–42, 103 (Fall 1973).

37. Walzer, *supra* note 32, at 319–22.

38. Protocol Additional to the Geneva Conventions of 12 August 1949, and Relating to the Protection of Victims of International Armed Conflicts, opened for signature Dec. 12, 1977, 1125 UNTS 3 [hereinafter Protocol I].

39. Christopher N. Crowe, *Command Responsibility in the Former Yugoslavia: The Chances for a Successful Prosecution,* 29 U. Rich. L. Rev. 191, 229 (1994). It remains to be seen whether the Hague Tribunal will consider Article 7(3) of its Statute to be significantly different from Article 86(2) of Addditional Protocol I, *supra* note 38.

40. Thomas Nagel, *Ruthlessness in Public Life, in* Public and Private Morality 75, 78–79 (Stuart Hampshire ed., 1978).

41. *Id.* at 90.

42. Richard H. Weisberg, Vichy Law and the Holocaust in France 65 (1996).

43. Jonathan Glover, Responsibility 176 (1970).

44. *Id.* at 178.

45. Prosecutor v. Erdemović, Case No. IT-96-22-A, Appeals Judgment (Oct. 7, 1997), discussed in note 48 *infra* [hereinafter Erdemović Appeal]. *See also* Theo-

dor Meron, *The Normative Impact on International Law of the International Tribunal for Former Yugoslavia*, 24 Israel Y. B. Hum. Rights 163, 180–82 (1995); Steven R. Ratner & Jason S. Abrams, Accountability for Human Rights Atrocities in International Law: Beyond the Nuremberg Legacy 123 (1997).

46. United States v. Von Leeb, 11 Trials of War Criminals before the Nuremberg Military Tribunals under Control Council Law No. 10, at 462, 509–15, 542–49 (1950) [hereinafter Trials]. *See also* United States v. Wilhelm List, *id.* at 757, 1236.

47. *Von Leeb*, 11 Trials, *supra* note 46, at 525–26.

48. Drazen Erdemović had been sentenced to ten years' subsequently reduced to five years imprisonment, following his guilty plea to one count of a crime against humanity, for participating in the mass execution of a large number of civilian Muslim men in the aftermath of the fall of Srebrenica. Erdemović invoked duress, alleging that when he had at first refused to join in the massacre, he was told that he himself would be shot together with the Muslims. See further *infra* notes 73–78 and corresponding text. Antonio Cassese argued that, where the accused has been charged with participation in a collective killing that would have proceeded irrespective of whether the accused was a participant, the defence has been allowed in principle in some cases, and that Erdemović had not enjoyed any real moral choice. Cassese stated the utilitarian argument. Erdemović Appeal, *supra* note 45, Separate and Dissenting Opinion of Judge Cassese, at 58. See also note 26 *supra*. The absolutist argument was framed by Judges Gabrielle Kirk McDonald and Lal Chand Vohrah, Erdemović Appeal, *supra*, Joint and Separate Opinion of Judge McDonald and Judge Vohrah, at 65.

Brackenbury, in contrast to Erdemović, was not required to participate in murder, but only to hand the Duke over. Thomas Nagel's comment on absolutism is apposite to his case, "not everything that happens to others as a result of what one does is something that one has done to them." Nagel, *supra* note 26, at 10.

49. T.S. Eliot, Murder in the Cathedral, Pt. II, at 77 (1935).

50. Boswell-Stone, *supra* note 4, at 125–26. *See also* Edward Hall, Hall's Chronicle 20 (1809) (photo reprint 1965); Satin, *supra* note 25, at 103–104; 3 Bullough, *supra* note 3, at 413–14. In both Holinshed and Shakespeare (*Richard II*, V.v.114–116), Exton demonstrates remorse for his actions.

51. Telling of the start of the episode, Holinshed writes that King Henry said: "Haue I no 'faithfull freend which will deliuer me of him, whose life will be my death, and whose death will be the preseruation of my life?' This saieng was much noted of them which were present, and especiallie of one called sir Piers of Exton." Boswell-Stone, *supra* note 4, at 125; Hall, *supra* note 50, at 20; 3 Bullough, *supra* note 3, at 413; Satin, *supra* note 25, at 103. A *Myrroure for Magistrates* (anon. 1559) suggests a more explicit order to Exton, explaining that "[t]o dash all dowtes [about his reign], he [the king] tooke no farther pause / But sent sir Pierce of Exton a traytrous knight / To Pomfret Castell, with other armed light." 3 Bullough, *supra* note 3, at 415, 422. In The First Fowre Bookes of the Civile Wars (1595), Samuel Daniel, like Shakespeare, is more subtle. He writes that "Henry desired Richard's death," so that

[h]e knew this time, & yet he would not seeme / Too quicke to wrath, as if affecting bloud; / But yet complaines so far, that men might deeme / He would twere done, & that he thought it good; / And wisht that some would so his life esteeme / As rid him of these feares wherein he stood: / And therewith eies a knight, that then was by, / Who soone could learne his lesson by his eie.

3 Bullough, *supra* note 3, at 434, 456-57. In a footnote, the editor, Geoffrey Bullough, notes that in the margin of the manuscript was written: "This Knight was Sir Pierce of Exton." *Id.* at 457, n. 1.

52. The character of a courtier ready to kill at the mere wink of authority is well described in a 1595 poem by Samuel Daniel, *The First Fowre Bookes of the Civile Wars*, 3 Bullough, *supra* note 3, at 434-60, which Shakespeare may have read:

> The man he knew was one that willingly
> For one good looke would hazard soule and all,
> An instrument for any villanie,
> That needed no commission more at all:
> A great ease to the king that should hereby
> Not need in this a course of justice call,
> Nor seeme to wil the act, for though what's wrought
> Were his own deed, he grieves should so be thought. . . .
> This knight, but o why should I call him knight
> To give impiety this reverent stile,
> Title of honour, worth, & vertues right
> Should not be given to a wretch so vile.

Id. at 457.

53. Christine de Pisan, Book of Fayttes of Armes and of Chyvalrye 13-14 (William Caxton trans., 1489, A. Byles ed., 1932) (written 1408-09); See also Meron, *supra* note 18, at 18-19, 27-28.

54. J. H. Hexter, The Vision of Politics on the Eve of the Reformation: More, Machiavelli and Seyssel 93, 82-93 (1973).

55. Shakespeare's *Richard III* calls attention to a courtier's responsibility to discourage crimes by leaders when King Edward complains bitterly that none of his aides had pleaded against his order to execute the Duke of Clarence (*Richard III*, II.i.107-33).

56. Writings on the Second World War demonstrate that orders to commit atrocities were often not accompanied by duress, at least, as Michael Walzer pointed out, not to the extent of implicating the risk of death. Walzer, *supra* note 32, at 314. In most cases, reluctance to carry out such orders resulted in a transfer to hardship posts and other harm to one's career. The Nuremberg Tribunal's *High Command Case* discussed the range of options available to German staff officers faced with an illegal order: they could issue orders countermanding the order, resign, or sabotage the order. Von Leeb, 11 Trials, *supra* note 46, at 511.

57. Michael Manheim, The Weak King Dilemma in the Shakespearean History Play 134 (1973).

58. Boswell-Stone, *supra* note 4, at 72.

59. Shakespeare's treatment of this episode owes much to Holinshed and to *The Troublesome Raigne of King John*, an anonymous play written in 1591. 4 Bullough, *supra* note 3, at 4, 22. Holinshed's account of the conversation between Hubert and Arthur and his story about Arthur's death originates in a contemporary Essex chronicle of Coggeshall, entitled *The English Chronicle of Radulph of Coggeshall*. F.M. Powicke, Ways of Medieval Life and Thought 27 (1949). *See also* 4 Bullough, *supra* note 3, at 15, 55-60. Holinshed's explanations for Arthur's death are, that (1) that Arthur died of grief; (2) that he was drowned in attempting to escape from Rouen; or (3) that he was killed by his uncle. Powicke, *supra* at 32, explains that the main authority for Arthur's disappearance is the annals

of Margam, a Cistercian abbey in South Wales. The story Frederick Powicke recounts, as described in the chronicle of Margam, suggests that John killed Arthur in a drunken fury. *Id.*

60. 4 Bullough, *supra* note 3, at 108.

61. *Id.* at 110.

62. *Id.*

63. *Id.*

64. *Id.*

65. *Id.* at 111.

66. *Id.*

67. Agreement for the Prosecution and Punishment of the Major War Criminals of the European Axis, *supra* note 27, at Art. 8.

68. See generally, Yoram Dinstein, The Defence of Obedience to Superior Orders in International Law (1965).

69. Hartmuth Horstkotte, *The Role of Criminal Law in Dealing with East Germany's Past: The Mauerschützen Cases, in* Democracy, Market Economy, and the Law 213, 215 (Werner F. Ebke & Detlev Vagts eds., 1995).

70. *Id.* at 216.

71. See e.g., Border Guards Prosecution Case, decision of Nov. 3, 1992, 100 ILR 366 (Fed. Sup. Ct.).

72. Horstkotte, *supra* note 69, at 221. For the decision of July 26, 1994, see 1994 Neue Juristische Wochenschrift at 2703. I am grateful to Professors Andreas Lowenfeld and Detlev Vagts for the translation from German.

73. Prosecutor v. Erdemović, Case No. IT-96-22-T, Sentencing Judgment, Nov. 29, 1996. *See also supra* note 48.

74. *Id.* at para. 80.

75. *Id.* at paras. 53–54.

76. *Id.* at para. 50. For the requirements regarding superior orders as a defence or as a ground for mitigation in U.S. practice, see U.S. Department of Defense, The Manual for Courts Martial, United States Rules for Court Martial 1984, No. 916(b); The Department of the Army Field Manual: Law of Land Warfare 27-10, Sec. 509 (Field Manual 27–10) (1956).

77. Case No. IT-96-22-T, *supra* note 73, at para. 91.

78. *Id.* at para. 111.

79. Manheim, *supra* note 57, at 95.

80. *Id.* at 99.

81. Herbert Morris, On Guilt and Innocence: Essays in Legal Philosophy and Moral Psychology 1–2 (1976).

82. *Id.* at 16. See H. Ansgar Kelly, *The Right to Remain Silent: before and after Joan of Arc*, 68 Speculum 992 (1993). J.G. Bellamy, The Law of Treason in England in the Late Middle Ages. 103, 137 (1970).

83. Morris, *supra* note 81, at 16.

84. Boswell-Stone, *supra* note 4, at 267.

85. 3 Bullough, *supra* note 3, at 111.

86. The historian Paul Murray Kendall presented King Edward as the architect of Clarence's murder and offered no suggestion that could point to Richard as the culprit. Furthermore, he described Clarence as a dangerous competitor to Edward and as largely responsible for much of what would befall him in the near future: once the "Duke of Clarence had grown ripe with secret hopes and private visions," he began to pose a threat to his brother, the king. Paul Murray Kendall,

Richard the Third 122 (1965). After Clarence arranged for the hanging of his former wife's servant, thus arrogating to himself authority he did not have, King Edward accused Clarence of "subverting the laws of the realm and presuming to take justice into his own hands," *id.* at 125, and ordered him imprisoned in the Tower.

Unlike the chroniclers, who accused Richard of complicity in the imprisonment and murder of Clarence either indirectly or directly, Paul Murray Kendall described Richard as dismayed by Clarence's fate and recounted how Richard in fact "pleaded with King Edward for George's life." *Id.* Ernest Jacob similarly rejected Shakespeare's imputation of responsibility to Richard for the death of Clarence. E.F. Jacob, The Fifteenth Century: 1399–1485 *in* the Oxford History of England 608 (Sir George Clark ed., 1961).

87. Kendall, *supra* note 86, at 126.

88. *Id.*

89. F.J. Levy, Tudor Historical Thought 72 (1967).

90. Shakespeare seems to have drawn inspiration for his story from literary sources, including George, Duke of Clarence, in A Myrroure for Magistrates (1559), *supra* note 51, at 301, and the anonymous poem, The True Tragedy of Richard III (ca. 1594) in 3 Bullough, *supra*, note 3, at 317. *See also* Satin, *supra* note 25, at 62–71. The former apportions the blame between Richard and King Edward, but places the primary responsibility for the actual murder on Richard. This poem may well have encouraged Shakespeare's desire to depict Richard as the principal culprit. The poet, William Baldwin, discusses Edward's order to imprison the Duke of Clarence in the Tower, and describes Richard's wish to use the opportunity to remove Clarence, a competitor for the Crown, and plot his end. Thus, according to this source, while Edward may have condemned Clarence to death, Richard incited the King, plotted the murder, and actually committed the crime. "George, Duke of Clarence," *supra* at 304–05.

Richard's responsibility is also highlighted in the Prologue to The True Tragedy of Richard III, in which Truth describes Richard as the person who actually drowned Clarence "in a butt of wine." Satin, *supra* note 25, at 63. In Richard III, Clarence decries the lack of legal proceedings and declares his innocence (I.iv.176–87). Shakespeare knew from the chroniclers that Clarence had been tried and convicted by Parliament, but he must have chosen to follow the literary sources to support the historically inaccurate claim of the total absence of judicial process. Thus, Shakespeare may have been echoing poet William Baldwin, who, speaking as the Duke of Clarence, states, "Take me for one of this wrong punisht sect, / Imprisoned first, accused without cause, / And doen to death, no proces had by lawes." George, Duke of Clarence, *supra*, at 301.

91. Kendall, *supra* note 86, at 398–402. *See also* Jacob, *supra* note 86, at 624; Boswell-Stone, *supra* note 4, at 387–94; and Satin, *supra* note 25, at 1.

92. Boswell-Stone, *supra* note 4, at 389. For Hall's version of this episode, *see* 3 Bullough, *supra* note 3, at 277.

93. Boswell-Stone, *supra* note 4, at 389.

94. 3 Bullough, *supra* note 3, at 278–79.

95. Hall, *supra* note 50, at 352.

96. Hall wrote,

Howbeit yf she coulde in no wise be intreated with her good wyll to delyuer hym, then thought he and such of the spiritualtie as wer present, that it were not in any wyse too bee attempted to take hym out againste her wyll, for it woulde be a thyng that should turne to the grudge of all men and high displeasure of God, yf the pryuilege of that place should be broken whiche had so many yeres bene kept, whiche bothe Kynges and Popes had graunted and confirmed, which ground was sanctifyed by Sainct Peter him selfe more then fyue hundreth yeres agone. . . . [A]nd therefore quod the Archebishop, God forbid that any manne shoulde for any yeartheley enterprise breake the immunitie and libertie of that sacred sanctuary that hath bene the safegard of so many a good mans life. . . .

Id. Leaving aside canon law, at least in the common law, Buckingham's and Holinshed's legal arguments may be serious. Although the privilege of sanctuary was one that belonged to a place rather than a person, it was available to felons, including traitors, and even minor malefactors and debtors. It is unclear, however, whether the common law recognized the privilege for persons who did not offend against the law and sought protection from other dangers. See J.H. Baker, *The English Law of Sanctuary,* 2 Ecclesiastical L.J. 8 (1990–92); 2 The Reports of Sir John Spelman 335–39, Selden Society Pub. No. 94 (J. H. Baker ed., 1978). However, the historian Polydore Vergil in De inventoribus rerum f. 55 (1528) expressed the view that a sanctuary also protected those who feared an attack. *Id.* at 340 & n.3. In a criticism of sanctuaries expressed in his History of King Richard III (c. 1513), Thomas More had Buckingham state that in unsettled times, a sanctuary could have given justifiable protection to political offenders. *Id.*

97. Satin, *supra* note 25, at 16.

98. In Hall, the Cardinal says: "but I trust quod he, we shall not nede it [to use force], but for any maner of nede I would we should not do it, I trust that she with reason shalbe contented and all thing in good maner obteined. And yf it hap that I brynge it not to passe, yet shall I further it to my best power, so that you all shall perceyue my good wyll, diligence, and indeauoure." Hall, *supra* note 50, at 353.

99. Nonetheless, Shakespeare was certainly aware of Hall's detailed account of the discussion between the Cardinal and the Queen. The Cardinal cajoles, promises, and repeats Buckingham's legal sophistry, assuring the Queen that no harm will befall the prince, and threatens that, in the absence of her consent, the prince will be forcibly removed: "they recon no priuilege broken, although they fetch him out of sanctuarie, whiche yf you finally refuse too deliver hym." *Id.* at 356. In response, the Queen pleads, invoking the prince's poor health, her need to care for him, the jeopardy to which he will be exposed and her right, even in the absence of sanctuary privileges, to be the guardian of her son. Finally, once the exasperated Cardinal pledges the Prince's safety with his own body and soul, the Queen yields. However, this is compulsion, not consent. On the immunity of churches in medieval ordinances, see Meron, *supra* note 18, at ch. 8.

Although Shakespeare's tale ends here, the chroniclers' story refers to the events following York's removal from sanctuary. Richard III was also concerned about the danger the princesses posed to his monarchical claims. According to the *Croyland Chronicle,* the history of the Croyland Monastery, Richard learned that the king's daughters were told to go abroad so that, "if any fatal mishap should befall the male children of the late king in the Tower, the kingdom might still, in consequence of the safety of daughters, some day fall again into the hands of the rightful heirs." Charles T. Wood, The Age of Chivalry 188 (1970). Richard responded immediately, apparently with the "purpose of ending [the] relative freedom of action for those in sanctuary," by appointing men to guard the church of Westminster, setting "a watch upon all the inlets and outlets of the monastery so that not one of the persons there shut up could go forth, and no one could enter, without his permission." Id. at 189.

100. Manheim, supra note 57, at 134.

101. Id. at 4. See also Katharine Eiseman Maus, Henry V, in The Norton Shakespeare 1445, 1446 (Stephen Greenblatt gen. ed., Walter Cohen, Jean E. Howard & Katharine Eisaman Maus eds., 1997), and David M. White, Shakespeare and Psychological Warfare, 12 Pub. Opinion Q. 68 (1948).

102. Lerner, supra note 14, at xxxix–xl.

103. Machiavelli, supra note 14, at 65.

104. Id. at 64.

105. Id.

106. Id. at 406–07 (ch. IV of The Discourses).

107. Meron, supra note 18, at 201–06.

108. Id. at 159–60.

109. Id.at 166–69. See also Gentili, supra note 21, at 212.

110. Geneva Convention (No. III) Relative to the Treatment of Prisoners of War, Aug. 12, 1949, Art. 13, 6 UST 3316, 75 UNTS 135.

111. See Instructions for the Government of Armies of the United States in the Field, General Orders No. 100, Art. 60, reprinted in The Laws of Armed Conflicts 3 (Dietrich Schindler & Jiří Toman eds., 3rd ed. 1988).

112. Theodor Meron, Francis Lieber's Code and Principles of Humanity, in Politics, Values and Functions: International Law in the 21st Century, Essays in Honor of Professor Louis Henkin 249, 252–53 (Jonathan I. Charney, Donald K. Anton & Mary Ellen O'Connell eds., 1997); and in 36 Colum. J. Transnat'l L. 269, 273 (1997).

113. Convention (No. IV) Respecting the Laws and Customs of War on Land, October 18, 1907, 36 Stat. 2277, 1 Bevans 631.

114. Gesta Henrici Quinti 92–93 (Frank Taylor & John S. Roskell eds., 1975) (1416–17).

115. The German philosopher Karl Jaspers addresses the issue of conscience and moral responsibility in The Question of German Guilt 63 (1947). By emphasizing that Hitler was unable to repent, Karl Jaspers concludes that Hitler was beyond the moral pale and unworthy of forgiveness. In such cases, there is no alternative to the use of force. However, Jasper's analysis of Hitler is not unassailable. It is true that Hitler was beyond the reach of ordinary moral judgement, but he was not a psychopath. Rather, he probably had his own perverted scale of values or his own morality. Incomprehensible as it is to people applying ordinary moral standards, Hitler's yardsticks not only justified to him the atrocities for which he was responsible, but probably did not even suggest that there was anything wrong with them.

116. Compare Saint Thomas Aquinas, Question 87, The Guilt of Punishment, in Summa Theologiae 39 (T.C. O'Brien trans., 1973).

117. Phyllis Rackin, Stages of History: Shakespeare's English Chronicles 6–8 (1990).

118. The Talmud clarifies in Makkot 24a that "Moses pronounced an adverse sentence on Israel—the visiting of the iniquities of the fathers on the children—

and it was revoked by Ezekiel." The JPS Torah Commentary: *Exodus* (Nahum M. Sarna translation and commentary) 110–11 (1991). Commentators note that a literal interpretation of the sins of the fathers concept must inevitably lead to the conclusion that repentance serves no purpose.

The thirteen attributes of God have been considered a poweful prayer at least since the time of the Talmud. *Tosafot* s.v. shalosh esrei midot enumerate these attributes of God, citing *Exodus* 34:6–7, while omitting any mention of visiting the sins of the fathers on their sons. The Thirteen Attributes occupy a central place in the traditional liturgy of Yom Kippur and the Selichot prayers, and are also cited in the weekday liturgy in the confession of the morning service (Artscroll Weekday Siddur, Nusach Ashkenaz 119a (1969).

119. Aquinas, *supra* note 116, at 39.

120. *Id.* at 41.

121. Aquinas, Question 81, Original Sin's Transmission, *in* Summa Theologiae, *supra* note 116, at 5.

122. *Id.* at 11.

123. *Id.* at 13.

124. Paul J. Glenn, A Tour of the Summa 163 (1960).

125. For example, when Jacques de Molay, Grand Master of the Order of the Temple, was about to be burnt at the stake by Philip IV The Fair of France, who persecuted the Templars to deprive them of their power and confiscated their properties, as he had persecuted the Lombards and the Jews, he is supposed to have cursed Philip and the Pope, both of whom died soon thereafter. Philip IV was succeeded by his sons, first Louis X, then Philip V and finally Charles IV, the last Capetian king. However, none had male heirs, except Philip IV's daughter Isabella, who married Edward II of England, triggering their son's Edward III's claims to the Crown of France and, eventually, the One Hundred Years War. As a result, the kingdom of France passed on to another dynasty, the Valois. For many in France, legends about the curse the Grand Master cast on the Capetians were not myth but, with the demise of the Capetians, became a reality.

126. Boswell-Stone, *supra* note 4, at 188.

127. Levy, *supra* note 89, at 227.

128. Because of his father's attainment, Richard could not inherit his father's title. He was knighted by Henry VI, restored to the dukedom of York, and, a few years later, to his other hereditary rights. Allison Weir, The Wars of the Roses 77–78, 83 (1995).

129. Some of Shakespeare's texts involve revenge or vengeance not for the acts of former generations, but for the acts of living persons, the targets of the revenge. Hamlet's obsession with revenging the murder and dishonour suffered by his father at the hands of Claudius is a primary example, one that results in a minor bloodbath. Although the New Testament prohibits such vengeance (Romans 12:19–20), the Old Testament does not. See Richard Posner, Law and Literature 58 (1988). Richard Posner describes *Romeo and Juliet* as a particularly powerful denunciation of revenge. *Id.* at 62.

EPILOGUE

1. 89 Am. J. Int'l L. 224, 226–27 (1995).

2. See Jeffrey Rosen, *The Social Police: Following the Law, Because You'd Be Too Embarrassed Not To*, The New Yorker, Oct. 20, 1997, at 170, 172–74.

INDEX